Rural Water Supply in Africa

Building Blocks for Handpump Sustainability

Peter Harvey & Bob Reed

Water, Engineering and Development Centre
Loughborough University
2004

WEDC

Water, Engineering and Development Centre
Loughborough University
Leicestershire
LE11 3TU UK

Harvey, P. A. and Reed, R. A. (2004)
Rural Water Supply in Africa: Building Blocks for Handpump Sustainability
WEDC, Loughborough University, UK.

A reference copy of this publication is also available online from:
http://www.lboro.ac.uk/wedc/

ISBN Paperback 1 84380 067 5

This document is an output from a project funded by the UK
Department for International Development (DFID)
for the benefit of low-income countries.
The views expressed are not necessarily those of DFID.

Designed and produced at WEDC
by Sue Plummer

About the authors

 **Peter Harvey** is an Assistant Programme Manager at the Water, Engineering and Development Centre (WEDC). He specializes in water supply and sanitation for low-income communities and disaster-affected populations. He has worked on water supply and sanitation programmes in Africa, Asia and Eastern Europe, and has particular experience of rural water supply in sub-Saharan Africa. His major interests include groundwater development and sustainability of water and sanitation services.

 **Bob Reed** is a Senior Programme Manager at WEDC. He specializes in water supply and sanitation for rural areas, low-income urban communities and refugees. He has considerable experience of training, design and project implementation in the Pacific, the Caribbean, Asia and Africa. In recent years he has focused on the provision of improved and sustainable water supply and sanitation systems for displaced populations.

The authors would like to hear from anyone who uses this book in the field with comments on its usefulness and areas which require improvement. Please forward comments or suggestions to the authors at the address overleaf.

About WEDC

The Water, Engineering and Development Centre (WEDC) is one of the world's leading institutions concerned with education, training, research and consultancy for the planning, provision and management of physical infrastructure for development in low- and middle-income countries.

WEDC is devoted to activities that improve the health and well-being of people living in both rural areas and urban communities. We encourage the integration of technological, environmental, social, economic and management inputs for effective and sustainable development.

Water, Engineering and Development Centre
Loughborough University
Leicestershire
LE11 3TU UK

Phone: +44 1509 222885
Fax: +44 1509 211079
Email: WEDC@lboro.ac.uk
http://www.lboro.ac.uk/wedc/

Acknowledgements

The financial support of the Department for International Development (DFID) of the British Government is gratefully acknowledged. The authors would also like to thank the following individuals and organizations for their valuable contribution to the development of this publication, especially the members of the Advisory Panel who guided the research.

Peer Reviewers
Department for International Development
Charlotte Engmann, CWSA, Ghana
John Kandulu, WaterAid
Rose Lidonde, WEDC
Dr. Jerry Ndamba, IWSD, Zimbabwe

Advisory Panel Members
Mansoor Ali, UNICEF
Vincent Allen, Consallen Pumps
Erich Baumann, RWSN/SKAT
Nick Burn, Intermediate Technology Development Group
Bent Kjellerup, Independent Consultant
Pola Kimena, MLGH, Zambia
Gordon Mumbo, WaterAid
Kevin Sansom, WEDC
Brian Skinner, WEDC

Editorial contributions
Kim Daniel

Design
Cover design and typesetting by Sue Plummer
Illustrations by Rod Shaw and Ken Chatterton
Photographs by Peter Harvey

We would also like to thank the following organizations for assisting the field research, without whose interest and participation this work could not have been undertaken.

Afram Plains Development Organisation (APDO), Ghana
African Medical Research Foundation (AMREF), Kenya
Busoga Trust, Uganda
Community Water and Sanitation Agency (CWSA), Ghana
Directorate of Water Development (DWD), Uganda
Department of Water Affairs and Forestry (DWAF), South Africa
Ministry of Local Government and Housing (MLGH), Zambia
Ministry of Water Resources Management and Development (MWRMD), Kenya
Network for Water and Sanitation (NETWAS), Kenya
Mouchel Parkman, UK
Partners in Development (PID), South Africa
Rural Water Development (RWD), Kenya
Sustainable Aid in Africa (SANA), Kenya
United Nations Children's Fund, (UNICEF), Zambia
WaterAid, Ghana
World Vision, Zambia

In addition, we wish to extend our thanks to all those people who have contributed to the development of this document through participation in international discussion groups, meetings and workshops.

The opinions expressed within this book are not necessarily those of DFID or the collaborators but are solely those of the authors.

Contents

Abbreviations

APM	Area Pump Mechanic
CBO	Community-based organization
CVM	Contingent Valuation Method
DFID	Department for International Development (UK)
ESA	External Support Agency
HIPC	Heavily Indebted Poor Countries
HPM	Handpump Mechanic
HTH	High Test Hypochlorite
IMF	International Monetary Fund
IWRM	Integrated Water Resource Management
KAP	Knowledge Attitude and Practice
M&E	Monitoring and Evaluation
MDG	Millennium Development Goal
MPA	Methodology for Participatory Assessment
O&M	Operation and Maintenance
PMV	Preventive Maintenance Visit
POOM	Private Ownership, Operation and Maintenance
PPOM	Public-Private Operation and Maintenance
PREPP	Participation, Ranking, Experience, Perception & Partnership
uPVC	unplasticized Poly-Vinyl-Chloride
RWS	Rural Water Supply
RWSN	Rural Water Supply Network (formerly HTN)
SARAR	Self-esteem, Associative strengths, Resourcefulness, Action planning and Responsibility
SSA	sub-Saharan Africa
SWAp	Sector-Wide Approach
UNICEF	United Nations Children's Fund
VLOM	Village Level Operation and Maintenance
VLOMM	Village Level Operation and Management of Maintenance
WAS	Water Assurance Scheme
WASHE	Water, Sanitation and Hygiene Education
WATSAN	Water and Sanitation
WEDC	Water, Engineering and Development Centre
WHO	World Health Organization
WSP	Water and Sanitation Program
WTP	Willingness to pay
WUG	Water User Group

List of boxes

List of figures

List of tables

List of photographs

Preface

There is no 'blueprint' for sustainable rural water supply. Sustainability is a complex issue made up of many factors or 'building blocks'. Water supplies will not be made sustainable by simply piling these blocks on top of one another. Instead, they must be considered carefully in relation to one another to build sustainable services. A holistic approach to planning and implementation is essential.

Any process that leads to sustainable services must be flexible and dynamic. Steps can be used to guide this process in the right direction but the local context in each specific case will create different obstacles for which different solutions will be required. When tackling the issue of sustainability it is important to relate the wider picture (concerning policy, governance, institutions and finances) to local conditions (regarding communities, the environment and technology).

Rural water supply projects of the past have resulted in limited levels of sustainability because of what they were — projects. Water supply has traditionally been seen as part of the discipline of engineering and consequently has suffered from the engineering mindset of 'design and build'. The reason this approach has had limited success is that water supply is about much more than the provision of physical infrastructure. Just as healthcare is seen as an ongoing service for which there will always be demand, so too is water supply. There is, therefore, a need for a paradigm shift from projects to programmes, and from facilities to services. Programmes should be viewed as ongoing implementation strategies that ensure the sustainable provision of water services. They should facilitate user choice and encompass long-term institutional support to communities, sustainable financing mechanisms, monitoring, evaluation and review.

Policy and strategies need to be developed in a way which recognizes the service-based nature of water supply and the need for government to play a crucial role, especially in providing support, co-ordination and regulation. There is a range of institutional frameworks and models that can be used for service delivery, and respective governments should be free from external pressure to select the most appropriate options for them. Appropriate legislative and regulatory frameworks that are compatible with government policy must also be developed.

The relative strengths and weakness of the private sector, non-governmental organizations, faith-based organizations and community-based organizations need to be assessed, especially with respect to long-term sustainability of the institutions themselves. Capacity building and institutional strengthening needs should be identified and addressed to increase efficiency and effectiveness for permanent change. This is an ongoing process which requires effective monitoring and assessment.

User communities must be granted true decision-making authority. This means that they should be given comprehensive information needed to make informed decisions, without being pressured to follow the preferences of the facilitator. Communities and households should be free to select technology and service levels that suit them. They should also be free to select the most appropriate management system for operation and maintenance (O&M), including the option not to manage this themselves.

Community management requires ongoing institutional support. It must not be assumed that once a community has been 'sensitized', 'mobilized' and 'harmonized' it can be left alone to manage its own water supply. It should also not be assumed that a sense of ownership will lead automatically to a sense of responsibility and willingness to finance and manage. If community management systems are to be sustainable they require ongoing support from an overseeing institution to provide encouragement and motivation, monitoring, participatory planning, capacity building and specialist technical assistance. Appropriate legislation may also be necessary to establish community-based organizations as legal entities which legally own the systems they manage.

Sustainable financing mechanisms need to consider O&M and longer-term rehabilitation needs. This is essential if systems are to remain operational indefinitely. Implementers should strive to instil in users a sense of the need to pay for a water service. The emphasis must be shifted from paying for maintenance of a facility to paying for the provision of safe, adequate and accessible water. This concept of paying for water may be difficult to instil in water users in poor rural communities, but has the potential to remove many barriers to sustainable community financing.

Despite increased emphasis on social and community aspects of water supply, technology does still matter. Technology options which are low-cost, easy to understand and easy to maintain and repair are likely to be more sustainable than those that require specialist skills or equipment. Where feasible, household water supply options remove many of the obstacles to sustainability created by community ownership. Wherever possible, a range of options should be presented to potential users. Local innovation that brings the technology closer to the people should also be encouraged in the interests of sustainability.

Operation and maintenance of systems is of key importance in sustaining water services. Despite its growing prevalence in recent years, community management of O&M has had limited success and is not the only available option. New and innovative maintenance systems require further investigation, especially those that encourage indigenous private sector participation. These maintenance and repair systems are at the heart of service provision, especially for point water sources, and should be linked to long-term rehabilitation needs where relevant.

The problem of supplying spare parts for rural water supply facilities such as handpumps has often been highlighted in the past. Private sector provision of spares is not, in general, a viable option on the basis of profit alone. Where spares supply is linked to other private sector activities such as technical services for construction, operation and maintenance, and the provision of pumps and equipment, it is much more likely to be sustained. Alternative approaches include links with advertising or the involvement of not-for-profit organizations. The spares supply problem can be reduced to an even greater extent through the use of local technical solutions which do not require imported components, whether from overseas or from the national capital.

Monitoring, evaluation and review are the mortar that holds the building blocks for sustainability together and ensure the integration of the different sustainability factors. Monitoring is an ongoing process that should cover all levels of operation (from national governments to communities) and all aspects of rural water supply programmes (e.g. policy, institutions, finances, technology and O&M). At its most basic, monitoring should determine whether or not communities have access to water. It should also aim to assess management, operational, maintenance and environmental performance, for which measurable indicators must be set. Monitoring is necessary to determine overall success rates for a given programme, area or technology, and identify problems early in order to find timely solutions and pre-empt failures. Effective monitoring involves much more than data collection. It is important that data are evaluated and reviewed to inform decision-makers and to improve performance.

Water supply provision in rural areas of sub-Saharan Africa is far behind that in urban areas. International and national targets set a significant challenge for the rural water sector, which is likely to be impossible to overcome unless existing and future systems can be made more sustainable. Since access to safe water is a human right, it is essential that sector professionals take the issue of sustainability seriously. This means accepting the successes and shortfalls of the past, learning from these and overcoming the fear of change. A co-ordinated approach to planning, implementation and monitoring is essential in order to ensure that water services lead to sustained benefits for poor rural communities.

This book is based on extensive research into the issue of rural water supply sustainability in Africa. The initial focus of the research was water supplies using handpumps but initial findings indicated that many of the issues affecting sustainability were not dependent on technology choice. Consequently, the scope was broadened to consider rural water supply in general, to find out what features of projects and programmes promote sustainability.

Chapter 1

Introduction

1.1 About this book

1.1.1 Target users

The primary target users of this book are those responsible for planning, implementing and supporting rural water supply programmes and projects in Africa. The book is designed for local and regional government personnel, non-governmental organization (NGO) field managers and practitioners, and private contractors. The book should also provide a useful overview of rural water service sustainability for policy-makers, senior technical staff within line ministries, donors and their advisers.

Other potential users include social science, engineering and environmental research or educational institutions in sub-Saharan Africa, and members of rural communities who have an interest in water service sustainability.

1.1.2 Aims and objectives

The primary aims of the book are to raise awareness of issues that affect rural water supply sustainability, provide options for addressing these, using examples, and describe how these options can be implemented.

This book does not prescribe a 'one size fits all' solution but encourages a flexible approach to decision-making in which the key factors influencing sustainability are considered. The overall objective of the book is to enable the reader to appreciate the interrelationship between different issues that affect sustainability and the importance of adopting a holistic approach to planning and implementation, in order to achieve sustainable outcomes.

The book is based on field research in Ghana, Kenya, South Africa, Uganda and Zambia, and extensive research and consultation on the issue of rural water

1

supply sustainability. The research aimed to collect and analyse experiences from rural water supply projects and programmes, particularly in Africa, to find out what features promote their sustainability. The research focused initially on water supplies using handpumps but initial findings indicated that many of the issues affecting sustainability were not dependent on technology choice. The scope of the research was therefore broadened to consider all relevant technologies. Data from a variety of sources were synthesized to identify barriers to sustainability and options for achieving sustainable rural water services. An e-conference with participants from more than 30 countries and a number of international meetings and workshops were held in order to guide the research and to develop a useful resource for the sector. This book is the product of international collaboration (for more information on the research see Annex F).

1.1.3 How to use this book

It may not be necessary for the reader to read the book from beginning to end, but an awareness of the interrelationships between different sustainability factors is essential. This chapter presents an overview of the key factors that affect sustainability, around which the following chapters are designed. The reader can then select which factors to investigate further. Each chapter ends with a series of steps which guide the reader through a process to select appropriate options for enhanced sustainability. These steps are not designed as a 'blueprint' that is guaranteed to produce sustainable outcomes, but as a way of addressing the key issues raised. Sources for further reading are suggested at the end of each chapter.

Throughout the book examples from case studies are used to highlight key points and illustrate good and bad practice with respect to sustainability. The Annexes contain supporting information and tools for advocacy and monitoring.

1.2 Rural water supply in Africa

1.2.1 Service coverage

Africa, despite having a much lower population than Asia, accounts for almost one-third of the global population without access to improved water supply, and has the lowest service coverage figures of any continent. Around 6 per cent of the global burden of disease is water-related, and diarrhoeal and related diseases are responsible for the death of two million people a year, most of them children under five (WHO/UNICEF, 2000). The provision of safe water supply, accompanied by adequate sanitation services and hygiene education, represents

1

an effective health intervention that significantly reduces morbidity and mortality related to diarrhoeal disease.

The Millennium Development Goal (MDG) agreed at the United Nations in 2000 is to halve by 2015 the proportion of people without sustainable access to adequate and affordable safe drinking water (Annan, 2000). This goal will be much harder to achieve in Africa than in the rest of the developing world due to the low levels of existing coverage (Figure 1.1) coupled with high population growth rates in some areas. This is further compounded by the fact that existing services demonstrate limited sustainability throughout the continent.

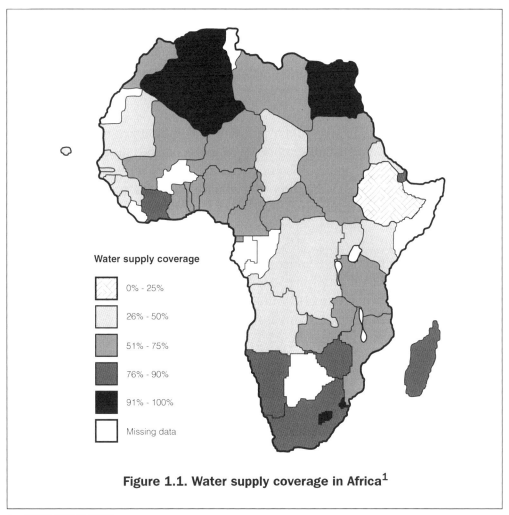

Water supply coverage

- 0% - 25%
- 26% - 50%
- 51% - 75%
- 76% - 90%
- 91% - 100%
- Missing data

Figure 1.1. Water supply coverage in Africa[1]

1. WHO/UNICEF, 2000

1.2.2 Why focus on rural supply?

According to the World Health Organization and the United Nations Children's Fund rural water coverage in Africa was 45 per cent in 2000, compared to 40 per cent in 1990, still leaving 237 million people unserved (WHO/UNICEF, 2000). Meanwhile, urban water coverage in Africa was much higher at 83 per cent in 2000, with only 37 million urban dwellers unserved. It is clear that rural areas of Africa are lagging significantly behind urban areas in water supply. This fact, coupled with high poverty levels in many rural areas and depressed levels of service sustainability, indicates a critical need for focused attention to the provision of potable water to rural communities in Africa. This book, therefore, addresses domestic water supply in the rural context only and many of the issues explored may not be appropriate for urban or peri-urban areas.

There are a number of reasons why the sustainability of water services in rural Africa is generally quite low. Some of these are related to environmental and technical issues, while many are related to social and management issues. The book will explore these different aspects in detail and present a range of options to make existing and future water systems more sustainable. Currently, many rural water supply projects and programmes focus on the goal of increasing service coverage through the implementation of new water systems and facilities. It is essential that this is accompanied by adequate attention to the crucial aspect of sustainability if any gains are not to be short-lived.

1.2.3 Water supply technologies

Rural water supply provision in sub-Saharan Africa (SSA) is typified by low-cost, simple technologies which can be operated, maintained and financed by poor rural communities or households. The choice of technology for improved water supplies, dependent on environmental, socio-economic and political conditions, includes:

- Protected springs;

- Handpump equipped boreholes and wells;

- Rainwater harvesting;

- Hand-dug wells;

- Gravity-fed systems; and

- Small-scale pumped systems.

1

Many of the issues addressed in this book are relevant to all these water supply technologies; and the importance of an open, flexible approach to technology selection is emphasized and promoted. There is no single technology option which can be used in all situations and each technology has specific advantages and limitations. Financial implications are important, both in terms of initial costs to the donor and community, and recurrent costs. In general, financial responsibility for ongoing operation and maintenance (O&M) of water systems lies with the user community. It is therefore essential that O&M costs are within the financial means of the users. Appropriate technical skills, tools and spare parts are also required to facilitate maintenance and repair. Whatever technology is selected, some level of O&M activity is necessary. There is an increasingly popular school of thought that the more simple the technology, the less the O&M requirements and the more sustainable it is likely to be (Lockwood, 2004; Sutton, 2003). While this is generally true, 'simple' technologies may not always be appropriate due to lack of user acceptability or restrictive environmental conditions.

The choice of technology in any particular situation is limited by the environment and, in particular, the water sources that are available locally. Many areas of SSA have few natural springs, and populations have traditionally relied on surface water or shallow groundwater. Groundwater provides potable water to an estimated 1.5 billion people worldwide daily (DFID, 2001) and has proved the most reliable resource for meeting rural water demand in sub-Saharan Africa (MacDonald & Davies, 2000). This is primarily because of the relative ease of access to water that does not usually need treatment prior to drinking. During the 1980s it became apparent that past policies had left a legacy of expensive and non-functioning water systems all over the world and consequently developing countries and donors began recognizing the importance of the handpump due to its low cost and ease of operation and maintenance, and the availability of shallow groundwater resources beneath much of Africa and Asia (Arlosoroff et al., 1987). Wells and boreholes with handpumps were therefore promoted as the most viable option for rural water supply in many developing countries. In the past two decades handpumps have become the principal technology for supplying water to over one billion people in rural areas in at least 40 developing countries (RWSN, 2004a).

Despite the popularity of the handpump, evidence suggests that it has failed to deliver satisfactory levels of sustainability. In 1994 it was estimated that 40 to 50 per cent of handpumps in SSA were not working (Diwi Consult & BIDR, 1994), and according to RWSN (2004b) there are currently approximately 250,000 handpumps in Africa, less than half of which are operational. This is backed up

1

by data from Uganda (DWD, 2002a) and South Africa (Hazelton, 2000) which indicate similar operational failure rates. An evaluation in Mali in 1997 found 90 per cent of pumps inoperable one year after installation (World Bank, 1997). Despite these low levels of sustainability, handpumps are likely to remain a major method of delivery of rural water supplies, as they are still considered the most appropriate and popular solution in many cases. For this reason, the book has a particular focus on the handpump but does not exclude alternative technologies.

1.3   Sustainability

The Cambridge Dictionary (2003) defines sustainable as 'able to continue over a period of time'; or 'causing little or no damage to the environment and therefore able to continue for a long time'. The key to sustainability would therefore appear to be to identify what enables a water supply to remain operational over a long period of time. However, it is important that the sustainability of a single handpump is separated from that of the project or programme under which it was installed. This book is primarily concerned about factors influencing project or programme sustainability, i.e. factors which facilitate the sustainable operation of a large number of pumps, rather than micro-issues affecting the function of a particular pump (or 'handpump function'). While these are obviously interconnected, and lessons can be learnt from pump-specific detail, it is important to focus on programmatic approaches and models that contribute to sustainability.

INTRODUCTION

The four success criteria linked to programme or project sustainability, as adopted by WELL (1998), are:

- Effectiveness;
- Equity;
- Efficiency; and
- Replicability.

Parry-Jones et al. (2001a) found a wide range of definitions for sustainability relating to water supply projects, but concluded that the most frequently recurring core issues in these definitions were:

- Minimal external assistance in the long term;
- Financing of regular operation and maintenance costs by users; and
- Continued flow of benefits over a long period.

Davis and Brikké (1995) defined a drinking water supply as sustainable if:

- The water consumed is not over-exploited but naturally replenished;
- Facilities are maintained in a condition which ensures a reliable and adequate water supply; and
- The benefits of the supply continue to be realized over a prolonged period of time.

This definition fits in with the findings above and is useful in setting out three simple requirements of a sustainable supply. These can be combined with the WELL success criteria to develop the following definition, which is adopted for this book:

A water service is sustainable if the water sources are not over-exploited but naturally replenished, facilities are maintained in a condition which ensures a reliable and adequate water supply, the benefits of the supply continue to be realized by all users indefinitely, and the service delivery process demonstrates a cost-effective use of resources that can be replicated.

A 'water service' means the ongoing provision of water of adequate quality and quantity to all people within a defined area of service. The 'users' include all those in the community which the systems serve, and the 'service delivery process' means the way in which systems are installed, operated, maintained and repaired. It is important to distinguish a 'sustainable' water service from a 'successful' one. A project or programme in which facilities are operational over a prolonged period of time due to heavy external financial and technical support may be successful, but the approach is likely to be very inefficient and impossible or difficult to replicate elsewhere. Under the definition such a project could not be said to be sustainable. The inclusion of equity as one of the criteria for sustainability is debatable, yet since water is now seen as a human right (World Water Council, 2002) it is essential that water services reach all, including the poor and vulnerable.

Sustainability is a complex, dynamic concept which is made up of many interrelated components. Once a general definition for sustainability is developed it is important to identify the factors that contribute to its achievement. For this reason, a number of sustainability factors have been identified which constitute 'building blocks' for sustainability.

Based on a review of previous studies and existing literature (Abrams, 1998; WELL, 1998; Mukherjee & van Wijk, 2002) eight factors have been identified as being critical to achieving sustainability of rural water supplies:

- Policy context;

- Institutional arrangements;

- Financial and economic issues;

- Community and social aspects;

- Technology and the natural environment;

- Spare parts supply;

- Maintenance systems; and

- Monitoring.

Sustainability cannot be achieved by focusing on one or two of these aspects in isolation. Some water supply projects and programmes stress the importance of single issues such as community ownership or supply chains or appropriate technology in order to achieve sustainability. These may all contribute to sustainability but do not provide the solution in themselves. It is essential,

1

therefore, that a holistic approach be taken which addresses all sustainability factors and the relationships between them.

1.3.1   Interdependence

Figure 1.2 illustrates the way in which sustainable services depend on all these 'building blocks' and that without any one of them the supporting wall of sustainability begins to weaken. Each layer in the wall depends on the layers below and supports the layers above. National and regional policies are likely to affect all other sustainability factors and provide the overarching context in which these factors must be viewed. Planning is heavily influenced by policy and must address all the 'building blocks' in the wall above. The focus of implementation is on technology and the natural environment, but this must consider other issues including O&M and monitoring. O&M includes maintenance systems and spare parts supply, and is dependent on all the blocks below, including technology choice, community aspects and institutional issues. Monitoring is of key importance for achieving long-term sustainability and will be influenced by, and should address, all other layers and blocks in the wall.

The sustainability factors or building blocks identified above address all the issues covered in our definition of sustainability including functionality, project effectiveness, equity, replicability, and efficiency. There is a great degree of interdependency between different factors, with monitoring addressing all other factors and acting as the mortar that keeps the building blocks together. The following chapters of this book describe the key issues which contribute to, and hinder, sustainability under each sustainability factor.

1.3.2   Measuring sustainability

In order to measure sustainability, or the effect of factors and issues on sustainability, the four success criteria adopted by WELL (1998) can be used. In discussing specific issues under the sustainability factors in the following chapters, these criteria will be revisited repeatedly.

Effectiveness is the degree to which rural water services and interventions meet their objectives. This comprises the functionality of the water supply facility, issues around water quantity and quality, and associated benefits such as improved health, time saved and income generated.

Efficiency represents the output produced per unit of resources. These include financial, human and physical resources for service delivery, operation and maintenance. Water services may operate successfully but overexploit natural

1

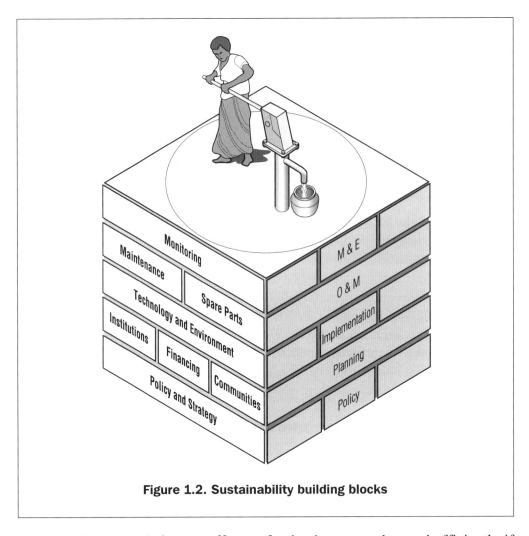

Figure 1.2. Sustainability building blocks

resources (e.g. water), human effort or funds; these must be used efficiently if services can be said to be sustainable.

Equity is the degree to which water services reach all members of communities, including the poor and disadvantaged groups. Issues related to vulnerability, poverty and gender are of key importance to ensure that equity is achieved. Water services must be affordable and accessible to all if they are to be equitable.

Replicability is essential to ensure the expansion of water services and to increase sustainable access to safe drinking water. This concept combines technical, environmental, financial and institutional issues. Flexible approaches that can be replicated are essential for sustainability.

Chapter 2

Policy and strategy

National policies and strategies need to be developed in a way which recognizes the service-based nature of water supply and the need for government to play a crucial role, especially in providing support, co-ordination and regulation. There is a range of institutional frameworks and models that can be used for service delivery, and respective governments should be free from external pressure to select the most appropriate options for them. Appropriate legislative and regulatory frameworks that are compatible with government policy must also be developed. This chapter aims to identify where policy may have an adverse effect on sustainability, how this impacts on existing roles and responsibilities, and what changes may be required.

2.1   Policies and strategies affecting water supply

The terms 'policy' and strategy' are often used interchangeably. For the purposes of this book the following definitions are used:

- 'Policy' is a specific statement that guides or directs decision-making; and

- Strategy' refers to an elaborate and systematic plan of action.

There is a wide range of government policies and strategies that affect rural water supplies, some directly, others indirectly. Many of these have a significant impact on the sustainability of water services, intentionally or otherwise.

2.1.1   National policies

A number of general national policies influence sustainability. Many African countries have developed similar generic policies due, primarily, to the influence of the International Monetary Fund (IMF) and World Bank. The most common of these are policies to promote:

- Decentralization and civil service reform;

- Privatization;

- Economic liberalization and free trade;

- Poverty reduction and health improvement; and

- Government co-ordination of donors and NGOs.

In addition, there are often policies specific to the water sector, such as:

- Community management of water systems; and

- Handpump standardization.

These policies and subsequent strategies, and how they impact on service sustainability, are addressed in the following sections of this chapter.

2.1.2 Poverty Reduction Strategy Papers

Poverty Reduction Strategy Papers (PRSPs) describe a country's macroeconomic, structural and social policies and programmes to promote growth and reduce poverty, as well as associated external financing needs. Many African governments have now developed, or are developing, PRSPs through a participatory process involving civil society and development partners, including the World Bank and the IMF. The emphasis placed on water and sanitation in these strategy papers varies enormously, from entire chapters devoted to the subject, to passing references alone.

The World Bank (2004) aims to assist policy-makers and sector departments to design PRSP water and sanitation strategies that actively address the needs of the poor. The approach used is to:

- Provide guidance on analysis of the linkages between poverty, water and sanitation;

- Assist in identifying problem areas that require intervention and in defining objectives;

- Provide a menu of possible public interventions, and a framework that assists in their prioritization;

- Assist in defining a monitoring and evaluation framework that allows re-evaluation of the linkages, appraisal of poverty outcomes, and assessment of whether the chosen intervention has been effective.

Sustainable rural water supply has a number of positive effects on poverty reduction, such as reducing the burden of disease and money spent on medical treatment; releasing time previously used for collecting water for other activities; and facilitating income generation through productive use of water. Where existing policy and strategy papers fail to emphasize these links, advocacy campaigns may be necessary to highlight the need to incorporate rural water supply strategies into national PRSPs.

2

2.1.3 Rural water supply strategies

Many African governments have ambitious targets for increasing rural water supply coverage in line with international targets such as the Millennium Development Goals. In general, these national targets include time-bound percentage coverage figures and set appropriate service levels in terms of litres per person per day, water quality standards and distance of water points from dwellings. Many African countries have developed rural water supply strategies in order to reach these targets. These strategies may be in the form of five or ten year operational plans, or may cover longer time periods. Current strategies from different African countries are typified by the following:

- The setting of minimum quantities of water per person per day;

- Water sector reforms that define water as an economic good and adopt an integrated approach to delivering water and sanitation services;

- A decentralized approach to service delivery in which the role of the public sector at all levels is mainly to monitor, regulate and facilitate the performance of stakeholders in O&M;

- A demand responsive approach to the delivery of community based water supplies, for which users are responsible for managing O&M to ensure sustainability;

- Private sector provision of all goods and technical services including the provision and distribution of spare parts; and

- Capacity building and sector reform.

In addition, some examples of recurring issues are:

- Integration of hygiene education with the provision of water and sanitation facilities;

- Gender mainstreaming at all levels of sector activities;

- Appropriate technology and research activities;

- Cost recovery in order to ensure sustainability;

- Monitoring stakeholder, system and sector performance; and

- Integrated Water Resource Management (IWRM) promoting economic use of water.

Many national strategies are influenced by external donors and international organizations, and hence there is a significant degree of uniformity of policy among different countries, at least on paper. As a result, despite local differences in culture, environment and politics, many effects of policy and strategy are region-, rather than country-, specific. These are explored in more detail in the following sections of this chapter.

2.1.4   Sector-Wide Approaches

The Sector-Wide Approach (SWAp) is a mechanism whereby governments and development partners agree on a strategy to achieve improvement in sector performance and more effective use of resources **through programmes rather than projects**. Various definitions of SWAp have been put forward, reflecting a range of views as to what is actually meant by this term. CIDA (2000) suggests the following definition:

'The sector-wide approach defines a method of working between Government and donors. The defining characteristics are that all significant funding for the sector supports a single policy and expenditure programme, under Government leadership, adopting common approaches across the sector, and progressing towards relying on Government procedures to disburse and account for all funds.'

SWAps have already been developed and implemented by a small number of countries in Africa and are likely to be developed by many more in future. At the heart of the strategy is **central budget support**, whereby donors give funds directly to central government which allocates funds for sector activities to local government. This is sometimes referred to as a 'basket fund' approach. While there is no fixed formula for their development, SWAps should always follow a highly consultative process to ensure that all stakeholders participate in the development of the approach. Typical features of SWAp include:

- It is developed on principles of partnership and collaboration and the goal of achieving sustainable access to water supply and sanitation services;

- All significant funding for the sector supports a single policy and expenditure programme;

- Government provides leadership for the programme;

- Common implementation and management approaches are applied across the sector by all partners;

- The programme progresses towards relying on government procedures to disburse and account for all funds.

2

One of the key features of SWAp is to improve the sustainability of services (DWD, 2002a). The shift from facility-driven 'projects' with a finite lifespan to service-based 'programmes' has significant potential to achieve this aim. The overall drive for greater efficiency and effectiveness should also contribute to service sustainability, as should greater co-ordination and consistency among implementing agencies. However, if these benefits are to be realized, it is essential that government bodies are accountable, that activities and outputs are adequately monitored, and that roles and responsibilities are clearly defined.

2.2   Roles and responsibilities

National policies and water supply strategies inevitably determine the roles and responsibilities of different sector stakeholders. Increasingly, African countries are adopting the following structure:

In the framework shown in Figure 2.1, decentralized government institutions take on an enabling role and are responsible for initial financing and regulation, facilitation and monitoring of sector stakeholders. The private sector is responsible for the delivery of technical services such as drilling, installation and spare parts supply; and community-based organizations (CBOs) are responsible for the management and financing of O&M. Actual O&M activities may be conducted by the private sector or communities themselves. This framework presents both opportunities and threats to sustainability which are outlined below and expanded in Chapter 3.

2.2.1   National government

National government is the principal policy-making body and should also be the leader, administrator and co-ordinator of sector activities. The appropriate line ministry or agency for rural water supply should be the key driver in developing and implementing sector strategies. These should include overall strategies for service delivery and monitoring of sector activities, but these should not be so

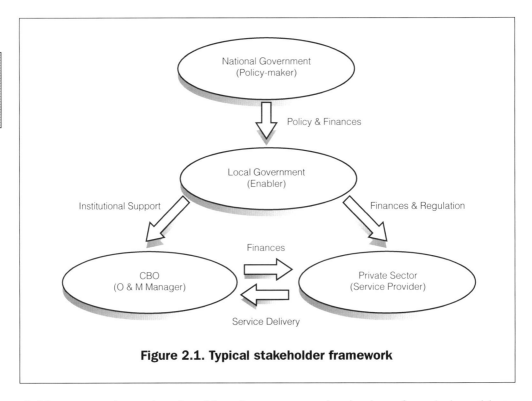

Figure 2.1. Typical stakeholder framework

rigid as to restrict regional and local government institutions from being able to develop sub-strategies suited to local context.

When national governments become reliant on financial support from external donors for virtually all investment in the water sector they may become locked into the dependency syndrome. This places a Government in a difficult position since they require financial support, yet inevitably lose some autonomy as a result of this. Government staff may be unwilling to say 'no' to, or disagree with, policy initiatives of major donors for fear of losing precious external funding. If policy is to be truly developed by governments they must develop the capacity to say 'no' and to seek ways in which to generate internal revenue for water supply provision. This is likely to lead to the promotion of low-cost solutions which can be sustained, rather than ongoing dependency on high investment solutions and the need for repeated rehabilitation.

2.2.2 Local government

Current PRSPs from many African countries promote decentralized government involvement in service provision, in partnership with the private sector.

Opportunities

Opportunities provided by decentralization policies are that local government:

- Provides a sustainable institution close to the communities served;

- Is strategically located to determine local needs and priorities; and

- Is ideally placed to develop and implement monitoring strategies.

Constraints

Current constraints to decentralization include:

- Insufficient resources, knowledge and expertise in local government institutions,

- Lack of local revenue/taxation and over reliance on central government funding;

- Underdeveloped private sector unable to provide services;

- A mismatch of knowledge and capacity between the private and local public sector;

- Increased layers of corruption at different levels of government;

- Lack of regulation to ensure transparency in public-private partnerships; and

- Central ministries of constituent sectors (health, water, environment, local government etc.) may be unwilling to devolve powers to local authorities.

The basic principle of decentralization can make a valuable contribution to sustainable rural water services, but only if the above constraints, which are considerable, can be overcome. Perhaps the most crucial constraint is that local government institutions often lack the resources and expertise to provide sufficient regulation and support to the private sector (Sohail, 2001). It is essential that institutions be provided with sufficient resources, the capacity of public and private institutions is sufficiently strengthened, and appropriate structures are developed to ensure accountability and transparency. If greater autonomy and responsibility is to be given to district level institutions then there is a need for a regional power base to support, monitor and regulate activities.

2.2.3 Community-based organizations

Many government strategies stipulate that rural water services should be community-based. This means that communities select a water supply technology, of which they become owners, are involved in its implementation, and are responsible for managing the operation and maintenance of their chosen technology (they may or may not actually conduct maintenance themselves). This assumes that communities are:

1. Given a range of technologies and information in order to make an informed choice;

2. Willing and able to manage O&M (this may mean that they use a third party to actually carry out maintenance and repair); and

3. Willing and able to finance the cost of O&M in the long-term.

These three criteria are prerequisites for sustainable community management and yet they are not often investigated fully before a water supply initiative commences, despite rhetoric to the contrary. Communities are rarely provided with sufficient information and options in order to make an informed decision regarding technology choice, and hence their willingness and ability to manage and finance O&M on a long-term basis is not firmly established. Community-based organizations (CBOs) usually take the form of committees which lack legal status, meaning they are often unable to take legal ownership of systems and facilities. These issues are addressed in more detail in Chapter 4.

It is also important to note that current strategies do little to address long-term rehabilitation needs apart from recognizing the fact that this is currently beyond the means of most communities, and the need for government to provide for this in the medium term. This issue is addressed in detail in Chapter 9.

Box 2.1. Community management policy[1]

The National policy for water resource management in Kenya states that:

'The basic solution to the problems in operation and maintenance of water supply schemes ... lies in the full involvement of the users'; and

'The Government will continue to promote the development of water systems that are self-sustaining and where the beneficiaries themselves are encouraged to take full responsibility for operating and maintaining systems.'

---

1. MWR, 1999

Box 2.1 presents a typical example of governments' views of community management, i.e. that sustained O&M comes down to the role of the community alone. The term 'self-sustaining' is slightly ambiguous but implies that communities should be capable of sustaining their water supplies all by themselves. Such assumptions are dangerous since experience to date shows that **successful community management requires ongoing institutional support**.

While community-based water services have demonstrated some high levels of sustainability, this is only the case where there is a strong institution (government or NGO) in place to support communities. If policies are to continue to promote community management they must also recognize the necessity for institutional support if water services are to be sustainable. It should be noted, however, that even this is no guarantee, since institutions themselves may not be sustainable.

The alternative is to develop policies and strategies that do not prescribe stakeholder roles but set out a more flexible framework. Chapter 7 presents a number of different models for operation and maintenance of rural water supplies, some of which fit the community management model while others do not. The model that is most likely to lead to enhanced sustainability levels will depend on the local context.

2.2.4   Private sector

Privatization is another key component of many African governments' poverty reduction strategies. While there is nothing inherently wrong with private sector involvement, it is important to recognize its limitations and some of the constraints to its promotion.

Opportunities

Opportunities provided by privatization policies are:

- Income generation for the indigenous private sector;

- Development and growth of indigenous private sector where it does not exist or is very weak;

- Increased potential for local revenue generation through taxation of business;

- Increased efficiency of service delivery by promoting competition; and

- Economic growth and employment.

Constraints

Constraints relating to privatization include:

- The local private sector is often underdeveloped and lacks required expertise, especially in 'software' areas;

- Private sector organizations may lack the capacity and skills needed to enter into and manage contracts;

- Private companies may be less likely to relate positively to communities;

- Tendering for contracts locally increases potential for corruption at this level; and

- The prioritization of profits over services may lead to social exclusion, especially affecting the poorest in society.

In order to overcome these constraints, proficient government regulation is essential including sound pro-poor strategies. Effective contract management strategies also need to be put in place to prevent over-pricing or sub-standard workmanship.

Box 2.2 presents the case where increased private sector participation has the potential to undo the progress made by the community-focused NGO approaches of the past.

Box 2.2. Privatization[1]

In Ghana and Uganda, decentralized government institutions are now encouraged to contract out to the private sector which currently lacks the necessary skills and expertise to deliver. This is especially the case for 'software' activities such as community mobilization, where the experience and skills of NGOs are fast becoming under-used. As a result, many lessons learnt from the past are likely to be lost and there is the danger that rural water supply is once again becoming facility-driven rather than demand-driven.

---

1. Harvey, 2003

Arguably, one positive effect of civil service reform programmes and downsizing is that skilled individuals who previously worked in government are driven into the private sector. This presents an opportunity for the private sector to develop in partnership with local government. For this to be successful, however, appropriate support strategies are required that focus on a limited number of areas, promote quality of workmanship and business viability, and develop appropriate monitoring mechanisms (Danert et al., 2003).

With the increasing move to budget support, local government regulation and private sector implementation, it is essential that services remain responsive to community demand (see Chapter 4). If the Millennium Development Goals are to be achieved, water supply coverage must be increased, but if more emphasis is placed on the facility than systems to sustain services, any gains will be short-lived.

Sometimes there is an unwillingness in the private sector to relate appropriately to the community and to properly involve them in relevant stages of the project cycle, especially if this is seen as time- or resource-consuming. It is therefore important that community-related requirements are built into contracts and that such activities are regulated.

Another downside of privatization is the increased potential for corruption. Corruption among external support agencies, NGOs, governments and the private sector remains a serious obstacle to sustainability since it reduces efficiency ('a cost-effective use of resources') and stifles opportunity for long-term solutions. It is therefore essential that privatization be accompanied by transparent regulation.

Opportunities for the private sector must be evaluated carefully and realistically, particularly concerning the provision of community/social expertise, and the provision of handpump spare parts, which is not often commercially viable as a stand-alone activity (see Chapter 8). An assessment of existing private sector capacity is also essential to determine what level of involvement is realistic and what needs to be done to increase this. Incentives for private sector participation must also be analysed; profit, 'making a living', professional pride and social status and esteem may all play a role in sustaining private sector involvement.

2.2.5 Non-governmental organizations

Where government policy promotes privatization, decentralization and Sector-Wide Approaches, the traditional role of non-governmental and not-for-profit organizations may be threatened. Traditionally, many rural water systems have been installed under projects funded by donors and implemented by NGOs, many of which are skilled in participatory approaches, appropriate technology development and innovative management strategies. If donors are now to commit funds to central government, which then allocates resources to local

2

government, which then contracts out service delivery and construction to the private sector, what role remains for the NGO?

At worst, NGOs will cease to operate, the experiences of local and international NGOs will be forgotten, and valuable knowledge will be lost. At best, NGOs can work in partnership with the public and private sectors to build capacity and share knowledge, or can reinvent themselves as private sector organizations to bid for contracts. The reality is, for the time being at least, that there is still a vital role for NGOs and not-for-profit organizations, since many African governments have not adopted SWAps or have a long way to go until they are effectively implemented. It also likely that charities and faith-based organizations will continue to implement water supply interventions using funds from charitable contributions. These should, however, be **implemented in a manner consistent with government policy**.

2.3   From policy to practice

Policies and strategies are written words on paper, but should be much more than that if they are to result in the desired goal of sustainable water services. In order for policy to be put into practice there must be:

• Institutions and personnel to drive policy implementation;

• Stakeholders that adhere to policy and strategy guidelines;

• Consistent regulatory and legislative frameworks; and

• Adequate financial resources.

2.3.1   Policy drivers

National governments must be responsible for developing and driving policy. For this reason it is essential that government institutions 'own' their respective policies and strategies. This means that they must believe these are best practice for the sector and that they should be in the driving seat from the onset of strategy development. National and regional government institutions should act in partnership with other sector stakeholders to develop appropriate strategies and should establish a national action committee to oversee its development and implementation (see Section 2.5). Without such a body charged with this task, it is likely to take an excessively long time before any changes to policy affect practice. Political will and commitment are essential.

2.3.2 Stakeholders

It is important that all sector stakeholders respect and adhere to government policy, and work within the strategy framework developed. External Support Agencies (ESAs) and NGOs must be willing to follow policy and strategies. Inconsistent practices of the past can often be put down to non-adherence to policy and the sidelining of government. Government institutions, from national to local level, have a responsibility to monitor and regulate ESAs and NGOs. They should also ensure that they do not bend policies due to external pressure as a result of an offer of increased investment.

2.3.3 Legislature and regulation

It is essential that regulatory and legislative frameworks correspond to policy and strategies, otherwise these will be impossible to implement. Where necessary, appropriate legislature will need to be introduced in order to enforce rules and regulations. This should consider issues of land and communal ownership and consequences for community-based water systems. Where community management systems are to be promoted it may be necessary to establish community-based organizations as legal entities. Regulatory frameworks for public-private partnerships are also necessary to ensure satisfactory standards of workmanship by private contractors and effective contract management. Anti-corruption legislation is also likely to be important for increased efficiency of decentralized systems.

2.4   Policy and technology

2.4.1   Handpump standardization

The 1970s and 1980s saw the development of 'Village Level Operation and Maintenance' (VLOM) handpumps that could be maintained at community level and whose specifications were available in the public domain (Colin, 1999). Many African governments were encouraged by external donors to use a small number of public domain handpumps to support the development of local manufacture and viable markets. This was based on the belief that limiting use to a few locally manufactured public domain handpumps would stimulate self-sufficiency and eventually create a demand for spares that would result in the emergence of distribution channels to meet it.

Two decades on, many governments have adopted handpump standardization policies, whereby usually only one or two public domain pumps are allowed to be used in the country. Such policies have had positive effects by minimizing the number of different handpump models in country and encouraging the provision of spare parts, but there is no evidence that sustainable supply chains have

2

developed as a result. Local manufacture also remains limited, with the majority of pumps and spares being imported. This may be due, in part, to limited incentives for local private entrepreneurs and lack of government support.

Advantages

Advantages of handpump standardization policies are that:

- The number of handpump models requiring specialist spares and skills in a particular country is reduced;

- The quality of pumps and components can be more readily assured since there is a standard against which they can be tested; and

- Opportunities are created for local enterprise where standardized pumps and spares are manufactured locally.

Disadvantages

Disadvantages of standardization include:

- Lack of competition among manufacturers to improve the quality of products;

- Lack of incentives for local innovators and entrepreneurs; and

- Inflexible attitudes to alternative technologies.

The term standardization' is understood by some to apply solely to public domain 'standardized' pumps, but the term is often used simply to describe a limitation of handpump choice in a particular country. Some countries have chosen to standardize on a range of pumps including proprietary or non public domain pumps. Whichever pumps are selected, it is important that standardization is carefully regulated and should allow flexibility so as not to stifle local competition, innovation and manufacturing. If this not the case, such policies simply sustain dependency on imported pumps and spare parts, the quality of which may be poor.

Another issue to consider is where there are large numbers of particular models of existing pumps which have not been selected as 'standardized' pumps by the government. Box 2.3 gives an example of this in which the sustainability of over 1000 water points is potentially threatened rather than enhanced by the standardization policy adopted in one country. This emphasizes the need for flexibility in policy development and implementation. The process by which standardization is introduced is also important, since where all interested parties are involved the policy is likely to be more successful.

Box 2.3. Handpump standardization[1]

The Government of Uganda has chosen to standardize on the Uganda versions of the India Mark II and Mark III pumps (known as the U2 and U3). These pumps are manufactured locally and adapted to suit local groundwater conditions and community needs. However, there are over 1000 existing Consallen handpumps in the east of the country. They have been installed by an NGO using private, DFID and EU funding, and currently demonstrate higher levels of reliability than the U2/U3, but despite proof of the ability to manufacture these pumps locally the Consallen was not selected as a standard pump for Uganda. In this instance it can be argued that standardization has done little to improve sustainability.

---

1. Harvey, 2003

2.4.2 Economic liberalization and tax-free aid

Many poverty reduction strategies in Africa promote economic liberalization which means the removal of trade restrictions. This makes it cheaper to import public domain pumps, such as the India Mark II and Afridev, and associated spare parts from India than to manufacture the same pumps locally, even where there is existing capacity to do this (see Box 2.4). The procurement procedures

---

Box 2.4. Economic liberalization and tax-free aid[1]

Kenya has existing capacity to manufacture the Afridev pump in-country but the commercial viability of this is threatened by the importation of cheaper Afridev pumps from Asia. Since import duty is waived for handpumps these imported pumps are cheaper in-country than those manufactured locally. Local companies simply cannot compete with these subsidized imports. If spare parts are imported separately from pumps, import duty must be paid, making the cost of these significant. However, there is no incentive for manufacturers to produce spares locally since the profit margins are negligible compared to that for pumps, which they are unable to sell. This situation is a result of economic liberalization, 'duty-free aid' and the cost-saving practices of donors.

---

1. Harvey et al., 2003

and tax-free status of some External Support Agencies (ESAs) and NGOs often compound the problem. Instead of buying locally, donors opt for the cheapest

2

price internationally and recipient governments waive import duties and other taxes which reduces costs further. This benefits the donor by reducing costs but undermines sustainability since it increases dependency on imported pumps and does not stimulate local private-sector provision of pumps and spares. Evidence suggests that the more local the purchase of the pump (for example at regional or district level) the more likely the retailer is to make sure spares are available locally (WSP, 2000; Harvey et al., 2003).

The key differences between the predominant current situation of imported pumps and the optimum situation of locally developed and manufactured pumps are summarized below:

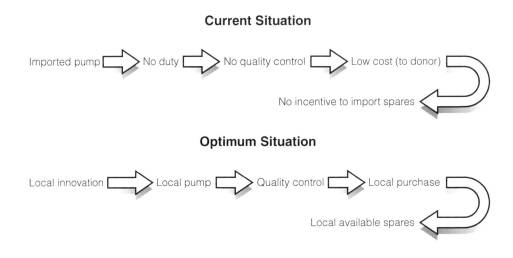

Where communities are presented with a real choice concerning technology they may also apply pressure for local provision and changes to policy. Technology choices presented to communities should include household options, low- and medium-cost communal options and different types of handpumps. They should also be informed of where equipment, pumps and parts are available (see Section 4.3).

Government policy can have a key impact on the sustainability of handpump-based water supplies by supporting local innovation and manufacture. This may mean imposing appropriate duties on imports while providing incentives for local enterprise. It may also mean greater restrictions on donor procurement practices (see Section 3.7). Currently, policies favour donors and foreign manufacturers more than they support sustainable services. Whether pumps are imported or produced locally, third party quality control is an important measure to ensure appropriate standards for equipment and components.

2.4.3   Government rhetoric

Even if not formalized in official policies and documents, government rhetoric can have a significant influence on water supply technology and sustainability. This may include the promotion of one particular technology, such as the handpump, or negative impressions concerning another, such as the Rope Pump. False promises or impressions created by politicians that government will provide and finance water supplies can also have a serious influence on sustainability. Research has shown (Reed, 1995) that where even the slightest perception exists that government will provide, communities are very reluctant to manage and finance their own services.

Box 2.5. Government rhetoric[1]

'Water - gathered and stored since the beginning of time in layers of granite and rock, in the embrace of dams, the ribbons of rivers - will one day, unheralded, modestly, easily, simply flow out to every South African who turns a tap. That is my dream.'

---

1.   Antje Krog, preamble to the South African Government's White Paper on Water Policy

Box 2.5 gives an example of government rhetoric from South Africa; while this describes what may be a worthy goal, the fact that a key strategic government document predetermines technology (i.e. piped water supply) is likely to support the idea that low-cost alternatives are sub-standard and threaten the sustainability of existing rural water supplies that rely on these.

2.5   Steps towards appropriate policy

The policies and strategies outlined above have considerable potential to affect the sustainability of rural water supplies. Figure 2.2 summarizes the steps that can be taken to develop appropriate policy and strategy. There is **no guarantee** that fulfilment of these steps will lead to policies resulting in sustainable water services. For this reason it is a dynamic process that may be repeated at regular intervals, in order to review and revise policy decisions.

Before this process can be embarked upon it is necessary to determine who should be responsible for driving it. Ideally, government should be in the driving seat and work in partnership with other stakeholders. A national action

2

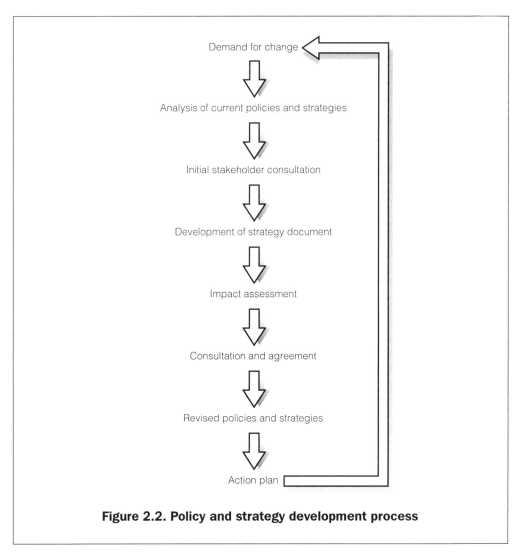

Demand for change

Analysis of current policies and strategies

Initial stakeholder consultation

Development of strategy document

Impact assessment

Consultation and agreement

Revised policies and strategies

Action plan

Figure 2.2. Policy and strategy development process

committee for rural water supply can be formed including representatives of all government ministries and departments involved, directly or indirectly, with water supply. The chairmanship of this committee should remain with the principal department responsible for water supply provision. A policy planning schedule can be developed in which the process is repeated at five-yearly intervals.

Step 1. Demand for change

The first step in developing appropriate policy and strategy for rural water supply is to assess the demand for changing current policies and strategies. Clearly, if there is nothing wrong with these, there is no need to develop new ones. Demand for change is most likely to arise if existing goals and targets are not being met or are unlikely to be met, levels of efficiency and effectiveness are inadequate, institutional capacities are insufficient, or overall sustainability levels are too low. It should be noted, however, that demand for change in itself does not necessarily mean that there is a need to change policy. It may be that change is needed in implementation or management instead. Or it may be that ESAs and NGOs, and even government agencies, simply are not following government policy. If this is the case, it is necessary to find out why. Legislative and regulatory frameworks may be incompatible with policy and prevent effective implementation. Demand for change can be best measured through a detailed monitoring and evaluation exercise to review current levels of sustainability and variables affecting these. A review of the water sector may also be necessary to assess sectoral trends locally, regionally and globally which may influence the development of new policies.

Step 2. Analysis of current policies and strategies

Assuming that there is a recognized need and demand for change it is then necessary to analyse current policy and strategies carefully. This should include rural water supply goals, policies and strategies, as well as national policies and strategies for other sectors which may affect the water sector. It is important to identify where policy may have an adverse effect on sustainability and how this impacts on existing roles and responsibilities. Table 2.1 can be used to identify policies which may hinder sustainability.

The sustainability snapshot tool can be used to identify sustainability problems in consultation with communities (see Section 9.4). It is also essential that legal and legislative issues be analysed fully, including overlaps and gaps in legislature. Any policy developed without appropriate consideration of legislative aspects runs the risk of being incomplete or at worst, irrelevant. Once the relevant policy issues have been investigated the issue(s) with the most negative impact on sustainability can be identified. On the basis of this, a range of possible changes to policy in order to rectify the situation can be considered.

Step 3. Initial stakeholder consultation

If the policy analysis indicates that current strategies are hindering sustainability then a consultation process should commence to lead to the development of an appropriate strategy. The first step in consultation is to identify stakeholders that should be involved in the process; these are likely to include government ministries and departments, external support agencies, other institutions/

Table 2.1. Policy and strategy analysis

Identified sustainability problem	Relevant policy issues and possible effects
Environmental or technical constraint to operation (e.g. groundwater quality/yield)	**Handpump standardization** - is the selected technology appropriate for the prevailing environmental conditions? **Decentralization** - is local government adequately monitoring the actions (siting, drilling, installation) of private contractors **Privatization** - does the private sector have the technical and human resources to successfully undertake the work?
Low user acceptability of facilities and low willingness to manage/ pay for O&M	**Decentralization** - is local government undertaking/facilitating sufficient community mobilization prior to implementation? **Privatization** - is the private sector undertaking sufficient community mobilization prior to implementation? **Community management** - do communities have the necessary incentives, knowledge and information to support O&M?
Lack of technical capacity to undertake maintenance and repair	**Decentralization** - is local government able to provide adequate support? **Privatization** - does the private sector have sufficient technical capacity to undertake O&M? **Community management** - do communities have the necessary skills and knowledge to undertake O&M?
Lack of technical resources (spares/tools) to undertake maintenance and repair	**Handpump standardization** - are tools and spares available for the selected technology? **Community management** - do communities have access to appropriate tools and spare parts? **Economic liberalization** - are local alternative technologies unable to compete with imported equipment?
Lack of finances for O&M	**Handpump standardization** - is the selected technology too costly for communities to maintain? **Privatization** - are private service providers setting tariffs too high for users? **Community management** - do communities have the necessary organizational capacity to finance O&M? Cost-recovery targets - do cost recovery targets place too much expectation on communities?

organizations and communities. A comprehensive consultation process is required to collect representative views of different types of communities, to ensure that these feed into the process. The stakeholders can then form a policy review committee and task groups to focus on specific policy issues. This process of consultation should include workshops and public hearings to facilitate dialogue.

Step 4. Development of strategy document

The next step is for the review committee and task groups to develop a strategy document. This document should outline the overall goals and targets, and identify the roles of key stakeholders and financial requirements in order to achieve these. It should also present an appropriate regulatory and legislative framework in which to operate. Key issues that should be addressed in a strategy document include:

- Overall objectives and goals;

- Desired outputs;

- Policy actions to achieve outputs (including roles and capacity building needs);

- Summary of indicators and milestones; and

- Investment and financing plan.

It may be useful to develop the strategy using a logical framework approach, a simple example of which is presented in Table 2.2. By incorporating measurable indicators into the framework this can be established as a monitoring tool to measure progress in strategy implementation. An appropriate framework should consider institutional, regulatory and monitoring arrangements, stakeholder participation, sustainable financing mechanisms and budgetary allocations, and technology development and selection.

Step 5. Impact assessment

Having produced the first draft of the strategy document it is then necessary to assess the likely impact of the new strategy on government institutions and other stakeholders, including communities. This should include an assessment of stakeholder capacities to fulfil respective duties. Financial, environmental and socio-economic impacts should also be investigated.

Step 6. Consultation and agreement

The results of the impact assessment should be fed into the strategy document and appropriate revisions undertaken. It is then necessary to enter a further stage of consultation to ensure that all stakeholders are in agreement, and to formally approve the proposed strategy. This may lead to further revisions of the strategy document and assessment of associated impacts. Communities should remain involved at this stage. This cyclical process should continue until agreement is reached.

Table 2.2. Logical framework for strategy document (example)

2

Sector objectives	Outputs	Policy actions	Indicators/ milestones	Investment plan
To increase sustainable access to water supply in rural areas	Institutional structures established for rural water supply at regional and district levels	Develop clear roles and responsibilities at all levels; form co-ordination committees; implement monitoring and regulatory framework	Co-ordination committees in operation by end of 2004; monitoring and regulatory framework fully operational by 2005	$$$
	District level co-ordination of rural water supply and institutional support to communities	Provide training at district and regional levels; inspect and monitor activities with respect to performance standards	Performance of regional and district co-ordination bodies in line with performance standards by 2006	$$$
	Increased private sector participation in construction and O&M (including spares supply)	Develop initiatives to develop efficient and competitive private sector; implement pilot studies for private sector service delivery	Turnover of private sector has doubled over 4 year period (2004-2008); 20% of water systems managed by private sector by 2008	$$$
	Sustainable community- and household-based water supplies, where all recurrent O&M costs are met by users	District co-ordination committees to implement regular monitoring schedule for all communities, to provide support and technical backstopping	Quarterly monitoring data compiled for all districts by 2005; sustainable financing in 80% of communities by 2006	$$$
	Increased number of new and improved water systems in rural areas	New systems to be installed and sources protected using demand-responsive approach	Proportion of people without sustainable access to safe drinking water to be halved by 2015	$$$
	Local development and promotion of appropriate technologies	Establish research and development fund and Implement pilot studies to field test existing local pumping technologies	Appropriate technologies used 10% more each year from 2004 at local level	$$$

Step 7. Revised policies and strategies

Following consultation, the strategy document should be finalized. If policies have been identified which need to undergo change, recommendations may need to be made for revisions in overall policy, as well as strategy. This will be easier to achieve for policies specific to the water sector than sector-wide policies, within which the strategy will need to fit.

2

Step 8. Action plan for strategy implementation

Once the strategy has been agreed upon by all stakeholders it is necessary to develop an action plan detailing how it will be introduced and implemented. This is likely to be an incremental process and the action plan should include a detailed time scale, with clear allocation of roles and responsibilities. It should also identify relevant legislative and regulatory issues which will need to be addressed in implementing the strategy. Provision should be made for ongoing monitoring and performance measurement to determine future demand for change, so that the process can be repeated as and when required.

2.5.1 Advocacy

Rural water supply planners, managers and practitioners have a key role to play in influencing government policy at district, regional and national levels. Some of the key ways in which professionals can advocate for changes in policy and strategy, that enhance sustainability, are illustrated in Annex A. The key advocacy areas addressed highlight the need for:

- Institutional support for sustainable community management;

- Private sector expertise in 'software' activities for sustainable privatization;

- A flexible approach to technology selection which promotes local sustainable solutions; and

- Import conditions and procurement practices which promote sustainable private sector provision of technology.

Further reading

Rosensweig, F. (1998) *Strategies for Decentralizing Rural Water Supply and Sanitation.* Paper prepared for the World Bank Conference on Community Water Supply and Sanitation. The World Bank: Washington, D.C.

Sara, J. and Katz T. (1998) *Making Rural Water Supply Sustainable: Recommendations from a Global Study,* UNDP-World Bank, Water and Sanitation Program, http://www.worldbank.org/watsan/rural.html.

World Bank (2004) *Poverty Reduction Strategy Paper Sourcebook.* http://www.worldbank.org/poverty/strategies/sourcetoc.htm.

Chapter 3

Institutional issues

There are many different institutional issues that influence rural water supply sustainability. In order to determine the most appropriate management options and partnership approaches the relative strengths and weaknesses of potential stakeholders need to be assessed, especially with respect to long-term sustainability of the institutions themselves. This chapter emphasizes the need for a paradigm shift from projects to programmes, the key importance of institutional support for the community management option and the importance of capacity building. It also outlines a number of different partnership models that can be applied.

3.1   The end of the project

The traditional approach to rural water supply in Africa has been that of a project with a finite life span. This is convenient for external donors and implementing NGOs but conflicts with the very principle of sustainability. A water supply is a service, and any service requires ongoing management. The focus on the facility or static infrastructure (which it is hoped that the users will keep going somehow) detracts from the importance of managing and maintaining a water service, which is a dynamic process.

Some donors have now recognized the limitations of the project model and are moving towards a programmatic approach, such as that promoted by the Sector-Wide Approach to planning (SWAp) where central government is the administrator. There remains a need to develop long-term strategies which recognize the importance of ongoing support, whether this be fulfilled by government, the private sector or NGOs. No longer is it acceptable for an implementing agency to install water supply facilities which are simply 'handed over' to the users, and then to leave, washing its hands of them. Unfortunately, however, this still happens far too often. Whether through central budget support or regional programmes it is important that donors, governments and implementers subscribe to the concept of rural **water supply services**. This does not mean that these services cannot be financed by the end-users but does recognize the importance of institutional management, monitoring and regulation.

3

Table 3.1. Advantages of programmes over projects

Sustainability factor	Project	Programme
Policy content	The influence on policy is minimized by the time-frame of the project	There is potential to develop advocacy strategies to influence long-term policy and strategy change
Institutional arrangements	Projects are often donor-driven and implemented by NGOs/consultants who leave the area after a finite period	Local government and sustainable institutions take the key roles
Community aspects	The need for a project 'handover' transfers all O&M responsibility to users who may not be ready for this	Sustainable partnerships can be developed over time and ongoing institutional support provided to communities
Financial and economic issues	Time-bound budgetary requirements limit sustainable financing mechanisms	Budgetary allocations can be made for institutional support for communities and long-term incremental strategies
Technology and the natural environment	Technology choice often remains rigid and there is no time to investigate longer-term solutions	Allocations for research and development can investigate alternative technologies and monitor environmental issues
Spare parts supply	The need for an exit strategy has led to the idea of a 'seed fund' for private spare parts supply - this has not worked	Incremental strategies can be developed to encourage spares supply by linking with other programme activities
Maintenance systems	Systems are often set up with no provision for ongoing monitoring and regulation	Ongoing and participatory monitoring of maintenance can be developed including stakeholder regulation
Rehabilitation strategies	There is insufficient time or incentive to develop long-term rehabilitation strategies	Long-term rehabilitation strategies can be developed addressing financial, technical and institutional requirements
Monitoring	Monitoring systems can be set up but there is no ongoing drive to sustain these	Sustainable monitoring systems can be developed to identify, pre-empt and solve problems

3.1.1 Advantages of the programme approach

The programme approach can contribute to sustainability in a number of ways that touch upon all the sustainability factors outlined in Chapter 1. This includes sustained management, financing and regulation, as well as appropriate policy-change, technology choice, maintenance, and long-term rehabilitation strategies. The advantages of rural water supply programmes over projects are summarized in Table 3.1.Many of the advantages identified concern the potential of programmes to deliver sustainable solutions. Simply changing to a programmatic approach will not in itself automatically result in these but provides an appropriate platform.

3

3.2   Forging partnerships

In order for programmes to be successful there is a necessity for productive partnerships between different sector stakeholders. Chapter 2 outlines the typical roles of government, community-based organizations and the private sector in many current rural water supply strategies. There are, however, several different ways in which stakeholders can forge partnerships for sustainable water services. These must address the following two programme components:

- Implementation - provision of improved water supply systems and facilities; and

- O&M - ongoing operation, maintenance and upgrade of systems.

It may be that different stakeholder partnerships are used for these two components.

3.2.1   Stakeholders

There are several different potential stakeholders who may be involved in rural water supply programmes. These include:

- External Support Agencies (ESAs);

- National and local government institutions;

- Non-governmental organizations (NGOs);

- Communities and community-based organizations (CBOs);

- Private sector companies and individuals; and

- Non-profit sector organizations (churches etc.).

External support agencies

Traditionally the water supply sector in sub-Saharan Africa has been heavily dependent on external support from international and bilateral donors. ESAs have significant influence on policy decisions and often work in partnership with governments. ESA support has advantages and disadvantages. It provides valuable financial resources but ESAs often dictate the terms under which funds can be used, which reduces government autonomy. Apart from budgetary support, ESAs can also play a key role in capacity building to enable sufficient government regulation and support to CBOs and the private sector.

Government

National and local government institutions are generally the most important stakeholders if services are to be sustainable. The role of government in rural water supply must be clearly defined at all levels and understood by all stakeholders. In many cases the principal role of government is that of co-ordination, particularly co-ordination of those ministries and departments that in one way or the other have something to do with water supply. Government staff, skills and practices have a significant impact on service delivery (Gross, et al., 2001) and therefore government capacity, especially at local levels, is of key importance.

Non-governmental organizations

In the past, NGOs have been the primary implementers of rural water supplies, and in some countries this remains the case. International and local NGOs rely on funds from ESAs or charitable contributions and normally implement water supply projects, where a given number of facilities are installed within a fixed period of time. The vast majority of NGOs have adopted the community management model and some, especially local ones, work within the same area over many years and become semi-permanent institutions.

Community-based organizations

CBOs are often water committees which are responsible for the management of water points but can also be development co-operatives, women's groups and institutions such as a community school or clinic. In general, CBOs are made up of volunteers who commit their time and energy for the good of the community. Many NGOs have concentrated efforts to form and build the capacity of CBOs in order to empower communities. Even where CBOs are not in existence, communities play a crucial role in sustainability since they are the end-users of water services.

Private sector

The private sector is sometimes known as the 'profit-making' sector, though in reality many indigenous 'for-profit' companies may barely get by financially. Private enterprise is increasingly playing a role in rural water supply in Africa. The private sector comprises private companies and individuals which provide services for profit or to make a living. These include drilling contractors, engineers, handpump mechanics and water vendors. While profit is the principal driving factor for such stakeholders, professional pride and esteem may also be important motivators that should not be overlooked.

3

Non-profit sector

The non-profit or not-for-profit sector is used to describe a range of stakeholders which are non-governmental but not traditional NGOs. The most common of these are faith-based organizations, such as churches and mosques, which provide services to communities not for profit but as a humanitarian act. These institutions are often long-term or permanent organizations which can fulfil specific support roles.

3.2.2 Conceiving and sustaining partnerships

Institutional partnerships for rural water services can involve any of the above stakeholders, and the number and nature of partners will depend on the local context. In order to form sustainable partnerships the following features (adapted from Karasoff, 1998) are critical:

- A shared vision and mission to provide a framework to guide future actions;

- Common goals that are mutually beneficial to all partners and that can be measured;

- Clear roles and responsibilities that best use the expertise of each partner;

- Shared responsibility and authority for attaining partnership goals;

- Shared decision-making using a process on which all partners agree;

- A joint plan that outlines goals, objectives, outcomes, strategies and measurable indicators (for monitoring); and

- Shared resources committed by all partners.

Good communications and time are key elements in setting up partnerships. Allowing time and encouraging dialogue facilitates understanding and smoother relations in the long term (Jones, 2001). Strong leadership, equitable governance structures and firm institutional commitment are also crucial to successful and sustainable partnerships.

3.2.3 Co-ordination committees

One effective way in which different stakeholders can work together is to form co-ordination committees at regional or district level. Such a committee is likely to consist of personnel from a variety of local government institutions which are directly or indirectly involved in or affected by rural water supply, as well as representatives of NGOs, private sector organizations and community groups. Traditional leaders can also have an important role to play, both in representing communities and in ensuring that government is made accountable, and should be included where possible. An example of such a co-ordination committee structure is the Water, Sanitation and Hygiene Education (WASHE) approach, as used in Zambia (Zambia-Water, 2004).

Political interference can be a major obstacle to equitable and sustainable provision of services. Where politicians attempt to influence local government strategies and actions for rural water supply, the presence of a co-ordinating committee can be a useful tool to resist such pressure on the basis of collective authority. This means that if local government officials are pressurized by local politicians to favour particular communities, they can resist this by informing the politician that the decision is not theirs alone, but has to be agreed by the committee which consists of various other partners.

3.3 Partnership models for service delivery

There are a number of possible partnership models for rural water services which provide different arrangements for operation and maintenance. These apply to the ongoing delivery of safe water and include:

- Community management;

- Public-private;

- Manufacturer-NGO;

- Primary healthcare;

- Least subsidy; and

- Government service.

The chosen institutional model will be heavily influenced by government policy but service sustainability can only be achieved if the partnerships that deliver them are also sustainable. It is therefore essential that all stakeholders have sufficient capacity and incentive to sustain their respective roles. Section 3.8 outlines a process that can be used to select the most appropriate partnership model for any given situation. Each of the six partnership models for service delivery (operation and maintenance) is described in more detail below. Specific maintenance systems which fit under different partnership models are explored in more detail in Chapter 7. The issue of spare parts supply is not addressed specifically but is covered in Chapter 8.

3

3.3.1 Community management model

The community management model, sometimes known as 'Village Level Operation and Maintenance' (VLOM), is by far the most common partnership approach adopted in sub-Saharan Africa. In the model depicted in Figure 3.1 local government acts as enabler and is responsible for regulation, facilitation and monitoring of sector stakeholders. The term 'facilitation' as used here does not refer to the payment of allowances but to providing an environment in which stakeholders are able to operate with minimal constraints. This may involve information provision, follow-up training and technical support. The private

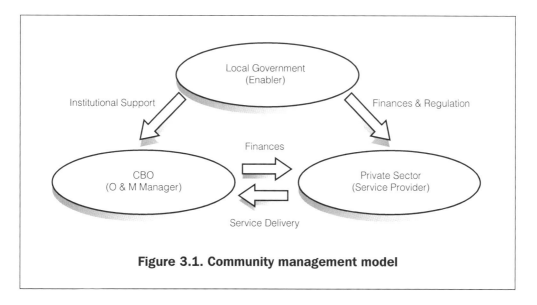

Figure 3.1. Community management model

sector is responsible for implementation, and CBOs are responsible for the management and financing of O&M. Actual O&M activities may be conducted by the private sector, such as Area Pump Mechanics (APMs), or community volunteers. Where local government institutions are especially weak the role of enabler is sometimes fulfilled by an NGO or ESA

Community management models require dynamic management and leadership at all levels (see Box 3.1), and it is important that government recognizes the need for effective facilitation and ongoing support to CBOs. Section 3.8 addresses this issue in more detail.

3

Box 3.1. Successful community managment[1]

The Water, Sanitation and Hygiene Education (WASHE) strategy adopted in Zambia is an example of a multi-layered, multi-disciplinary model which recognizes the need for institutional support for community management. WASHE committees exist at national, provincial, district and village levels and provide a framework for strategy development, training, capacity building, O&M and monitoring. This model works most effectively where there is dynamic management at all levels; where leadership is weak, handpump sustainability levels are usually low.

---

1. Harvey and Skinner, 2002

3.3.2   Public-private partnerships

The public-private model (Figure 3.2) is used here to describe the institutional framework where the private sector manages water services for which the users pay. This differs from community management in that the community may or may not own the water facility and has no responsibility for management. The users are expected, however, to pay the private service provider all ongoing O&M costs.

The public-private model still requires the government to act as facilitator and regulator (though NGOs can also fulfil this role) but the onus is on the private sector organization to provide a water service and collect revenue from the users, who in effect finance the service.

This is the typical model used for urban water supplies, although many urban systems remain subsidized by government. The term 'public-private partnerships' (PPP) is used increasingly in the water sector in Africa, but to date, most PPPs relevant to the rural sector apply to the delivery of improved water systems and facilities only, rather than the operation and maintenance of these. There are some successful examples of ongoing private sector service provision

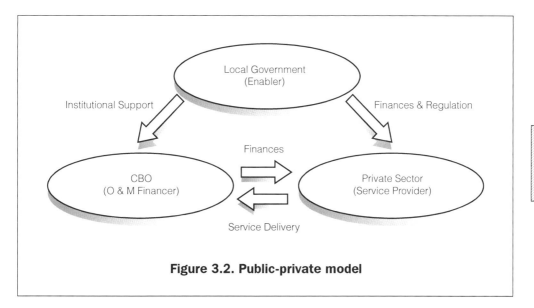

Figure 3.2. Public-private model

(see Box 3.2) but so far this has been limited, in part by the low number of attempts.

Box 3.2. Public-private partnerships[1]

One example of a public-private partnership is the handpump lease concept. This has been successfully implemented in Lubango, Angola, since 1990, when several hundred handpumps were handed over directly to the local water company. Since that time the company has taken care of the maintenance and repair of these handpumps in the peri-urban and rural zone. Each family pays an equivalent of US$0.40 to the pump caretaker each month and the revenue raised pays the pump caretaker's salary and the water company.

---

1. van Beers, 2001a

3.3.3 Manufacturer-NGO model

The manufacturer-NGO model (Figure 3.3) is a variation on the community management and public-private models based on a relationship between an implementing agency and a private manufacturer.

In this model the NGO (which could be replaced by local government) takes the lead role but has a strong partnership with a private manufacturer which provides hardware (e.g. handpumps and spare parts), technical advice and training. This can be a local manufacturer or an international manufacturer working through

3

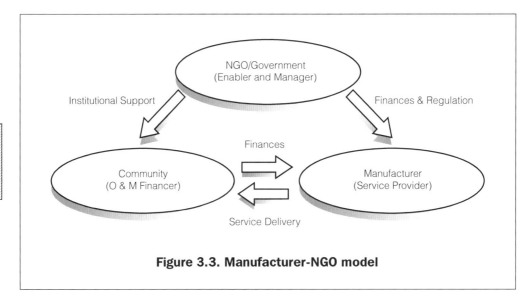

Figure 3.3. Manufacturer-NGO model

local agents. This partnership benefits the implementing agency because it has a private supplier of goods and services it can rely on, and benefits the manufacturer because it has a continued demand for its products over the long term. It also benefits the water users in that they receive ongoing institutional support and have access to appropriate equipment and services. The only major constraint is that the sustainability of the partnership depends largely on continued provision of new water systems by the NGO or Government in order to sustain the interest of the manufacturer in selling more products.

Box 3.3. Manufacturer-NGO model

Private manufacturers are interested in long-term profits and will be much more likely to offer technical services and ensure spare parts supply where there is a clear long-term demand for their products. Appropriate regulation and quality control will also ensure that the manufacturer provides high quality equipment. This will only work where donors and implementing agencies select manufacturers on the basis of quality, value for money and after-sales service, rather than simply the cheapest purchase price.

3.3.4   Primary healthcare model

The primary healthcare model (Figure 3.4) is a relatively rare partnership in which the provision of water supply falls under the auspices of primary healthcare under the Ministry of Health. This model relies on a primary

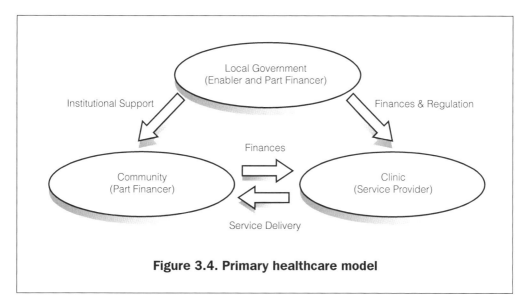

Figure 3.4. Primary healthcare model

3

healthcare institution which is responsible for delivering healthcare services through clinics and community visits. Working alongside doctors, nurses and traditional birth attendants and healers are water technicians who are responsible for implementation of new water systems and maintenance of existing facilities. They are also responsible for undertaking repairs to healthcare vehicles and other mechanical or electrical equipment. These technicians are paid by the healthcare institution while communities pay for the cost of spare parts provided by them.

The fact that water supply is coupled with the provision of healthcare leads to improved efficiency in service delivery and greater awareness of links and potential links between water and disease (see Box 3.4).

Box 3.4. Primary healthcare and water[1]

Under the primary healthcare scheme in Maryland County, Liberia, if a clinician noted a pattern of water-related illness from a particular area he or she might ask whether the village pump was working OK. If the answer was that it was not, he or she might inspect it or call for a technician. Similarly, the water technicians arranged the delivery of equipment such as pumps and rigs based on the travel arrangements of nurses and healthcare staff visiting communities by pick-up.

---

1. Allen, 1996

3.3.5 Least subsidy model

The least subsidy model (Figure 3.5) is a relatively new approach which recognizes the need for government to provide some subsidy for rural water supply services.

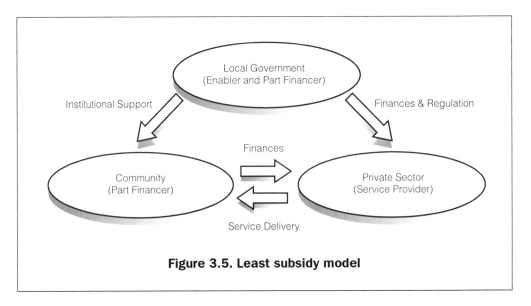

Figure 3.5. Least subsidy model

This model can be implemented when private companies bid for the minimum or least subsidy from government to provide water systems at agreed service levels for a period of, say, 10 to 15 years. These private companies need to assess and negotiate the community contribution they will get for O&M. The government then pays the minimum subsidy to the company and the communities pay their water tariffs. This model has not been tried for rural water services in Africa to date but its application to other sectors in Latin America demonstrates considerable potential, and for this reason it is included here (see Box 3.5).

Box 3.5. Least subsidy bidding[1]

Private telecommunications operators in Peru bid for the minimum government subsidy they require to provide pay phone service in targeted rural areas. Part of the subsidy is paid on award of the contract, part once the equipment is installed, and the rest in semi-annual installments for several years, contingent on compliance with performance standards.

---

1. Cannock, 2001

A variation on this model is for individual means-tested water subsidies whereby the poorest households receive a government subsidy and pay less for water. The subsidy may be funded entirely by the government or from other users. This has been successfully implemented for urban water services delivered by the private sector, for example in Chile (Gómez-Lobo, 2001) but has not yet been transferred to the rural sector.

3.3.6 Government service model

The government service model is largely a thing of the past but is still applied in some countries such as South Africa. The government service model (Figure 3.6)

3

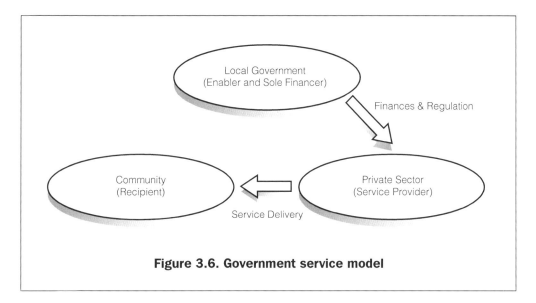

Figure 3.6. Government service model

accepts that the government is solely responsible for rural water supply provision and funds all initial and ongoing costs associated with this. The private sector may be used to deliver technical services but the community is not expected to contribute to the cost of O&M and there is no attempt at cost-recovery. With the 'free basic water' policy in South Africa this model is used in some areas with limited success (see Box 3.6).

3.3.7 Selecting an appropriate partnership model

Table 3.2 summarizes stakeholder roles for the six different categories of partnership model for both initial implementation of the facility (system) and operation and maintenance. In each model, regulation is conducted by the local government. This is important whether service delivery is the responsibility of NGOs, private companies or communities. All models are based on the assumption that local government is the ideal level to enable, finance and

---

Box 3.6. Government services[1]

In Kwazulu-Natal, South Africa, District Councils are responsible for O&M of handpumps, and contract out repair and maintenance to private contractors. Once a problem is reported by a community the time lag before the handpump is repaired can vary from several weeks to several months or years. The reasons for such lengthy delays are inadequate budgeting, bureaucratic procedures, and the inefficiency of repairing a single pump at a time, which results in councils waiting until there are several pumps in need of repair in a given area before contracting a company to attend to these.

3

1. Harvey and Kayaga, 2003

Table 3.2. Possible partnership frameworks

Model	Regulator	Financer		Manager	Implementer	
		Facility	O&M		Facility	O&M
Community management	National and local Governement	NGO/Local Government	Community	NGO/Local Government and Community	NGO/Private sector	Private sector/ Community
Public-private	National and local Governement	Local Government	Community	Private sector	Private sector	Private sector
Manufacturer-NGO	National and local Governement	NGO	Community	NGO & Community	Private sector	Private sector/ Community
Primary healthcare	National and local Governement	NGO/Local Government	Community	Local Government/ clinic	Local Government/ clinic	Local Government/ clinic
Least subsidy	National and local Governement	Community/ Local Government	Community/ Local Government	Private sector	Private sector	Private sector
Government service	National and local Governement	Local Government	Local Government	Local Government	Private sector	Private sector

regulate activities. This assumption is based on the fact that local government is, in most cases, the most sustainable institution, i.e. it should remain operational in the area indefinitely. There are cases, however, where an alternative institution such as a local NGO or faith-based organization may be better equipped to fulfil this role. This is particularly likely in areas of instability, such as those subject to civil war and political upheaval, but also where decentralization policies and strategies are not in place or where implementation of these is weak and ineffective.

The most appropriate partnership model will depend on the context, but given the short-comings of community management approaches there is a strong need to investigate alternative approaches such as public-private, least subsidy and primary healthcare partnerships.

3

3.4   Regulation

Whichever partnership model is chosen, stakeholder activities need to be regulated. In its broadest sense regulation means a 'sustained and focused control exercised by a public agency over activities that are valued by a community' (Ogus, 1994). It is a set of functions rather than a rigid sense of rules. Government policies set out the general legal framework and rules, and it is the role of the regulator to interpret these in relation to practical circumstances. The term 'regulation' is most commonly used to refer to public sector regulation of the private sector. It can also include, however, regulation of NGOs, community-based organizations, co-ordination committees and government agencies.

According to Trémolet and Browning (2002) regulatory functions include:

• Economic regulation (of price, service quality and competition);

• Environmental regulation (of water abstraction and discharge); and

• Public health regulation (of drinking water quality).

Regulation should ensure that the price that users pay for water is fair, that there is a high quality of workmanship for construction of facilities, that service standards for O&M are acceptable, that water systems do not result in detrimental effects on the environment (or other water systems), and that water quality is consistent with national (and/or WHO) guidelines.

Local and regional government institutions are best placed to regulate NGO, CBO and private sector activities. This involves monitoring activities (see Chapter 9) and, on the basis of this, identifying where intervention is required and acting accordingly. Contracts with private contractors should be devised to ensure service quality standards and to permit the enforcement of fines or penalties for failure to meet standards. Partnerships arrangements with implementing agencies such as NGOs should also ensure that standards are met.

For private sector service delivery, in particular, effective government regulation at local level is essential. Where government structures are ill-defined or capacity is weak this creates a significant barrier to private sector participation. Government institutions must also be regulated, normally by other government bodies, to ensure accountability and transparency of operations.

3.5   Ongoing institutional support for community management

The community management model remains by far the most widespread for rural water supply in sub-Saharan Africa, and yet has failed to deliver the levels of sustainability that were initially anticipated. As described above, experience suggests that there may often be better alternatives to community management and the authors aim to encourage pilot studies that test new and innovative models. It is accepted, however, that community management is currently the most common model implemented and is likely to remain so for the short-term future at least.

While community management is based on the well-intentioned principle of encouraging ownership and empowering communities, it also acts as a convenient concept for shifting responsibility for ongoing operation and maintenance, and hence sustainability, of services from facility-provider to end-user. Community 'sensitization' or 'mobilization' is designed to instil a sense of ownership and responsibility, but this does not automatically lead to a willingness to manage or finance a water supply over a prolonged period of time. Consequently many facilities fall into disrepair soon after installation or as soon as anything goes wrong with the pump.

The assumption that supporting community-based O&M (such as VLOM) is a less onerous task than running a centralized maintenance system has not been borne out in the field (WHO, 2000), and at present there is little evidence to suggest that governments have facilitated VLOM effectively on their own (Colin, 1999). This may be because Government authorities and support agencies do not understand the need for appropriate support systems, perhaps in part because the development of the VLOM concept created complacency (Ockelford, 2002). There has been a widespread misconception that services can be managed autonomously by communities, and that governments can be side-stepped in the process of service delivery by external support agencies (Carter, 2002). This may explain why there is often a lack of understanding among governments.

There remains a strong need for re-examination of assumptions surrounding community management and a new approach to institutional support to communities. Carter et al. (1999) defines a 'sustainability chain' for community water supply consisting of motivation, maintenance, cost recovery and continuing support. Even stronger institutions than at present are needed to promote and support community management, and adequate funding is still required for agencies to be able to perform their essential supportive role (Davis & Brikké, 1995). This is backed up by new strategies developed by implementing agencies that recognize the need for institutional support and the need to budget for this accordingly (Nedjoh et al., 2003). Such support is not a stop-gap or short-term measure, but should be ongoing.

3

The term **'scaling-up community management'** is now increasingly used to refer to the need to increase sustainability and coverage by creating institutional frameworks for community managed services, using a learning approach which includes all relevant stakeholders and allows for local context (Schouten & Moriarty, 2003). This requires political support and involves calculating the full costs of implementing the community management model; promoting appropriate low-cost technology; building capacity at all levels; and providing adequate financing from communities, government and the private sector (Lockwood, 2004).

3.5.1 What comprises 'support'?

The first step is to recognize that support is required if community management is to deliver sustainable solutions. The second is to determine what that support should entail. Appropriate institutional support comprises the following components:

- Encouragement and motivation;

- Monitoring and evaluation;

- Participatory planning;

- Capacity building; and

- Specialist technical assistance (including financial support where required).

Institutional support is best provided by a local government institution (for the reasons given in 3.3.7), although where this is not possible an NGO or stakeholder group can fulfil this role. One way in which appropriate institutional support can be provided is by means of a district water and sanitation team (or D-WASHE) which may include water, environmental health and/or community development staff. Monitoring and evaluation strategies are essential to determine the status of water facilities, financial and human resources, and environmental issues. Based on monitoring results, participatory planning exercises should be undertaken with communities experiencing difficulties. These can address technical problems or difficulties experienced by CBOs, such as lack of willingness to pay among users or lack of competent mechanics. Such teams can also provide specialist technical assistance if required, for which there is likely to be some charge made to communities. The last important aspect is the need for capacity building and institutional strengthening. This applies to CBOs and local government institutions themselves.

It is important that external support agencies (ESAs) work in partnership with government institutions from the onset of programmes. The capacity of institutions must be considered if they are to be able to fulfil the necessary support role effectively, and appropriate institutional strengthening may be required at various stages.

3.5.2   Financing institutional suppport

This institutional support obviously has a cost associated with it, and appropriate investment strategies are required to meet this. Figure 3.7 illustrates the forecast of the coverage level of safe drinking water based on sustained investment in the rural water sector including as well as excluding a budgetary allocation for institutional support for community-based O&M.

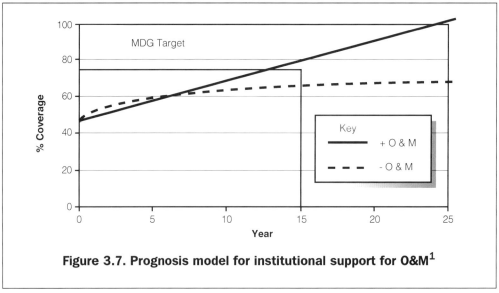

Figure 3.7. Prognosis model for institutional support for O&M[1]

1. Adapted from Nedjoh et. al., 2003

This is based on a prognosis model developed by the Community Water and Sanitation Agency (CWSA) in the Volta Region of Ghana (Nedjoh et al., 2003) but has been adapted for generic application. The broken line illustrates the scenario where investment is made for increasing service coverage but no money is used for O&M support, while the continuous line illustrates the scenario where 6 per cent of total investment is used for O&M support. This is based on the annual investment of $2 million per year for a region with a total population of approximately 1,200,000 people, half of whom have access to water in year zero. The model indicates that without O&M support the coverage level would increase from 50 per cent and stabilize at around 67 per cent, whereafter the breakdown rate would equal the rate of new constructions. To reach a higher coverage level, significantly higher capital investment would be needed.

The MDG target of halving those without access to safe drinking water by 2015 is superimposed on the graph, assuming that there was 50 per cent water coverage in the year 2000 (year zero). With O&M support this target could be achieved with appropriate investment levels, and 100 per cent coverage achieved by 2025. After this the capital investment could be reduced greatly to cover only the breakdowns. Without O&M support the MDG target would not be achieved.

3.6 Building institutional capacity

In order for the different partnership models described to be successful it is essential that the different institutional stakeholders have sufficient capacity to fulfil their respective roles. Capacity building and sustainability are closely related. Without adequate, appropriate capacity at different levels of government and at local level, services will not be sustainable (Abrams, 1996). Capacity building is a broad term, for which a range of definitions have been developed. It can apply to the water sector in a particular country or region, or it can apply to specific institutions, organizations or communities. The following definition (adapted from Abrams, 1996) is applied to institutional capacity.

Capacity building is the process whereby an institution equips itself to undertake the necessary functions of governance and service provision in a sustainable fashion. The process of capacity building must be aimed at both increasing access to resources and to changing the power relationships between the parties involved. Capacity building is not only constrained to officials and technicians but must also include the general awareness of the local population regarding their services.

Capacity building comprises the following components:

- Human resource development;

- Institutional reform and restructuring;

- Development of an appropriate operating environment;

- Provision of physical and financial resources;

- Impact assessment and follow-up training.

3

Human resource development can consist of formal education, training and individual professional development to develop a strong institutional skills base. Institutional reform and restructuring addresses the need for changes in organizational structure, management strategies and operational systems to enhance efficiency and effectiveness. This goes hand-in-hand with developing an operational environment in which the staff of the institution is able to perform its duties effectively and efficiently. There is also likely to be a need for the provision of physical and financial resources for equipment and facilities. Lessons learnt by other stakeholders and external organizations should feed into this process through effective information exchange where possible.

In assessing the capacity building needs of different institutions, in order to improve sustainability, it is useful to consider individually ways to increase effectiveness, efficiency, equity and replicability. Capacity building is an ongoing, dynamic process since staff may be transferred and knowledge forgotten. It should include periodic assessment of the impact of past capacity-building initiatives, so that plans can be made for current and future needs.

3.6.1   Government capacity

Government institutions have a key role to play in rural water supply programmes, especially in an enabling role as policy-maker, facilitator and regulator. However, government departments are often criticized for adopting bureaucratic procedures and practices which hinder efficiency and effectiveness. The availability of qualified and skilled staff varies considerably and there are often reported skills gaps.

There are, therefore, common capacity-building needs for local government institutions which include the following:

- Training of government personnel in 'hardware' and 'software' aspects of programmes and streamlining workforce.

Photograph 3.1. District Water Office, Uganda

- Development of transparent contractual frameworks and formats to facilitate effective private sector involvement.

- Development of efficient monitoring systems which provide appropriate support to communities and useful data.

- Development of appropriate information and knowledge management systems in collaboration with other stakeholders.

- Development of strategies for research in technical and non-technical areas, which may lead to higher levels of sustainability.

Knowledge development is essential and this should include information gathered through monitoring on district and regional conditions and services. Local staff must be aware of the service conditions in the area for which they are responsible.

3.6.2 Private sector capacity

The focus of many institutional strengthening initiatives focuses on government, while accompanying strategies often place considerable responsibility on the

3

private sector. It is therefore essential that the private sector has sufficient capacity to fulfil the roles assigned to it, and specific actions may be required to ensure this. In particular, private companies and individuals often require adequate knowledge and expertise in:

- Community consultation techniques;

- Tariff development and cost-recovery strategies;

- Latest technical innovations; and

- Data management.

While private sector organizations should perhaps pay to build their own capacity, government as regulator should ensure that companies have the necessary skills and resources prior to awarding contracts, and should assist them by facilitating access to appropriate training and advice.

3.7   Procurement

One way in which institutions can influence sustainability is to develop appropriate procurement strategies. Currently, many governments and NGOs purchase technical equipment, such as handpumps, directly from manufacturers. In general, these manufacturers are outside the country and sometimes orders pass through the central procurement departments of ESAs and NGOs. This practice threatens sustainability in a number of ways:

- The procurement of pumps is separated from that of spare parts, creating little incentive to private enterprise to provide spares.

- Reliance on imported goods makes no contribution to the local economy, especially where import duties are waived.

- There is minimal opportunity for local innovation to develop appropriate and sustainable technologies.

- There are likely to be extensive time delays from order date to delivery date.

- There is likely to be a lack of direct quality control (resulting in high levels of rejected parts) and limited consultation with the manufacturer.

For these reasons, the argument for local procurement is a strong one.

3.7.1 Buy local

Whether pumps are manufactured in country or not, governments and donors should buy as local as possible, e.g. in a district capital rather than the national capital. Where local retailers sell pumps they are more likely to ensure that they also stock spare parts, making these available close to communities (WSP, 2000; Harvey et al., 2003). Institutional strategies should, where possible, incorporate the following components:

- In-country quality control of equipment;

- Purchase of handpumps at district level; and

- Support to grassroots innovation and manufacture.

Annex A includes advocacy tools that can be used to promote local procurement.

3.8 Institutional steps towards sustainability

In order to ensure that institutional aspects have an optimum positive effect on water service sustainability there are six key steps which should be followed.

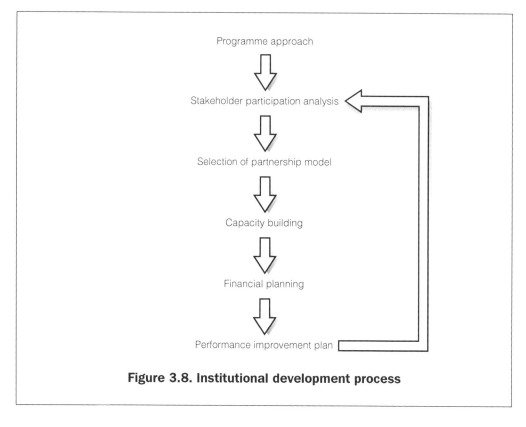

Figure 3.8. Institutional development process

Figure 3.8 summarizes a dynamic process that can be used to develop sustainable institutional arrangements for increased service sustainability. This is not a 'blueprint' for success but an indicative process that may be adopted and adapted on an ongoing basis.

This process can be conducted at a national or regional level, and should be co-ordinated by a planning committee comprising representatives of relevant government ministries and departments, and external support agencies involved in water supply.

Step 1. Programme approach

The first step is to recognize that rural water supply should be **delivered as a service and managed as a programme**. The project-based facility provision approach of the past has failed to deliver adequate levels of sustainability throughout the sub-continent. Any programme should last indefinitely and include provision for ongoing regulation and monitoring. Programmes should incorporate the provision of new water systems, upgrade and expansion of existing systems, and ongoing operation and maintenance of all systems.

Step 2. Stakeholder participation analysis

The second step is to investigate the interests, incentives, disincentives and capacity of each relevant stakeholder, in order to assess their willingness and ability to be involved. This is likely to be carried out at district or regional level, although findings should be reported at national level to influence national institutional strategies. The analysis will help to define stakeholder roles and lead to the selection of the most suitable institutional model. Table 3.3 presents an example of such an analysis considering local government, the private sector, NGOs, CBOs and individual users.

Individual users are considered separately from community groups or organizations to recognize the fact that there may be individuals within a community who have different incentives, disincentives and capacity to those of the organization or the community as a whole.

This analysis should be conducted through consultation with all stakeholders and an assessment of their respective capacities. A large sample of communities (e.g. at least 100 for a district with 400 communities, i.e. 25 per cent), and a number of private sector organizations, NGOs and local government offices (e.g. District Water Offices) should be involved in the consultation exercise. This exercise is

Table 3.3. Stakeholder participation analysis

Stakeholders	Incentives for stakeholder participation	Disincentives for stakeholder participation	Capacity of stakeholder to participate
Local government	Political goodwill Political votes Government/ESA policy	Overstretched resources Political influence	Limited human resources Limited financial and technical resources
Community groups (CBOs)	Time saving Reduced burden Improved health Income generation	Lack of community cohesion/stability Alternative priorities	Limited human resources Limited financial and technical resources
Individual users	Time saving Reduced burden Improved health Income generation	Lack of transparency or trust Lack of equity	Limited financial resources
NGOs	Humanitarian satisfaction Donor funds	Governmental procedures Finite time commitment	Project-based funding limits ongoing support
Private sector	Profit Professional pride and esteem	Less profit than alternative commercial activities	Dependent on geographical area, commercial activity and nature of population

3

useful to obtain a perspective for all parties involved and identify opportunities and limitations.

Step 3. Selection of partnership model

Once the particular incentives and capabilities of different stakeholders have been assessed these can then be matched to the requirements for different partnership models mentioned in Section 3.3. Firstly, the dominant partnership model(s) that exist in the country should be assessed to examine where and why they might be inadequate. Subsequently a decision can be made as to whether to improve the existing model(s) or opt for something new. Table 3.4 presents what is likely to be required of each stakeholder for each institutional model to operate successfully.

If any stakeholder is unable or unwilling to undertake their responsibilities for a particular model then an alternative should be sought. The final choice of institutional model should be made through a consultation exercise in which all relevant stakeholders actively contribute.

Table 3.4. Partnership model stakeholder responsibilities

Model	Government	Community	Private sector
Community management	Quarterly monitoring Regulation of CBOs (roles may be performed by NGO)	Management of O&M Payment and collection of revenue Financial management	Provision of spare parts (role may be performed by NGO)
Public-private	Quarterly monitoring Regulation of private sector (and NGO)	Payment of revenue Routine maintenance	Provision of water services and associated equipment Collection of revenue Financial management
Manufacturer-NGO	Quarterly monitoring Regulation of private sector (roles may be performed by NGO)	Management of O&M Payment and collection of revenue Financial management	Provision of water services and associated equipment
Primary healthcare	Provision of water services and associated equipment	Payment of revenue Routine maintenance	
Least subsidy	Quarterly monitoring Payment of subsidy to water service provider and regulation	Payment of revenue Routine maintenance	Provision of water services and associated equipment Collection of revenue Financial management
Government service	Sole responsibility for financing water services Quarterly monitoring	Routine maintenance	Provision of technical services and equipment

Step 4. Capacity building

Even where institutions are relatively strong there is still likely to be a need for capacity building. Once roles and responsibilities are clearly defined the necessary skill gaps should be identified for all stakeholders to identify obstacles that may prevent them from fulfilling their respective roles. Appropriate capacity building measures should then be implemented to rectify any shortcomings. These may include training of community members in book-keeping, financial investment options or maintenance activities; training of government staff in financial and contract management and monitoring and evaluation; or training private sector organizations in community liaison and tariff collection. These activities take time, especially those involving communities. Communities should not be rushed just because the implementing agency wants to construct facilities quickly in order to meet targets.

Step 5. Financial planning

It is essential that governments and donors make adequate budgetary allocation for regulatory and support activities. The cost of quarterly monitoring visits to all communities, including social and technical assessments, should be budgeted for, as should all costs associated with capacity building activities. Financial models should also be developed for long-term rehabilitation and upgrading. (Chapter 5 contains more information about financial issues.)

3

Step 6. Performance improvement plan

The final step is to develop a performance improvement plan which takes the key outputs of all the steps so far to form a time-bound action plan to improve performance of stakeholders and the effectiveness of institutional partnerships. This plan can be developed through a problem-tree approach whereby the key problems or barriers to sustainability related to institutional issues are identified, and objectives are then developed to overcome these.

Any institutional issues should be assessed to ensure that these do not have an adverse affect on efficiency or sustainability and, if they do, solutions should be developed to overcome them. For example, if procurement practices and procedures are identified as having an adverse effect, measures should be taken to promote local procurement and link services and equipment.

Further reading

Building Partnerships for Development (BPD) Resource Centre. http://www.bpd-waterandsanitation.org/english/resource.asp.

Danert, K., Carter, R.C., Rwamwanja, R., Ssebalu, J., Carr, G., and Kane, D. (2003) 'The Private Sector in Water and Sanitation Services in Uganda: Understanding the context and developing support strategies.' *Journal of International Development,* 15 (8) 1099-1114.

Jones, D. (2001) *Conceiving and Managing Partnerships: A guiding framework.* Practitioner Note Series, Business Partners for Development, Water and Sanitation Cluster: London.

Lockwood, H. (2004) *Scaling Up Community Management of Rural Water Supply.* Thematic Overview Paper, IRC: Delft, The Netherlands. (can be accessed at http://www.irc.nl/content/view/full/8857)

Ockelford, J. and Reed, R.A. (2002) *Participatory Planning for Integrated Rural Water Supply and Sanitation Programmes.* WEDC, Loughborough University: UK. (can be accessed at http://wedc.lboro.ac.uk/projects/new_projects3.php?id=3)

Trémolet, S. and Browning, S. (2002) *The Interface between Regulatory Frameworks and Tri-Sector Partnerships.* Business Partners for Development, Water and Sanitation Cluster: London.

3

Chapter 4

Community issues

User communities must be granted true decision-making authority. This means that they should be given comprehensive information needed to make informed decisions, without being pressured to follow the preferences of the facilitator. Communities and households should be free to select technology and service levels that suit them. They should also be free to select the most appropriate management system for operation and maintenance (O&M), including the option not to manage this themselves. This chapter highlights the importance of community and social issues in sustaining water supplies, and different ways in which these can be managed and supported. The willingness and ability to manage supplies and willingness and ability to pay for water among communities are considered, and the importance of equity, impact and gender are also emphasized.

4.1   Community and household water supplies

Most rural water supplies in sub-Saharan Africa are community-based. That is to say, most water systems are owned, operated and managed by a community rather than an individual or household. This fact alone may be one important reason why the sustainability of such systems is so often poor. Community members are often less willing to contribute a modest amount to the cost of a community water supply than they are to pay a significantly greater amount for a private household supply (Sutton, 2003). The obstacles to sustainability created by conflict within communities can also be reduced greatly through the development of household options.

4.1.1   Household and small-group water supplies

Many African countries report low coverage rates for access to safe water, yet the many millions of people who are 'unserved' rely on water from traditional sources that they have found or developed for themselves. These include hand-dug wells, scoop-holes and surface water sources such as rivers and streams.

Such water sources may be household-based or used by small groups (often consisting of several families). There are several ways in which household and small-group water supplies can be promoted and improved to provide sustainable access to safe water. These include:

• Improvement of existing traditional sources;

• Promotion of traditional well construction;

• Household water treatment;

• Rainwater harvesting; and

• Provision of credit systems for small user group subsidy/investment.

Where appropriate, household and small user group technologies can be upgraded to safer water sources, thus offering greater security to the poor and reducing dependency on remote technologies. Point water sources, such as handpumps, are designed on the basis of a user population of 200-300 people, which may result in implementers amalgamating groups to make a 'community' unit of adequate size (Sutton, 2003). This may marginalize users who live further away from the new source and may lead to disagreement or conflict between different traditional groups (e.g. families, clans and villages) within the artificially created 'community'. It may also result in the installation of a handpump mid-way between villages, several hundred metres from the nearest user and with no clear ownership (Harvey & Skinner, 2002). The number of users using a traditional source, or the number of people within a discrete village community, may be considerably less than 200 people. Small-scale options should, therefore, be considered alongside more technologically advanced community options. Comprehensive information on all feasible options should be provided to community members in order for them to decide on the most appropriate technology and service level for them.

4.1.2 Community water supplies

Household and small-group water supplies may not always be feasible, particularly where users currently have to walk excessive distances to collect water. Since one aim of improving access to safe water should be to reduce the time and energy required to collect water, new water sources closer to communities are often required. This often means that there is a need to exploit groundwater, i.e. water held in rocks and soils underground. Where possible, hand-dug wells for households or small groups can be constructed, but where groundwater levels are deeper, drilled boreholes may be the only option. Due to the high cost of such intervention, boreholes cannot be drilled for every household or extended family group, and must be developed for the entire community. There may also be instances where a gravity-fed or pumped water system is the technology selected by the users. Again, for there to be an efficient use of resources, such schemes need to be developed for the whole population in an area.

The vast majority of rural water supplies implemented by support agencies, whether NGO or governmental, are community-based. Communities may be clearly defined villages, or a collection of scattered households in a rural area. In either case, it is essential that all members of a community are provided with the knowledge to determine which of those options that are environmentally and technically feasible is the most preferable for them.

4

4.1.3   Health and hygiene

While there are many potential benefits of an improved water supply, improved health remains one of the most important. This can only be achieved if accompanied by appropriate hygiene practices such as safe collection, handling and storage of water. Inappropriate water handling and storage can result in water from a protected source becoming as unsafe as water from an unprotected source. Health and hygiene awareness are therefore crucial if benefits from improved water services are to be maximized. If rural water supplies are to benefit all users equally it is important that all community members (women, children and men) are made aware of the links between water, health and hygiene.

4.2   What constitutes a 'community'?

In addressing community participation it is important to ascertain what we mean by the term 'community'. Communities may be distinct groupings of people that have developed over generations, may be defined by artificial geographical boundaries, or may be determined by the service provided itself. Rural communities are most commonly defined by village but even this term has different meanings in different settings. In relation to water supply, a community is likely to be defined by the area which a given water system can realistically serve. This is not necessarily the same as a pre-existing community defined by ethnic or family groups. Many communities will, therefore, be made up of people of different:

• Gender;

• Families/clans;

- Ethnic groups;

- Religious groups;

- Socio-economic groups;

- Professions; and

- Literacy and education-levels.

It is a common mistake to assume that all people within a given community are the same and have a strong sense of communal identity and cohesion; this is often not the case. The social cohesion of any given community may have a significant impact on sustainability of services. It should not be taken for granted that a group of people has the internal resources, common interest, or sense of solidarity to either initiate action or sustain the management of a facility (DeGabriele, 2002). It is therefore essential that practitioners working with communities recognize the need to identify different groups and sub-groups within those communities. This is important to ensure equity and to improve effectiveness. Some communities consist of several distinct ethnic groups, some of which may be migratory, such as pastoralist farmers and herdsmen, with very different needs and priorities to settled populations. Conflict resolution may be necessary in some instances and facilitating agencies should be adequately trained in this area.

In recognizing that a community is not homogeneous the first step is taken in undertaking effective community consultation. The needs and wishes of community members are likely to vary considerably and in order to respond to these a structured, inclusive approach must be taken. Where there are already community-based organizations these may be used in the planning process, but care should be taken to ensure that no community members are excluded from such bodies and that they are truly representative. Also, where there is a proliferation of committees in a community (e.g. for education, health, agriculture, environment, natural resource management, religion etc.) some community members may be suffering from 'committee fatigue' since each committee relies on the same pool of influential/active persons. It is essential to establish the 'community' as a decision-making entity that ensures equity. This process alone involves consultation with all members of the community and may take considerable time, depending on community dynamics. Sutton & Nkoloma (2003) suggest **community mapping** (see PRA in Section 4.3.2, and Section 9.4.1) as a method to allow discussion of a broad range of issues, and identification of the positive aspects of the community as well as the problems.

4.3 Community participation

The importance of community participation in rural water supply is often emphasized, yet perceptions of what this means vary greatly. Community 'participation' might include any of the following:

- Prioritization and vocalization of community needs;

- Selection of appropriate facilities, technologies and locations;

- Financial contribution to capital costs;

- Provision of labour for construction of systems and facilities;

- Management of operation and maintenance;

- Setting and collection of water tariffs; or

- Physical maintenance and repair activities.

Community participation can be simply tokenistic, but if used appropriately has great potential to contribute to sustainable water supplies. Thorpe (2002) argues that participation should start as early as possible (from problem identification) and that if there is the need for a 'handover' from agency to community then the process is already flawed since the community should already 'own' the project. Community participation (including the simplest level of involvement) from early on enhances the future sense of ownership, but ongoing motivation is required for continuing participation (Batchelor et al., 2000). This is of key importance; just because a community has participated in the planning process does not mean that it will sustain participation in ongoing service delivery. **Community participation does not automatically lead to effective community management**, nor should it have to. Services that are not to be managed by the community should still follow on from effective community consultation and participatory planning. Community **participation** is a prerequisite for sustainability, i.e. to achieve efficiency, effectiveness, equity and replicability, but community **management** is not (see Section 4.4).

The key stages of the planning process which involve community participation are:

- Community established as a body with decision-making power;

- Demand assessment;

- Option identification; and

- Informed decision-making.

4.3.1 Community mobilization

The terms community 'mobilization' and 'sensitization' are often used to describe the process by which an implementing agency works with a community to encourage and enable it to participate. The terms are overlapping and are sometimes used interchangeably, but there are subtle differences. Community sensitization is a process by which community members become aware of the benefits of an improved water supply. This generally involves education and awareness raising, and is usually stimulated by an external agency.

Community mobilization is a process to facilitate participatory decision-making, planning and implementation, and can be stimulated by a community itself, or by others. It is a process which begins dialogue among members of a community to determine who, what, and how issues are decided, and to provide an avenue for everyone to participate in decisions that affect their lives.

An essential component of community mobilization is to define the 'community' and to establish an appropriate mechanism for decision-making which may include the establishment of a community body or committee. Capacity building is also an important aspect to ensure that the community has sufficient knowledge, skills and resources to participate.

Community mobilization may take considerable time and should not be rushed. Some communities may become actively involved in water supply activities within a matter of weeks; others may take several months or years. Community mobilization is an important component of community participation, since it is the process by which a community becomes involved.

4.3.2 Community participation techniques

There are many techniques that can be used to mobilize communities and facilitate their participation in demand assessment, option identification and informed decision-making. The following are probably the most widespread.

4

Rapid Rural Appraisal (RRA) is a method used by outsiders to acquire information about a community quickly and is best used for initial assessments. It consists of systematic, semi-structured activities conducted on-site by a multidisciplinary team with the aim of quickly and efficiently acquiring information about rural life and rural resources. Techniques include direct observation and asking questions about what is seen; guided interviews; group discussions with informal or selected groups; inspection of aerial photographs; and identifying and learning from key informants (Chambers, 1983).

Participatory Rural Appraisal (PRA) prioritizes local knowledge over outsider knowledge and aims at strengthening the analysing and decision-making power of communities. PRA is of key importance in facilitating community members to make decisions for themselves. PRA techniques include community mapping, ranking, voting (using 'pocket charts') and diagramming. Focus group discussions with different groups within a given community can be used to ensure that all individuals and groups have a voice and can contribute to the planning process. This is especially important for addressing equity issues concerning poverty and gender. PRA is a facilitating process that focuses on local people's capabilities as well as their knowledge, and enables them to be the analysts, planners and actors, and then in turn facilitators (Chambers, 1997).

Methodology for Participatory Assessments (MPA) is a comprehensive method for social assessment which can be carried out within a short time frame (three to four months) and can be used in all phases of the project cycle including planning, implementation and monitoring (Dayal et al., 2000). It recognizes the importance of gender and poverty-sensitive approaches and monitors key indicators of project sustainability and demand-responsiveness. MPA uses a participatory methodology in which stakeholders assign scores for the various indicators, so that each participatory exercise results in a picture, diagram or map of information for all participants to see and use to draw conclusions.

Self-esteem, Associative strengths, Resourcefulness, Action planning and Responsibility (SARAR) is a flexible participatory approach which is 'learner centred'. It was developed as a means of helping community members (the 'learners') take greater control of their lives and their environment by developing their skills in problem solving and resource management. SARAR focuses on the development of human capacities to assess, choose, plan, create, organize and take initiatives, based on people's self-esteem, the associative strength of the community, and their resourcefulness. It emphasizes the importance of action planning and clear responsibility for following plans through (Srinivasan, 1990; Rietbergen-McCracken & Narayan, 1998).

Knowledge Attitude and Practice (KAP) is a tool which can be used to obtain information about existing practices related to water supply, existing attitudes towards water, and the level of knowledge about water in a community. From this, the needs of the community regarding improving their water supply can be determined. The KAP approach aims to determine what people do and, more importantly, think, and uses techniques such as focus group discussions, interviews with individuals, household questionnaires and community observation transect walks (Duncker, 2001).

For more information about participatory techniques, see the references at the end of this chapter.

4.3.3 Demand assessment

Many Government and ESA strategies emphasize the importance of adopting a 'demand responsive' approach to the delivery of services. The term 'demand' has different meanings to different people. Wedgwood (2003) identifies three interpretations commonly used by different stakeholders:

- **Felt needs**: the 'felt needs' or aspirations of communities; service delivery might be driven by political or equity considerations to meet this demand.

- **Consumption**: engineers in particular tend to see demand as directly proportional to consumption; consequently, water supply schemes are designed according to volumes of water supplied per household. The cost of these schemes, maintenance and financial sustainability of the schemes are often sidelined. There is also a danger that environmental issues such as over abstraction of groundwater may be ignored.

- **Effective demand**: effective demand can be defined as 'demand for goods and services which is backed up with the resources to pay for it'.

While all these definitions are valid, that of 'effective demand' is perhaps the most useful. Demand does not mean that communities must literally demand an improved water supply before this should be considered. It simply means that communities should be able to demonstrate a desire for and commitment to a new service. Deverill et al. (2002) defines demand as *'an informed expression or desire for a particular service, assessed by the investments people are prepared to make, over the lifetime of the service, to receive and sustain it.'*

Demand is usually measured by a community's ability to contribute to initial costs and to demonstrate a willingness to pay (WTP) for ongoing O&M costs. Therein lies part of the problem; this definition of demand does not guarantee sustainability and may not even be a valid indicator. An initial contribution to the cost of a new facility, whether in cash or kind, does not necessarily demonstrate demand within a given community since this may be made by an individual sponsor or be seen as a one-off event. Studies have shown that there is no proven link between a capital contribution and long-term sustainability (IRC, 2002; Harvey et al., 2002b). Also, the ability of users to demonstrate appropriate levels of willingness to pay does not guarantee that this will be sustained. (WTP is addressed in more detail in Section 4.7.)

4

The first step in demand assessment is to assess **the need for a particular service**. Often it is assumed that communities need improved services when in actual fact their priorities are completely different. In order to assess 'demand' it is necessary, through consultation with different community groups, to identify the reasons that community members may desire an improved water supply. These include:

- Reduced time used to collect water;

- Reduced distance to water point;

- Reduced incidence of water-related disease;

- Increased water quantity;

- Improved water quality; and

- Increased opportunities for income generation.

A participatory appraisal is necessary to identify community priorities before any activity to establish a water system is embarked upon. Sustainability is directly related to the value that a given community or individual places on their new water supply. This 'added value' depends upon the above factors, but not necessarily in equal measure. Where the users recognize the health and economic benefits resulting from an improved water supply, this may contribute significantly towards sustainability, but is not a guarantee of it (DeGabriele, 2002). In many cases communities are well aware of the health benefits of an improved water supply but this is not a strong enough argument to ensure that they sustain it.

It is recognized widely that optimum sustainability of systems often depends upon the **lack of availability of alternative water sources** (Breslin, 2003; Harvey & Skinner, 2002; Sutton, 2002). Where water is a basic requirement for survival which is not currently easily accessible, support can build on existing demand. The challenge is to ensure sustainability where water is not perceived to be a major concern (Mawunganidze, 2002). Box 4.1 demonstrates the contrast between similar communities with and without easy access to alternative water sources.

Box 4.1. A tale of two villages[1]

In western Kenya there were two villages within a few kilometres of one another; both had handpumps installed at roughly the same time by the same agency, had very similar agricultural-based populations, consisted of the same ethnic group and received the same mobilization and training from the implementing agency. Five years after installation the handpump in village 1 was still functioning, having broken down and been repaired by the community several times, while the handpump in village 2 broke down approximately three years previously and had never been repaired. In investigating all the variables in the two villages it was discovered that the only major difference between them was that village 2 was located within 200m of a stream, from which the villagers now collected water, while the nearest alternative water source to village 1 was more than 3km away.

---

1. Harvey et al., 2003

Where existing demand for water is insufficient the demand for an improved water supply may be stimulated by developing and promoting options which embody the characteristics that people find most desirable, at a price they are willing to pay (sometimes known as social marketing). This is, however, a sometimes difficult and drawn-out process, and there is a danger that such stimulated demand is superficial and will not be sustained.

4.3.4 Option identification

Once the implementing agency determines that a community demonstrates sufficient demand for an improved water supply, it must then determine what options should be made available to them. Technology should not be predetermined in any rural water supply programme, and the final choice of technology should be made by the community from a range of feasible options. The range of options developed by the agency and offered to communities depends on the following issues:

- Technical factors;

- Financial constraints;

- Policies, plans and legislation;

- Institutional capacity;

- Social and cultural norms;

- Perceptions and priorities; and

- Environmental factors.

The first four of these issues affect the programme rather than individual communities, but social and cultural norms, perceptions and priorities, and environmental factors are likely to be community-specific and determined through community consultation and participation. Information on various aspects of the existing sources of water used by community members, and how they use them, are needed to inform the planning process (Ockelford & Reed, 2002), and may help to determine the most appropriate technical solution. A short feasibility study should be conducted by the implementer to gather information on existing practice, and environmental and technical issues.

Technical factors are crucial since these include the availability of hardware locally, skills required for O&M, and spare parts. Communities need to be encouraged to select **feasible options rather than fashionable options**. Hard questions need to be asked concerning what they are prepared to commit physically and financially for an indefinite period in order to sustain the proposed service. Communities must be made aware that they will not simply get a new facility when theirs finally needs replacement. Where there is a lack of data concerning ongoing O&M and replacement costs, detailed estimates should be made as realistically as possible, allowing for generous margins of error (see Chapter 5), and communicated to potential users. Monitoring of existing systems is required to improve the accuracy of such estimates. WaterAid's experience in

Mozambique has shown that where full information is provided, better off communities closer to towns tend to opt for handpumps while isolated rural villages have increasingly chosen protected wells (Breslin, 2003). Communities must be given real freedom to select their own technology, however low-cost, not pushed towards the implementer's preferred choice.

Often environmental, technical and financial factors severely constrain the range of possible technologies. Even where there is little realistic choice, however, **the importance of the discussion lies as much in the process (sharing the decision-making) as in the final ability to choose**. For this reason, communities should always make the final decision regarding their water system, even where there may be only one or two realistic options.

By presenting technical options it is very easy to raise community expectations unintentionally and care should be taken to prevent the generation of inappropriate expectations or assumptions among community members. It is essential that the implementing agency or facilitator only provides information on technology options for which they will be able to fulfil their responsibilities (see Box 4.2).

Box 4.2. Communities may not always get what they ask for[1]

Fesi is a large village in Kpando district, Ghana, with a population of over 2000. The community was offered a range of technology options and opted for a piped system, for which they had the necessary funds to meet the appropriate community contribution. However, five handpump-equipped boreholes were implemented instead, due primarily to budget constraints of the implementing agency. The WATSAN committee though satisfied with the operation of the handpumps was unhappy because the system did not respond to their needs.

---

1. Harvey et al., 2002a

4.3.5   Informed decision-making

Communities can only make appropriate decisions if they are provided with sufficient information. Ideally, communities should be empowered to make their own decisions regarding:

* The choice of technology to be used;

* Where water points should be located; and

• What O&M management system should be adopted.

Where various technology options are offered or available, it is essential that communities are provided with sufficient information to make an informed choice of appropriate technology for them (Deverill et al., 2002). Where a community makes an inappropriate choice, the cost of sustaining that technology may create additional pressures on already stretched resources and is likely to result in failure.

In order to do this, communities require clearly communicated information on different technologies and associated costs, environmental conditions, O&M and management needs, benefits and constraints. These information needs are summarized in Figure 4.1.

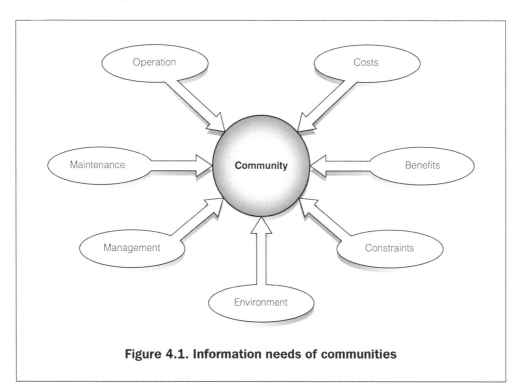

Figure 4.1. Information needs of communities

As well as selecting technology, communities should also participate in determining appropriate locations for water points. This may involve siting a borehole or tapstand. In order to do this, communities should be provided with accurate information on environmental conditions and constraints. A suggested methodology for borehole siting is presented in Section 6.2.5.

Ideally, communities should also be offered a range of management options, though in practice this rarely happens. Communities which are willing to finance a new water supply should not necessarily have to manage it. Alternative O&M management systems are addressed in Chapter 7.

4.4   Community management

As discussed in Chapter 3, the community management, or VLOM, model is the most widespread institutional model used to manage rural water supplies in Africa. VLOM became widespread in the 1980s and yet has undoubtedly delivered only limited success to date. Initially the model relied on community volunteers to maintain and repair their own pumps, but over time it was recognized that not all communities were capable of delivering the required technical inputs. There was also no evidence to suggest that where the local community had been mobilized to repair their own facility (e.g. handpump) higher levels of sustainability were achieved. While the downtime was often reduced (compared to a more central approach) the frequency of breakage often increased. As a result, VLOM was expanded to VLOMM (Village Level Operation and Management of Maintenance) to allow for cases where external pump mechanics conducted repairs, but the community kept responsibility for management. The terms VLOM and VLOMM are now used interchangeably.

4.4.1   WATSAN committees

Research has shown that community participation in maintenance is not critical to sustainability but strong leadership for community management is (Batchelor et al., 2000). Community management usually relies on the formation of a water,

WATSAN or WASHE committee which is responsible for all management issues related to water supply in the community. The members of such a committee vary considerably but implementers and facilitators usually encourage the participation of women and young people, as well as men. Functional literacy and numeracy among committee members have been shown to have a positive impact on the effectiveness of community management (Mumbo, 2001), and are often included in selection criteria, but, in general, these criteria should not be allowed to exclude women. Care should also be taken over the use of the term 'committee' since this may have different meanings and connotations in different languages or cultures. The status, roles and responsibilities of the 'committee' must therefore be clearly communicated.

4

Good governance at the community level during the project cycle is positively correlated with a more sustained water supply (IRC, 2002). It is important that community-based organizations (CBOs), such as water committees, are trusted and respected by general members of the community if they are to be effective. It is interesting to note that where projects use existing community management structures the sustainability of the water point is better than where a new committee is set up (Batchelor et al., 2000). Existing community structures may include other CBOs, such as community co-operatives or development committees, or traditional leadership structures. Local chiefs or tribal leaders often have a major influence within communities and their involvement may be the difference between success and failure.

4.4.2 Water user groups

An alternative to a WATSAN committee is a Water User Group (WUG) which is a larger group of individuals, usually 25 to 50 households, who voluntarily join together to participate in improving and maintaining their water supply on a sustainable basis. Some basic attributes of WUG are that membership should be voluntary; the WUG should have its own identity/name which is different to that of the village or sub-village; membership should be open to either a cluster of households, a public institution or a CBO; the WUG should be registered with the District Council as a legal entity; members should have a clear and supportive basis for legal ownership of a water point and right of occupancy; and affairs should be run on principles commonly agreed upon in a Memorandum of Understanding (van Miert & Binamungu, 2001). The necessary legal framework is the primary difference between the approaches for WUG and traditional committees. Legal recognition of a WUG and legal ownership may be difficult to achieve in some instances, but provide a number of potential benefits:

- Legal ownership of assets increases the sense of responsibility for upkeep of facilities;

- Rights and responsibilities are backed up by regulatory provisions to penalize offenders/intruders;

- WUGs have official support from political leadership (legal protection) at district, ward and village levels; and

- WUGs have full control over use of assets including operation and maintenance.

4.4.3   Sustaining management

Most problems with community management do not occur immediately after the commissioning of an improved water supply but sometime later, normally within one to three years. The reasons for the breakdown of management systems are numerous, but common causes are cited below:

- Community management often relies on voluntary inputs from community members, which people may do for a while but are reluctant to do in the long term.

- Key individuals on the water committee leave the community or die.

- The community organization charged with managing the water supply loses the trust and respect of the general community.

- Failure by community members to contribute maintenance fees leads to disillusionment among committee members who abandon their roles.

- Communities have no contact with local government (or the implementing NGO) and feel that they have abdicated responsibility; they therefore feel abandoned and become demotivated.

Ongoing institutional support and regular monitoring can help to pre-empt some of these problems and find solutions. Simple examples of this might be to restructure the water committee or to identify incentives for participation such as a 'sitting allowance' for committee members. An overseeing role (rather than a management role) may be more acceptable to some communities (Sansom et al., 2001). This means that the CBO oversees O&M but works in partnership with government and private sector stakeholders, whereby the community reports any problems but is not expected to find solutions to these alone. All the stakeholders potentially require professional support (see Section 3.5), and the support given to communities needs to be in the context of the roles of the other parties, such as government institutions and private sector.

One approach that has been used to help sustain community management is to pay WATSAN committee members a 'sitting allowance' from the revenue raised for water supply. This will be most successful where payment systems and amounts are transparent and are clearly conveyed to and agreed by the community as a whole. Committees must also be accountable to the community.

4.4.4   Relinquishing control

Simply because a community owns a water supply facility, made an initial contribution to its installation, and finances O&M does not mean that it must manage it. Implementers should take a flexible approach to management and investigate alternative options to the VLOM approach. Private or public sector management options (as presented in Chapter 7) may provide more sustainable frameworks in some cases. Such options should be discussed with communities who may be only to happy to relinquish control. This should not be seen as disempowerment since the community still has the freedom to express its preferences and, if it chooses, regain control.

4.5   Ownership

There is a widespread perception that 'ownership' is a prerequisite for community management and is the key to sustainability. The prevailing wisdom supports the idea that ownership of the water supply facility will lead to a responsibility for its management, which will lead to a willingness to manage, which in turn will lead to a willingness to meet ongoing O&M costs. In reality, research has shown that there is no automatic relationship between these aspects (Harvey & Reed, 2003). This can be represented by the following pathway, where the crossed-out arrows indicate a perceived link rather than an actual link:

Just because a community owns a facility does not necessarily mean that it acquires a sense of responsibility for its management, nor does it guarantee a willingness to manage or pay for its operation and maintenance. It is essential that implementers are disabused of this common misconception. While these links may exist in some cases, ownership in itself is not the 'key' to sustainability. The reverse of this can also be said to be true, i.e. the fact that a community is willing to pay for O&M does not necessarily mean that they have a strong sense of ownership.

4.5.1 Community versus individual ownership

The issue of communal ownership is very different to individual ownership, yet it is a common mistake to view them in the same way. Where an individual owns a handpump, for example, responsibility for its maintenance is clear and he or she is likely to ensure that it keeps going to maintain a ready supply of water. Where a community owns a handpump the same logic does not necessarily hold true, for the following reasons:

- There may be no definition of what constitutes the 'community' and it may have no clear or legal identity.

- The location of the facility is unlikely to be equidistant from all users and hence true equity is impossible to achieve.

- The ability to pay for the service may vary greatly within the community and the fact that each household should contribute the same amount may be seen as 'unjust' by some.

- Disagreements and distrust between different families or individuals can make the very concept of 'community' difficult to accept.

- The facility or system may be installed on land which belongs to an individual or the government, resulting in a widespread perception that it does not truly belong to the community.

- Some members of a community may believe that water supply should be a government service and disagree with the concept of community ownership and responsibility.

Box 4.3 illustrates the difference between individual and communal ownership.

4.5.2 Legal ownership

Where the water facility remains the legal property of the government, or is situated on land that does not belong to them, communities may feel 'used' as they are asked to manage and maintain a facility that is not legally theirs. Legal ownership of a point water source, such as a handpump, will only be vested in the community if there has been a clear transfer of assets from the implementing agency to the community. This requires the community to be a legal entity, as defined in the WUG approach. Legal ownership may also require the introduction of a by-law that enables a community or group to acquire the right

---

Box 4.3. Individual vs. communal ownership[1]

The Ubombo Family Wells Project in Maputaland, Kwazulu-Natal, South Africa, demonstrates the difference between individual and communal ownership. Here, individual families own hand-augured tubewells equipped with bucket pumps. Each family made a 12 per cent contribution to the total cost of the installation, meets all ongoing O&M costs and carries out maintenance when required. Communities in the area which had been offered handpump-equipped boreholes had rejected these, even though they would not have to pay for O&M, and expressed preference for household tubewells and bucket pumps. This is because the users understand the technology, recognize the high level of reliability and have a high sense of ownership and responsibility.

4

1. Harvey and Kayaga, 2003

of occupancy of a piece of land on which the water supply facility is located and of adequate surrounding land to allow access for all users (van Miert & Binamungu, 2001). This may not always be possible or appropriate, especially where land is owned by private individuals.

4.5.3   Land ownership

It is difficult to generalize on issues of land ownership for the whole of the sub-continent; rural land in sub-Saharan Africa can be owned by individuals, communities, traditional leaders or the government. It is important, however, for implementers to identify who legally owns the land that water systems are to be installed upon, and how this may affect ownership and responsibility for the service. For example, a water facility installed on privately owned land which is 'donated' to the community may lead to all sorts of problems if the land owner later changes his or her mind. In cases where individuals and communities have unsecured tenure on property this may affect their sense of stability and hence the sustainability of 'community-owned' facilities. Issues surrounding land ownership, including government policy, regulatory and legal frameworks need to be investigated locally, and appropriate reform advocated where required.

4.5.4   Does ownership really matter?

It is crucial to note that ownership is not in itself the answer to sustainable community-managed water services. Rather, it is a complex issue which requires in-depth consultation to understand. Where ownership issues are difficult and it is unlikely that a community will establish a strong sense of ownership of a particular facility (due to legal, land-ownership or community constraints) it may be more effective to abandon the desire to achieve community ownership and to develop a **sense of responsibility** for financing the upkeep of the facility. Instilling an understanding of the need to pay for water is one way in which this might be achieved.

4.6 Poverty

4.6.1 Ability to pay

Most rural water supplies serve poor communities. The question of whether such communities are actually able to pay for operation and maintenance of low-cost technologies is often raised, but research suggests that 'willingness' to pay is usually a more important issue than 'ability' to pay (Harvey et al., 2002b). The assumption that poor people have no resources at all inevitably leads to unsustainable subsidies and is usually inaccurate since many people are already paying a high price for sub-standard services (Evans, 1992).

Most communities do have resources and hence the ability to pay (at least something) for maintenance; however, the way in which those resources are managed will influence the ability of communities to **access** resources when needed. In agriculture-based communities, money may be more readily available following harvests than at other times of the year. It is therefore important that different ways of storing resources are investigated so that funds can be raised when needed. Where transparency and accountability are in place, maintenance funds may be stored in a bank account or with a treasurer. However, where currency devaluation or excessive bank charges deter communities from using bank accounts, alternative storage mechanisms may be used successfully, such as storing agricultural produce, community livestock or purchasing 'consumable' spares in advance of breakdowns (Box 4.4). The community should then have the ability to facilitate repairs at all times of the year (assuming they have the right spares in stock of course). Some communities also pay pump menders in kind (e.g. with a bag of maize) rather than in cash.

Box 4.4. Investing maintenance funds[1]

Due to restrictive bank charges the WATSAN committee in Philipo village, Petauke District, Zambia decided to invest their maintenance funds in spare parts rather than in the bank. Over a period of several months they had bought handpump riser pipes, rods, cylinder and cup and washer kit ready for future use.

---

1. Harvey and Skinner, 2002

In some situations the ability of the community to pay for maintenance may be severely limited or inadequate. Regional climatic events, such as drought, have a large negative impact on agricultural productivity so that the resources available to communities are severely limited. In such situations the ability to pay will be a key constraint to sustainability.

As discussed in Chapter 5, full cost-recovery of operation and maintenance from rural communities in Africa, at least on a large-scale, has not been achieved to date. This indicates that O&M is routinely subsidized by external support agencies or governments. This in itself is not a threat to sustainability provided that the subsidies themselves are sustainable. For example, if local government institutions such as district councils are able to routinely provide finances for transportation and storage of spare parts, this will be a considerable contribution to long-term sustainability.

An initial cash contribution is not a prerequisite for project sustainability; in fact, a study by IRC (2002) indicated that an initial contribution is actually **negatively** related to the sustainability of the water supply. The ability to pay such a contribution does not necessarily mean that there will be the ability or willingness to pay ongoing maintenance costs, especially since an individual, politician or contractor sometimes makes this payment on behalf of the community. Community participation, good governance and user satisfaction will have a greater influence on sustainability (IRC, 2002). Where a community is to be the legal owner of a new system it remains appropriate that they should make an initial contribution, but this may not be necessary where this is not to be the case. In either situation, an initial contribution is unlikely to be a crucial deciding factor (see Section 5.3).

4.6.2 Impact on poverty

Increased sustainability of water supplies can impact positively on poverty within communities by:

- Improving health through the provision of water of improved quantity and quality;

- Increasing available financial resources by reducing the burden of disease and hence money spent on hospital fees and drugs;

- Releasing time previously used for collecting water for other activities;

- Increasing skills in construction and mechanics through ongoing training of community masons and pump repairers; and

- Facilitating income generation activities through productive use of water; for example through watering of livestock, brick/block making or irrigation.

Where water supplies fail, the negative impact on poverty within communities may be significant. **A non-functioning handpump is a stark symbol of unfulfilled expectations and unchanging poverty**. If communities are provided with sufficient information to make their own decision regarding technology choice, they are likely to opt for low-cost options which they are willing and able to sustain. This should avoid excessive pressure on existing financial resources which would lead to increased poverty and inevitable failure.

4.7   Willingness to pay

Willingness to pay (WTP) is not necessarily directly linked to poverty but potentially has far greater impact on service sustainability. There are various definitions of willingness to pay but the one used most widely states that 'WTP is the maximum amount that an individual states they are willing to pay for a good or service' (DFID Demand Assessment Seminar, December, 1997). The term willingness to pay can be confusing as users may not be 'happy' paying a certain tariff; but they are willing to pay this amount rather than go without (Webster, 1999). Willingness to pay among communities is influenced by a number of factors, including the following (identified by Evans, 1992):

- Service level and standard;

- Perceived benefits;

- Level of income;

- Price and relative cost;

- Time saved;

- Characteristics of existing sources;

- Community cohesion;

- Perception of ownership and responsibility;

- Transparency of financial management; and

- Institutional framework.

Assessing this willingness to pay at the onset of the planning process is a key factor in determining whether the water supply is likely to be sustainable. While the level of income will influence this, it is only one of many factors.

It is important to note that men and women may have separate access to and control over resources and it should not be assumed that men are the principal providers in paying for water supplies (Evans, 1992). The willingness to pay among women may therefore be equally or more important than that among men. It should also be noted that there are often inequalities or contrasts within communities whereby some sections of the community subsidize others, either willingly or reluctantly. There are many cases where only certain sections of, or individuals within, a community contribute to a maintenance fund. In general, this is accepted by those contributing, who in effect subsidize their neighbours, although there are some cases where this leads to heated disagreement.

4.7.1   Measuring willingness to pay

There are three ways of estimating WTP:

- Observing prices that people pay for goods in various markets (e.g. water vending, buying from neighbours, paying local taxes).

- Observing individual expenditures of money, time, labour etc. to obtain goods - or to avoid their loss. This method might involve an assessment of coping strategies and involve observations, focus group discussions and even household surveys.

- Asking people directly what they are willing to pay for goods or services in the future.

The first two approaches are based on observations of behaviour, or revealed preferences, while the third technique is based upon stated preferences and includes costed option ranking and the contingent valuation methodology.

Costed option ranking is a methodology developed under an approach known as PREPP - 'Participation, Ranking, Experience, Perception and Partnership' (Coates et al., 2001). The purpose of this ranking exercise is to determine local consumer preferences for potential improved service options compared with the existing water services and sources. The group is presented with pictures showing a mix of two types or categories of service option: potential options with estimated annual costs for water and the most popular existing sources and costs. It is essential that costs are accurate and not underestimated (more details on costing different water supply options are presented in Chapter 6). This process makes it possible to identify the consumer's first, second and third preferences for a range of service options as part of a negotiated demand process. Issues related to storage, shared resources and sustained willingness to pay are explored via pictures and the sharing of experiences.

A more in depth method is the Contingent Valuation Method (CVM) in which facilitators carry out house-to-house surveys to determine the maximum amount that respondents would be willing to pay for the proposed improvement in water services in the context of the existing institutional regime within which households are free to allocate their financial resources (Whittington, 1998). This method has been increasingly advocated by economists and sector specialists as a useful tool for gathering reasonably accurate data about how much a household can afford and is willing to pay for particular water supply options presented to them (Cummings et al., 1986). This approach has been used primarily in an urban context and the cost of WTP surveys is currently somewhat prohibitive. There is, therefore, a need to develop a simplified version which can be applied to rural areas. The process supports community participation and enables an informed choice at the household level as well as for the community as a whole (for more information refer to Wedgwood & Sansom, 2003.)

Unfortunately, what no existing methods do is ensure that the measured willingness to pay is sustained.

4.7.2   Sustaining willingness to pay

Services which rely on the users to finance ongoing running costs will only be sustainable if the willingness of users to pay is sustained. Community members who are willing to finance O&M costs in the initial stages may soon become unwilling to do so. There are a variety of possible reasons for this reduced willingness to pay:

• Lack of transparency and accountability among the WATSAN committee;

• No faults with the facility and therefore no clear reason for paying;

• Dissatisfaction with water supply (location, time to queue, water quality/ quantity);

• Competition from cheaper water sources;

• Change in individual priorities.

This demonstrates that the problem with WTP surveys is that they can only measure the stated willingness of an individual at a particular given time. In order to sustain the necessary willingness to pay, however, there are a number of measures that can be taken.

Institutional support for communities

Perhaps the most effective mechanism that can be used to sustain willingness to pay is appropriate institutional support for communities, as described in Section 3.5. Where communities are regularly visited by an overseeing institution to monitor systems this reaffirms the need to contribute to O&M. The institution can advise communities on how to make best use of unspent funds through investment, can regulate WATSAN committees to ensure transparency, and can help to rectify any causes of dissatisfaction with a particular water system. Quarterly monitoring visits provide an ideal mechanism to identify problems early and find sustainable solutions.

Paying for water

The second measure that can assist greatly in sustaining willingness to pay relies on a major mind-shift among community members. **If water supply users understand that they must pay for water, rather than to maintain a system, many of the obstacles to sustained community financing disappear**. Such a mindset needs to be established early on in the community consultation process and, where there are existing facilities installed under different programmes, this is likely to be difficult to achieve. New programmes, however, have the opportunity to develop awareness and place the emphasis on 'water' rather than the 'facility'. If users accept from the outset that they have to pay for water from an improved water supply and that this will always be the case, financing is more likely to be sustained, providing that the service supplied meets the standard demanded by the users.

4.8   Gender

4.8.1   Impact of gender on sustainability

It is generally believed that sustained services are more likely to result from project interventions when they respond to the demand of all potential users - the poor, better off, women, and men - and empower the users to take greater control over their services throughout the project cycle (Narayan, 1995; Gross et al., 2001). However, some studies have indicated that consideration of gender and poverty makes no significant difference with respect to the sustainability of services (Batchelor et al., 2000; IRC, 2002). Such findings need to viewed with care, since the definitions of sustainability used by different individuals and organizations vary. The 'handpump function' (or borehole function) is sometimes used to measure sustainability and is related to two key factors: the frequency of breakdown and the average downtime (Batchelor et al., 2000). This handpump function is therefore a measure of technical sustainability but not of overall sustainability, as defined in Chapter 1.

Equity

Equity is one of the key success criteria linked to project sustainability. If sustainable projects are to demonstrate equity, then consideration of gender and poverty must be a prerequisite. It is important to note that water supply services which do not consider gender and the poor may perform well technically, but may leave an important segment of the population unserved and have less impact on the abandonment of less safe water sources (IRC, 2002). Since women form the greatest proportion of the poor and are also on average poorer than men (Reed, 2002), it is especially important that their needs and wishes are addressed.

Tokenism

Recent research has shown that many communities have female members in their community Water and Sanitation (WATSAN) committees, which demonstrates an increased awareness of the need for the involvement of women (Harvey et al., 2002b). However, the presence of women is often a requirement of the implementing agency rather than a community initiative, and as a result their involvement may be tokenistic (see Box 4.5).

Box 4.5. Gender roles in community WATSAN committees[1]

Visits to communities in Ghana found that men dominated WATSAN committee meetings and were responsible for specific roles such as chairperson, treasurer and secretary, while women were simply described as committee members. The influence of women in the decision-making process was therefore questionable, and was certainly not clear.

---

1. Harvey et al., 2002a

Studies in Malawi and Mozambique indicated that the presence, or absence, of women committee members did not affect the sustainability of the handpump (Bachelor et al., 2000), but their actual involvement is not documented. Societies and communities cannot be changed overnight and it remains important to determine realistic yet meaningful roles for different groups. The implementing/

facilitating institutions, whether government or NGO, must become genuinely gender sensitive before communities can be expected to be so. The first challenge, therefore, is how to make institutions truly gender sensitive so that they are not satisfied with women's tokenistic involvement (Regmi & Fawcett, 2001). It may then be possible to evaluate fully the impact of the involvement of women on project sustainability.

The benefits of women's participation in project planning and implementation of rural water supplies have long been argued. Perhaps the most important aspect in relation to sustainability is that women are often concerned about the operation of their water supply and are motivated to do something about it because it directly affects them. Field research in Zambia involved informal discussions with women in many communities, many of whom demonstrated a great interest in water supply issues and a high awareness of associated health implications (Harvey & Skinner, 2002). Some communities also reported that women made more successful treasurers than men, because they were trusted more by those contributing to the maintenance fund. Women can be equipped to take on important roles through focused training by the implementing agency.

4

It is difficult to generalize about the roles that are best fulfilled by men and women respectively. What is perhaps most important is that all community members, of whatever age and gender, are given an opportunity to actively participate, while respect for traditional and cultural practices is maintained. This must be assessed locally and may vary between geographical areas, ethnic groups and individual communities.

4.8.2 Impact of water supply on gender issues

It is interesting to note that water supplies that are not designed to consider gender and the poor may appear to perform well technically, but may leave an important segment of the population unserved and have less impact on the abandonment of less safe water sources (IRC, 2002). Since our definition of sustainability (Section 1.3) states that the benefits of the water supply should be realized by 'all users', rural water supply programmes should consider differences in gender roles, activities, needs and opportunities in order to ensure service equity.

Both women and men make competent pump repairers, but women repairers are not always accepted by community members who have decision-making powers (Harvey & Skinner, 2002), and there often appears to be a higher acceptance of women in non-technical roles such as environmental health assistants and pump caretakers (responsible primarily for keeping the pump surrounds clean). The

Photograph 4.1. Woman and child at handpump, Zambia

role of women in the upkeep of water points, however, redefines their position at the lowest level of water management and is of little consequential value in determining gender equity (Joshi & Fawcett, 2001). Regmi & Fawcett (2001) argue that it is important for local men and male technicians to be made aware that water has not only a technical dimension but also social dimensions, while Reed (2002) asserts that school boys and girls should become aware of the wider interrelated issues if gender stereotyping is not to be reinforced. While these are valuable goals, striving to achieve gender equity and empowerment of women may sometimes divert attention from trying to implement a sustainable water supply. Water supply programmes should first and foremost provide potable water to the target communities. It is essential that locally appropriate and culturally sensitive measures are taken to ensure equity in service provision and long-term sustainability. This means that gender and poverty issues must be considered and addressed within the planning process but does not necessarily mean that the implementation of an improved water supply must result in gender equity.

4.9   Social steps towards sustainability

Community and social issues undoubtedly have a considerable influence on the sustainability of water systems and services regardless of what management system is used. Figure 4.2 outlines the steps that should be taken to ensure that social factors have the maximum beneficial impact on service sustainability. This process should be carried by the implementing agency at community level.

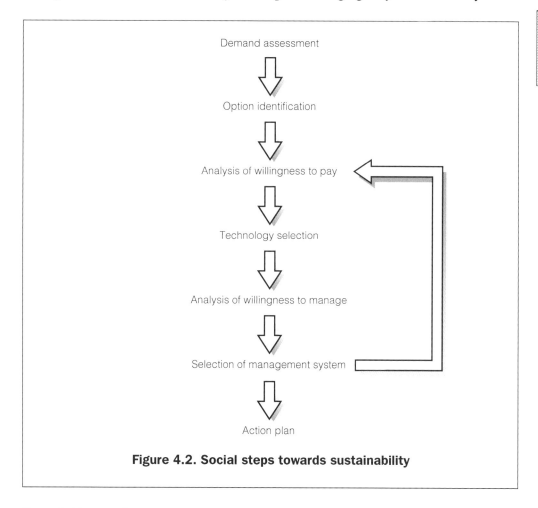

Demand assessment

Option identification

Analysis of willingness to pay

Technology selection

Analysis of willingness to manage

Selection of management system

Action plan

Figure 4.2. Social steps towards sustainability

Step 1. Demand assessment

The first step in the process is to measure community demand for an improved water supply (see Section 4.3.3). This can be achieved by conducting a series of consultations with different groups and individuals within the target community to identify the reasons that community members desire an improved water supply. From the consultation process a range of incentives and priorities can be determined and the expected 'added value' that a new water supply will bring can be measured. At this stage it may be possible to determine whether there is adequate demand for a water supply although this will be more firmly established after Step 3.

Step 2. Option identification

The next step is to present a range of water supply options to the community. The options available will depend primarily on environmental conditions, existing water sources, financial feasibility and community priorities expressed during the demand assessment.

Step 3. Analysis of willingness to pay

A simplified willingness to pay survey should then be conducted to assess the maximum amounts that community members would be willing to pay for each of the different technology options presented to them, both towards initial costs and ongoing O&M costs. O&M costs must be estimated as accurately as possible and this is easiest where detailed records are kept of O&M requirements (see Section 5.2). This will determine the relative demand or preference for each option. The most basic way in which to do this is to ask individuals about their preferences and at what price they would be willing to 'buy' the water, based on the level, quantity and quality of service. There is a danger that respondents will not answer truthfully, and what they say they will pay does not reflect what they would actually pay. Techniques such as PREPP (see Section 4.7) can be applied to try to eliminate biased responses; in particular, the way that the options are presented to the respondent, and how the willingness to pay question is asked are important. It is impossible, however, to remove a certain degree of error from the process.

Step 4. Technology selection

The information collated in Steps 2 and 3 should then be combined so that the community members are able to select their preferred water supply technology from a range of options, based on the advantages and disadvantages and related sustainability issues for each. The stated willingness to pay should be matched against the projected costs of O&M (see Chapter 5) to determine which options the community can afford. The final choice of technology should be made by the community as a whole and a consensus of opinion should be sought. The key determining factors are generally low cost and the environmental conditions.

Step 5. Analysis of willingness and ability to manage

Once the technology has been selected the willingness and ability of the community to manage their chosen system should be assessed. In order to do this the management requirements for the selected technology should be presented clearly to the community. This should include a projected breakdown of requirements for operation, maintenance, tariff collection and financial management. Simply asking community members whether they would be 'willing' or 'able' to undertake activities may be the first step but this is likely to provide incomplete or inaccurate information. Evidence of other community-based activities or organizations should be reviewed and it should be made clear that if they are unwilling or unable to manage their selected system this does not mean that the community will not get an improved water supply. Roles for men and women should be investigated and active participation of people of both genders and from a variety of age groups should be encouraged but not enforced. Migration patterns in and out of the community, for example for seasonal work, should be investigated and the likely impact of this on community management structures assessed.

4

Step 6. Selection of management system

The management system selected will depend on the willingness and ability of the community to take on responsibility for management and the range of options available. This may be influenced by the location of the community with respect to private sector organizations, and by existing management systems in operation in the surrounding area. Possible management options might include:

- Community management using pump maintenance volunteers from within the community;

- Community management using private area pump mechanics;

- Community-private sector management whereby the CBO collects revenue and pays this to a private service provider which is responsible for managing O&M; or

- Private sector management where the private service provider collects revenue and manages O&M.

Roles and responsibilities must be clearly defined for each option so that the community is able to make an informed choice. Estimated costs and cashflow predictions, including implications for each stakeholder, should be presented to the community. If the selected management system has implications on cost - for example, the selected privately managed system might be slightly more expensive than the community managed one - then the willingness of the community to pay must be matched against this to ensure that the cost is still within the assessed range. Where this is not the case the whole process may need to be repeated from the willingness to pay stage.

Step 7. Action plan

The final step in the process is to develop an action plan in conjunction with the community to determine a time frame of activities to implement the improved water supply, select individuals/groups to be involved, and develop an appropriate management system.

Further reading

Dayal, R., van Wijk, C. and Mukherjee, N. (2000) *Methodology for Participatory Assessments: With communities, institutions and policy makers.* Water and sanitation Program, The World Bank: Washington D.C.

Gosling, L. and Edwards, M. (1995) Toolkits: *A practical guide to assessment, monitoring, review and evaluation.* Save the Children: London.

Rietbergen-McCracken, J. and Narayan, D. (1998) *Participation and Social Assessment: Tools and techniques.* The World Bank: Washington D.C.

Schouten, T. and Moriarty, P. (2003) *Community Water, Community Management - From system to service in rural areas.* ITDG Publishing/IRC.

Sutton, S. and Nkoloma, H. (2003) *Encouraging Change: Sustainable steps in water supply, sanitation and hygiene.* TALC: St. Albans, UK.

van Miert, T. and Binamungu, D. (2001) *The Shinyanga Experience: Water user group concept as a sustainable management system for hand pump wells.* SKAT: St. Gallen, Switzerland.

Wedgwood and Sansom, K. (2003) *Willingness-to-pay Surveys - A Streamlined Approach: Guidance notes for small town water services.* WEDC, Loughborough University: UK.

Chapter 5

Financial issues

Sustainable financing mechanisms need to consider O&M and longer-term rehabilitation needs. This is essential if systems are to remain operational indefinitely. Implementers should strive to instil in users a sense of the need to pay for a water service. The emphasis must be shifted from paying for maintenance of a facility to paying for the provision of safe, adequate and accessible water. This concept of paying for water may be difficult to instil in water users in poor rural communities, but has the potential to remove many barriers to sustainable community financing. Financial issues discussed in this chapter include costing operation and maintenance, community financing, institutional financing, and subsidy.

5.1   Budgetary responsibilities

The first step in ensuring sustained financing is to determine stakeholder responsibilities for different costs associated with rural water services.

5.1.1   Cost allocation

Associated costs for rural water supply can be divided into the following categories:

- Needs assessment and community mobilization;

- Technical services for facility provision;

- Technical services for O&M;

- Institutional support for O&M;

- National and regional planning, co-ordination, monitoring and evaluation; and

- Upgrading, rehabilitation and expansion.

Where community saving or investment schemes are used there is also a need to consider inflation and currency depreciation. There are stakeholders who can finance these activities and also those who can implement them. The commonest options are summarized in Table 5.1.

Needs assessment and community mobilization are usually funded by the implementing agency, whether ESA, NGO or government institution. The cost of this may be significant and it is essential that adequate budgetary allocation is given to such 'software' activities as well as the associated 'hardware'. The degree of community mobilization and hence funding required will depend on the selected management option. Programmes using community management will require greater inputs than those adopting alternative strategies.

Table 5.1. Budgetary responsibilities

Activity	Financier	Implementer
Needs assessment and community mobilization	ESA, NGO or Local government	NGO, Local government or Private sector
Techical services for facility provision	ESA, NGO or Local government or Community	NGO, Community or Private sector
Technical services for O&M	Community and Local government or NGO	Community or Private sector
Institutional support for O&M	NGO or Local government	NGO, Local government or Private sector
National and regional planning and co-ordination	National and Regional government	National and Regional government
Upgrading, rehabilitation and expansion	NGO, Local government (and ideally Community, though this rarely occurs at present)	NGO or Private sector

Technical services for facility provision are usually implemented by the private sector and include system design and construction, borehole drilling, and pump installation. This can also be financed by ESA, NGO or government, although some government institutions lack sufficient financial and technical resources and rely heavily on external support (see Box 5.1).

It is now the norm for the technical services for O&M to be financed by users, usually through the collection of maintenance fees. These services are conducted

---

Box 5.1. Government dependency[1]

'Because of the nature of the equipment required we can never wholly fund and support handpump projects. ...NGOs are the livewire in providing water and sanitation services to the rural people. Without them the process would not work because we are not technically equipped.'

---

1. Mr. K. Ba-Innimayah, District Co-ordinating Director, Afram Plains District, Ghana

by either the private sector (including individual artisans or mechanics) or community volunteers. This cost covers routine maintenance and repair; more complex needs may be beyond the financial capacity of the community.

Another important cost is that of institutional support for O&M. Monitoring, regulation and facilitation requires adequate human and financial resources. It is likely to be unrealistic to expect communities to finance this, in which case local government requires adequate funding to fulfil this role. Where government institutions are particularly weak NGOs can take on the responsibility, although this is not ideal.

Most programmes lack financing strategies for rehabilitation and replacement costs. Ideally, these costs should be met by the users with minimal assistance from local government. This can only be achieved, however, if strategies are developed early on and financing mechanisms are clear and transparent.

5.1.2   Cost recovery

Cost recovery refers to the practice of charging users the full (or nearly full) cost of providing services (MacDonald & Pape, 2002). Full cost recovery means reimbursement to service providers of both recurring and non-recurring costs associated with construction, operation and maintenance of a water service. Costs include, but are not limited to, the costs of community mobilization, planning, design, administration, construction, equipment, and O&M expenses. Full cost recovery for rural water services in Africa is rarely, and probably never, achieved, because:

- The cost of facilities is significantly beyond the means of most rural communities; and

- The political and humanitarian desire for improved access to water, and definition of water as a 'right', mean implementers are reluctant to seek full reimbursement.

Implementation

Cost recovery for construction and installation of new water systems and facilities is, in practice, negligible. Communities are often requested to contribute 5 to15 per cent of initial capital costs, which does not even cover the cost of the facility itself (e.g. handpump, apron and borehole). The costs of mobilization, administration, management and transportation generally remain hidden. Even where communities make a financial contribution this may sit in a fund for future maintenance or institutional support, and is intended to demonstrate ownership rather than to recover actual implementation costs.

It is generally accepted that **user financing of implementation costs for improved rural water systems is an unrealistic goal**. Even in developed countries this is more commonly funded by governments than water consumers. In a rural African context, therefore, increased access to water currently relies on investment from governments and humanitarian donors.

Operation and maintenance

Cost recovery for ongoing service delivery and recurrent O&M costs is a much more achievable target, although this rarely reaches 100 per cent, due to hidden costs such as subsidy of spare parts provision, supply chains and institutional support. Rather than using the term 'cost recovery' this can be summarized as 'paying for water', i.e. the cost of ongoing provision of water from an existing system.

Expecting users to pay all direct O&M costs is a realistic target which implementers should strive to meet. Direct O&M costs comprise those for maintenance, repair and replacement. Cost recovery targets for private sector O&M systems should incorporate appropriate profit margins. Such systems have the added potential benefit of financial support to decentralized government institutions through local taxation.

Upgrade, rehabilitation and expansion

Ideally, water tariffs should cater for future system upgrade, rehabilitation and expansion costs as well as ongoing O&M costs. Currently, this occurs very rarely. One of the main constraints to this is the need for a transparent, secure and sustainable method of storing and investing money for future use. Community-managed financing mechanisms are rarely able to fulfil these requirements. Private sector service providers could potentially do this but require sufficient incentive and regulation. The second key constraint is insufficient ability and willingness to pay for these costs among users (see Section 5.2.3). In many cases it may be unrealistic to expect communities to finance these costs and this highlights the need for a supporting institution to provide backstopping (see Section 3.5). This also applies to emergency needs such as the results of sabotage or natural disasters.

5.2 The cost of sustainability

If rural water services are to be sustainable the following three categories of cost must be (a) calculated, and (b) funded:

- Direct O&M costs;

- Institutional O&M costs (including monitoring and evaluation); and

- Rehabilitation and expansion costs.

5

5.2.1 Costing O&M

When considering stand-alone water supply options such as handpumps, the main consideration when determining direct O&M costs is to incorporate recurrent repair costs and future replacement costs. Without considering the need for saving specific sums of money to replace major component parts, the sustainability of most water systems is undermined. One way is to set aside equal amounts every year, taking into account interest rates; this is known as amortization (Deverill, et al., 2002). These amounts can form part of the O&M tariffs charged. A four-stage process can be used to determine appropriate tariffs. Note that this considers the replacement of the handpump only, not the borehole (see Section 5.3).

1.   The first step is to calculate recurrent O&M costs, which include replacement of minor components such as seals and bearings, routine preventive maintenance such as greasing or tightening parts, and any wages associated with O&M. Table 5.2 gives an example of components, costs and estimated frequency of replacement for an India Mark II handpump.

    The annual maintenance cost may vary considerably, even for the same technology, and depends on the local environment and chosen maintenance system. For example, handpumps operating in areas of deep, aggressive groundwater may have much higher O&M costs than those operating in shallow, neutral conditions. Also, private sector maintenance systems may produce slightly higher costs than community-based systems, to allow for adequate profit for the service provider. The only reliable way to obtain guidance for costs in specific local conditions is through appropriate monitoring (see Chapter 9).

Annual maintenance cost, M = Cost of minor components + Labour costs + Profits

Table 5.2. Example of recurrent O&M costs for an India Mark II handpump[1]

Component	Estimated frequency of replacement (f) Years	Unit cost (U) US$	Annual cost (U/f) US$
O-ring seal	2	1.60	0.80
Cup leather	2	1.00	0.50
Chain	3	3.60	1.20
Handle axle	3	6.00	2.00
Axle bearing	3	7.50	2.50
M12 x 10 nut	1	1.50	1.50
M12 x 50 nut	1	1.50	1.50
Foot valve rubber	3	6.00	2.00
Piston valve rubber	2	1.00	0.50
Grease	1	2.50	2.50
Transportation costs	N/A	N/A	5.00
Pump caretaker wage	N/A	N/A	15.00
Total annual maintenance cost, M =			**$35.00**

1. Based on data from World Vision, Ghana. This is an example only; f and U will depend on local economy, quality and age of equipment, environmental conditions and usage pressure.

2.   The second step is to calculate the current replacement costs and the projected life-span of major components which are likely to need to be replaced. Depending on the technology and environment this may be based

on the replacement of the entire facility (e.g. handpump) or specific components of that facility. Table 5.3 gives an example of the major components of an India Mark II handpump which may need replacing after a five year period of use, and their respective costs.

Table 5.3. Example of 5 year replacement costs for an India Mark II handpump[1]

Component	Unit cost US$
Handpump cylinder	115.00
Foot valve	8.00
Handpump tank	22.00
Handpump head	81.00
10 connecting rods	80.00
Apron and drainage repairs	30.00
Total replacement cost, R =	**$336.00**

1. This is an example based on data from World Vision, Ghana, which identifies components requiring replacement five years after installation, assuming that stainless steel riser pipes are used. Where pipes are likely to be subject to corrosion these should be included in the cost estimate.

Once calculated, the estimated replacement cost should be compared to the total current cost of a complete handpump. In some cases the cost of a complete handpump may be lower than or similar to that of the component parts, particularly where pumps are ordered in bulk. If this is the case the entire handpump could be replaced after five years rather than the major components listed.

Current replacement cost, R = Current cost of complete facility or major components

n = Estimated number of years before replacement

The value of n may be greater than 5 and will depend on the particular technology, model, manufacturer and conditions under which it is operating.

3. The next step is to calculate the annual amount or **annuity** which needs to be put aside each year to meet future replacement costs. This is based on an Annuity Factor (AF), which is a function of the expected life-span of the

equipment in years (n) and the interest rate (r) in the local economy (Wedgwood & Sansom, 2003). This does not consider inflation but allows for devaluation, which is especially important for imported components and overrides inflation effects in many developing countries. The following equation can be used:

$$\textbf{Annunity, A} = \frac{\text{Current replacement cost, R}}{\text{Annuity factor}(\text{AF}_{r,\,n})}$$

Annuity factors are based on number of years and interest rates and can be read directly off financial cost tables. Such a table is presented in Annex B. In order to adjust for inflation the annuity can be multiplied by the cumulative inflation rate.

4.   The final step is to calculate the average annual cost of O&M per household. Ideally, the annual amount paid each year (or saved in a communal/private fund) should be slightly higher than the calculated annuity to allow for unforeseen events and inflation. A contingency factor of 20 per cent can be used to compensate for this and will ensure that the users have saved enough to compensate for future price changes for the required component. The household tariff per year, H, can be estimated using the following equation, where N is the number of households in the community:

$$\textbf{Annual household tariff, H} = 1.2 \times \left[\frac{M + A}{N}\right]$$

This is based simply on the total number of households using the facility. To ensure equity, household tariffs can be modified by three factors: the distance to the source, the number of people in the household, and 'special' factors such as poverty or disability (Deverill, et al., 2002). Box 5.2 gives a worked example for a handpump water supply.

The household tariffs calculated for low-cost technologies, such as handpumps and gravity-fed systems, are generally very low and normally below $0.50 a month. The process above can be repeated after five years to assess whether an increase in tariff is required based on the costs at that time. Alternatively, tariffs may be calculated for a twenty year period from the start of the service, accounting for repeated replacement of major components and/or pumps.

Box 5.2. Setting household tariffs for a handpump water supply[1]

Using the example for the India Mark II handpump above:

Total annual maintenance cost,	M = $35
Current replacement cost,	R = $336
Estimated number of years before replacement,	n = 5 years
Approximate interest rate,	r = 20%
Annuity factor (read from table, Annex B)	$AF_{r,n}$ = 2.83

Annuity, A = R/ $AF_{r,n}$ = 336 / 2.83 = $119

Number of households,   N = 50 (300 people)

Annual household tariff, H = $1.2 \times \left[\dfrac{M + A}{N} \right]$ = $1.2 \times \left[\dfrac{35 + 119}{50} \right]$ = **$3.70**

This can then be divided by 12 to convert to a monthly household tariff of **$0.30**.

---

1. Example only

5

Ongoing monitoring and regulation is essential to make appropriate adjustments for changing circumstances. The above process does not include costing for rehabilitation and expansion, which is considered in Section 5.2.3.

5.2.2   Costing institutional support

An ongoing issue raised in this book is the need for institutional support for community-based management systems or for regulation of the private sector. Such support obviously has an ongoing cost associated with it and yet this has been largely ignored in the past. Nedjoh et al. (2003) argues that local government institutions should earmark funds for monitoring and O&M and suggests that 6 per cent of investment funds for increasing access to rural water supply should be allocated to this. This is based on an ongoing programme to construct 100 new water points per annum, in an area with 500 existing water points. Obviously, institutional costs will vary considerably from location to location and it may be that a direct relationship with expansion investment is not always appropriate. It is essential, however, that the cost of institutional support is estimated and that appropriate budgetary allocation is made for this. Table 5.4 presents an example breakdown of costs for institutional support which shows the aspects which should be considered and estimated cost ratios for these. These costs are based on consultation with government agencies and NGOs in the countries visited under this research project and are indicative rather than accurate.

Table 5.4. Example breakdown of costs for institutional support[1]

Activity	Annual cost per 100 communities US$
Monitoring and evaluation • quarterly monitoring visits to all communities	3,000
Participatory planning • liaison with problem communities to develop solutions	2,000
Specialist technical assistance • advice and intervention for unforeseen technical problems	2,000
Capacity building • training of stakeholders (staff, communities, private sector etc.)	3,000
Total annual cost per 100 communities	**$10,000**

1. Unit costs are likely to reduce with an increase in the number of communities to which institutions provide support; this is an example only.

The above costing example equates to US$100 per supported community per year. Such a cost is not excessive and for 100 communities is roughly the cost of one handpump-equipped borehole in many African countries. The figure quoted could be reduced considerably further where institutions support a greater number of communities, where communities develop increased self-sufficiency, or where support from other stakeholders (e.g. non-profit organizations) is available. What is vitally important is that institutions attempt to estimate costs and budget accordingly.

Support costs need to be determined locally and appropriate long-term funding mechanisms sought. Where possible, local government institutions should develop budgets which recognize the need for such expenditure on a long-term basis. Even where water supply management systems are not community-based, institutional support costs are likely to remain at similar levels. In public-private models community-based costs may be replaced with those related to regulation of the private sector. The added advantage of this model is that taxation of the private sector can contribute to funding this support.

5.2.3   Rehabilitation and expansion costs

The cost of long-term rehabilitation should also be assessed where possible. This does not refer to the replacement of equipment or components but to larger scale measures, such as borehole rehabilitation or upgrade of pumps and systems. For the example of a handpump-equipped borehole it is important to recognize the borehole as part of the water system as well as the pump. Eventually the borehole itself may need rehabilitation due to problems such as siltation, insufficient yield and corrosion of screens/casing (see Chapter 6). Such measures may entail considerable cost and this must be **met by the supporting institution and/or the users of the system**.

Currently, most rehabilitation, upgrade and expansion costs are met by the supporting institution, whether government or NGO. Many government policies and strategies do not recognize the need for rehabilitation or, if they do, accept that they will have to finance this. The five year Rural Water and Sanitation Operation Plan in Uganda states that:

Government will support major rehabilitation expenses in the interim, in the long-term it is expected that communities will also take over these expenses.' (DWD, 2002b).

5

While this is a long-term strategic 'expectation', it is a gross overestimation to assume that communities will be able and willing to finance major rehabilitation costs where they often fail to finance the simplest repairs. It is most likely that this will only be achieved, in Uganda and elsewhere, by adopting an incremental process where costs are clear from the beginning. If communities of users are to be expected to finance rehabilitation, even in the 'long-term', appropriate financing mechanisms must be established in advance. Using the method described in Section 5.2.1, the 'rehabilitation annuity' needs to be estimated in addition to that for replacement. This can be done using the same equation and the current cost of the rehabilitation measure that will eventually be required.

Rehabilitation annuity, A_R $= \dfrac{\text{Current rehabilitation cost}}{\text{Annuity factor}(AF_{r,\,n})}$

The 'rehabilitation annuity' can then be combined with the recurrent maintenance costs and replacement annuity to calculate the household contribution needed to finance recurrent O&M, medium-term replacement and long-term rehabilitation. This is demonstrated in the following equation:

Annual household tariff, $H = 1.2 \times \left[\dfrac{M + A + A_R}{N} \right]$

Box 5.3 uses the previous example of the India Mark II handpump to illustrate the impact of incorporating rehabilitation costs in household water tariffs. By incorporating the need for borehole rehabilitation in twenty years' time, the monthly household tariff increases by almost two-and-a-half times from the previous value of $0.30. This may not seem a large amount but has a significant impact on planning and may affect the users' willingness to pay for the service.

Box 5.3. Setting household tariffs to cover rehabilitation costs[1]

Using the earlier example for the India Mark II handpump:

Current rehabilitation cost, R = $1000
(for airlift and hydrofracturing - see Section 6.5.3)

r = 20%   n = 20 years   N = 50 households

$AR = R / AF_{r,n} = 1000 / 4.67 = \$214$

$$\mathbf{H} = 1.2 \times \left[\frac{M + A + A_R}{N}\right] = 1.2 \times \left[\frac{35 + 119 + 214}{N}\right] = \$8.83$$

This can then be divided by 12 to convert to a monthly household tariff of **$0.74**.

---

1. Example only

The biggest problem with this method is the difficulty in estimating future rehabilitation needs and when that rehabilitation will be required. There is always an element of unpredictability about any system and what the users may demand in the future. For example, in future it may be that a borehole becomes contaminated and is beyond rehabilitation, meaning a new one must be drilled, or that a community decides it wants a newly available technology. In such situations, adequately financing rehabilitation from the outset is almost impossible.

An alternative approach to that shown in Box 5.3 is to insert the total original cost of the water system in place of the current rehabilitation cost. For example, a handpump-equipped borehole at a cost of US$5,000, with a projected life-span of twenty years, results in a monthly household tariff of $2.42, almost ten times that which does not account for rehabilitation at all (see Box 5.2). The best option may be to work in a degree of flexibility in tariff-setting which allows for some funds to be put aside to contribute to future rehabilitation costs. It remains likely, however, that the majority of these costs will continue to be met by governments or external support for the foreseeable future. A water tax which consolidates taxation funds for upgrading and rehabilitation may be one way in which appropriate finances can be generated.

5.3   Community financing

In the interests of efficiency, effectiveness, equity and replicability (i.e. sustainability) it is now generally accepted that rural communities and users should finance the cost of running their own water supplies. It is also commonplace for communities to be expected to contribute to the initial cost of their chosen technology or system. This inevitably places considerable responsibility on the shoulders of the users and makes community financing a crucial issue in the quest for sustainable rural water services. It is also essential, however, that communities trust those who are responsible for providing services.

5.3.1   Capital contribution

Many implementing agencies demand a cash contribution from the recipient community of 5 to15 per cent of the total installation cost. This is often seen as a clear indicator of demand, important to confirm ownership, and an indicator of the community's ability to organize and collect payments (Deverill et al., 2002). However, some studies have shown that a higher demand for a water supply service as expressed through initial payments in cash and/or kind is actually negatively related to sustaining the service (IRC, 2002). This may be because a small percentage contribution leads to high cost solutions which are expensive to sustain. The ability of a community (or its sponsors) to make an initial contribution to project inputs does not necessarily reflect an ability, or willingness, to pay for operation and maintenance costs over time. There is also the danger that once communities have 'paid' for their facility they consider that they have already fulfilled their responsibility.

The importance of a capital contribution by the community remains open to debate. Evidence suggests that contributions in kind, such as the contribution of labour or materials, result in similar levels of ownership and responsibility to those arising from cash contributions. Also, where community sensitization is effective, some communities may demonstrate equally high levels of ownership even where they made no initial contribution to the water supply facility at all.

5.3.2   Financing O&M

A World Bank monitoring and evaluation exercise in Karnataka, India, found one of the key issues adversely affecting sustainability to be the fact that the full cost of O&M was not yet being recovered from users (WSP, 1999). Available literature would suggest that nowhere is there full cost-recovery of operation and maintenance from rural communities, since the cost of spare parts, distribution, storage and technical support is often subsidized. Participants at the 1987 Interlaken consultation on progress in the Water Decade supported the view that full cost recovery should be the long-term goal, but that a transition period may be necessary before this can be achieved (Evans, 1992). It would appear that such a transition period is ongoing and little progress has been made towards its successful completion. There are a number of key measures that need to be fulfilled to ensure sustainable community financing:

- Determine ongoing costs and package this information in a way that communities can understand in order to make informed decisions.

- Convince people to pay for water through appropriate community sensitization.

- Establish transparent and efficient financial management systems.

- Sustain willingness to pay among communities through ongoing institutional support and promotion of income generation.

- Develop incremental strategies to phase out unsustainable subsidies, and/or develop mechanisms for sustainable cross-subsidy.

Costing O&M is the first step to ensure that communities are aware of ongoing costs and the financial commitment required to sustain their water systems. This allows them to select the most appropriate technology and system for them. Whatever financing system is to be used it is essential that users are aware of typical costs from the outset, and that those responsible for management are assisted in setting realistic and adequate water tariffs.

Box 5.4. Attitudinal poverty[1]

'This community has been used to so many free things. The free mobile clinic by the catholic diocese, free handpump and many other things...this has made us with time, believe that we are so poor and everything for us is, and should be, free. We are poor, indeed very poor and we cannot afford anything, even to eat is a struggle.'

---

1. Headmaster, godNyango Primary School, Kenya

Convincing people to pay for water is often not easy in communities, especially where there is a history of receiving services for free (Box 5.4). Past activities may have reinforced the perception of poverty and helplessness among communities, which retard efforts to encourage them to pay. Changing attitudes can be difficult in such situations but is not impossible, especially where trained social mobilizers work with the community over a period of several weeks or months

Accountability and transparency can go a long way to convince community members to contribute to a maintenance fund (Tayong & Poubom, 2002). It is important that users can see where their money is going and how it is being used, if they are to be convinced to contribute and to continue contributing. This is why it is sometimes easier to raise funds for the installation of a new facility than for its maintenance. Users may be unclear about why they should pay and what their money is being used for. If the principle of paying for water can be instilled, however, this dilemma disappears.

5

5.3.3 Revenue collection

There are many different mechanisms by which maintenance funds can be collected and stored, and locally appropriate systems should be developed through consultation with communities. The most common funding systems are:

* Reactive financing;

* Monthly tariffs; and

* Pay-as-you-fetch.

Reactive financing simply means that when a system fails or breaks down the community or better-off households club together to pay for repair. ***Monthly tariffs*** are perhaps the most widespread system whereby each household (or adult) in the community is expected to contribute a given amount each month. ***Pay-as-you-fetch*** systems require a caretaker to be present at the facility at all times (except when it is locked) to collect water tariffs from the community. Users pay a fixed amount per container. In some cases the caretaker operates the pump for customers and receives 20 to 30 per cent of the revenue raised as salary.

The advanced collection of maintenance funds does not necessarily shorten the downtime of a given handpump (Batchelor et al., 2000), although seasonal cash flow variations may have a big impact on whether finances can be raised rapidly (van Miert & Binamungu, 2002). Where household tariffs are paid monthly and funds are stored safely such systems can be highly successful. The most common problem encountered, however, is that willingness to pay among households is difficult to sustain and this often reduces over time. Pay-as-you-fetch systems are undoubtedly the most successful in terms of revenue generated but are only possible where there is a year-round cash economy (Box 5.5).

Box 5.5. Pay-as-you-fetch or sell-as-you-grow[1]

Two districts in Ghana were observed to have strikingly different approaches to the collection of maintenance fees. In Kpando district in the Volta Region there was a relatively strong cash economy and a 'pay-as-you-fetch' approach was used whereby users paid 50 cedis per 18 litre bucket ($0.35/m3) at the handpump. In the Afram Plains, Eastern Region, the population was heavily dependent on agriculture and income patterns were more erratic. Here a local NGO facilitated contact with prospective buyers to market agricultural produce on behalf of the community to pay for repairs and spare parts.

---

1. Harvey et al., 2002a

Where the pay-as-you-fetch system cannot be used household collections are the normal means of collecting water revenue. This can be conducted by WATSAN committee members, Water User Groups or private service providers. This can be a time consuming process, particularly where non-payers need to be chased up. Traditional leaders and respected community members can play an important role in exerting pressure and deciding where exemption or subsidy is appropriate (see 5.4.2).

5.3.4   Storage and investment of funds
In order to ensure year-round rapid repair it is important to have an appropriate mechanism for storing funds in advance of breakdown. Options for investment and storage of funds include:

*   Community bank account;
*   Community co-operative;
*   Advance purchase of spares; and
*   Private contractor.

Where a WATSAN committee is charged with the management of the water supply there is usually a treasurer to keep account of the money collected from the community and how this is spent. Some communities are encouraged to open bank accounts to store the money but this has a number of constraints. Communities are often situated a long distance from the nearest bank, bank charges rapidly eat away at the investment or currency devaluation negates the link between funds and imported parts. An alternative strategy is for the treasurer to keep these funds for when they are needed, which relies on considerable self-discipline and the trust of the rest of the community.

Rather than use a bank account communities can opt to run a co-operative whereby the water funds are used to purchase livestock or to support a community farm. Communal agricultural produce can then be sold when funds are required. This has the added advantage of avoiding devaluation effects. Similarly, funds can be used to purchase 'consumable' spare parts in advance of breakdown, though large stocks may be needed to guarantee that the correct spares are always available (Box 5.6).

5

Box 5.6. Goats, maize or spares[1]

Some communities in Zambia pay area pump mechanics in bags of maize rather than in cash. Others collect maintenance funds to purchase a 'community goat' which is then sold to raise cash when money is needed for repair. Other communities invest their maintenance funds in spare parts and over a period of time buy handpump riser pipes, rods, cylinders and cup and washer kits ready for future use.

---

1. Harvey and Skinner, 2002

Privately-managed O&M

Whether systems are managed by the community or the private sector many of the same issues surrounding community financing apply. For rural water supplies which are managed by a private contractor or individual rather than the community, the concept of 'paying for water' needs to be instilled. Where this occurs users regularly pay the contractor to run and maintain the system and are less concerned about where the money goes and what it is used for, so long as the water supply continues to operate at the desired service level. The storage of funds becomes the responsibility of the private company which removes one level of complexity at community level. This does not, however, remove problems which may occur due to seasonal cash-flow fluctuations. Private contractors will also need to meet overheads such as administration and taxation costs and meet profit targets. These costs must be included in estimating total O&M costs and setting household tariffs. However, where a company is responsible for a large number of systems for many communities, the impact of these costs on each community becomes very small.

Sustaining willingness to pay was discussed in Chapter 4, and is a common problem restricting sustainability. A key measure to ensure sustained financing of O&M is to use water to generate income (see below).

5.3.5 Income generation

Where water directly leads to income generation the problem of community financing may become significantly less. For this reason, opportunities for income generation should always be investigated. Possible ventures include livestock watering, irrigation for market gardens, block making, beer brewing and food processing. Where communities and individuals rely on an improved water supply to generate revenue, as well as for its other benefits, they will have a much larger incentive to keep it operating and should have finances available to enable ongoing O&M (see Box 5.7). Those who benefit financially from a system may be asked to pay a higher tariff than those that do not. For example, cattle owners may be expected to pay more than other community members if they have access to water for their animals as well as their families. Experience shows, however, that there are few examples of successful income generation from systems designed primarily for the supply of drinking water (Kjellerup, 2004).

Box 5.7. Water-led income[1]

In Kandiga village, Ghana an improved water supply brought economic independence, especially to women. As a result of improved access to safe drinking water many women earned the vital cash they needed to pay for food and school fees through selling groundnuts and making butter from shea nuts or brewing pito (a local drink). This also created the necessary resources and incentives to ensure the sustainability of their water supply.

---

1. Wheat, 2000

5.4 Pro-poor financing strategies

In our original definition of sustainability one of the four success criteria identified was 'equity'. This means that all members of a community regardless of gender, age, race, religion or wealth should benefit from an improved water supply. The United Nations Committee on Economic, Cultural and Social Rights issued a statement in November 2002 declaring access to water a human right and stating that water is a social and cultural good, not merely an economic commodity. Many government strategies now recognize this fact and aim to increase access to water for all. In order to achieve this, however, it is important to find ways in which to serve the poorest and most vulnerable, while ensuring adequate cost recovery from the users.

5.4.1 Government subsidy

One way to ensure that the poor are adequately served is to offer direct subsidies to poor communities. These are likely to be partial rather than total subsidies, and in effect this is often what happens since users rarely meet the full cost of O&M. A formalized version of this is the bidding for least subsidy approach (Figure 5.1).

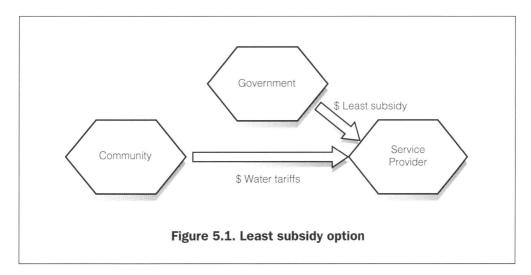

Figure 5.1. Least subsidy option

Here it is accepted that governments provide some level of subsidy and private service providers bid for the lowest level of subsidy that they believe they require to deliver a sustainable water service over a set period of time. The remainder of costs are recovered by the private company from the users. This approach can be adopted for both the delivery of new improved water supplies and ongoing services.

Direct government subsidy can also take the form of household subsidies whereby the poorest households in a community are wholly or partially exempted from paying water tariffs and the government pays their contributions. Although this has been applied to urban water supplies (Gómez-Lobo, 2001) the required bureaucracy makes this an unlikely solution for rural populations.

5.4.2   Community cross-subsidy

Many poor rural people are currently subsidized by other more affluent members of their community. Community management systems often recognize that some households are unable to afford water tariffs or maintenance funds and therefore exempt them from payment. This is a sensitive issue since it may give rise to internal disagreement or envy and is open to abuse. It is, however, highly effective where community management is strong and allows the poorest and most vulnerable to be supported and protected by the rest of the community. The service provider in this case may be a CBO or private sector individual/ organization (see Figure 5.2).

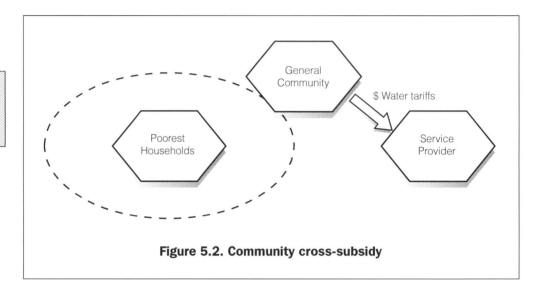

Figure 5.2. Community cross-subsidy

This system of cross-subsidy within a community is difficult to formalize and relies upon the goodwill and objectivity of the management committee. Transferring such an arrangement to a situation where the community's water supply is not managed by the community would present significant problems. It is much harder for an 'outsider' to assess community dynamics and poverty levels and to levy different households different amounts.

5.4.3   Hidden subsidies

Some subsidies for operation and maintenance of rural water supplies are indirect or 'hidden'. These include support for spare parts supply, storage and distribution, and monitoring, regulation and institutional support for communities. Here, the service provider may be a local mechanic who obtains spare parts from a local NGO or subsidized dealer (see Figure 5.3). It may be accepted that some level of such subsidy is needed, particularly for institutional support, but where possible, attempts should be made to phase out hidden subsidies over time and these costs should be worked into financial plans.

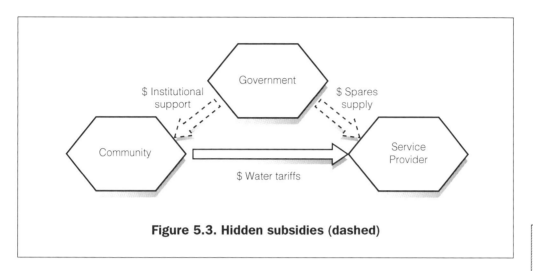

Figure 5.3. Hidden subsidies (dashed)

5.5   Steps towards financial sustainability

If water services are to be sustainable financially it is essential that all associated costs are assessed fully and that appropriate financing mechanisms are established accordingly. Figure 5.4 outlines the general steps that need to be taken in order to achieve financial sustainability, though this is not designed as a rigid 'blueprint'. A holistic assessment of the sector may be necessary prior to the first step in order to determine the number of systems involved and hence economies of scale for monitoring and O&M support costs.

This process can be conducted at a national or regional level, and should be co-ordinated by a planning committee comprising representatives of relevant government ministries and departments, and external support agencies involved in water supply.

Step 1. Target setting

The first step in the process is to set clear time-bound targets for implementation of new water systems, upgrading, expansion and rehabilitation. These targets are likely to be linked to rural water supply coverage figures and will include the estimated number of new systems for each relevant technology type and the respective populations served. Targets should also be set for keeping existing water systems and facilities operational, or for upgrading or expanding these. All water supplies within the programme area should be included in the target-setting exercise to ensure that service coverage figures are accurate.

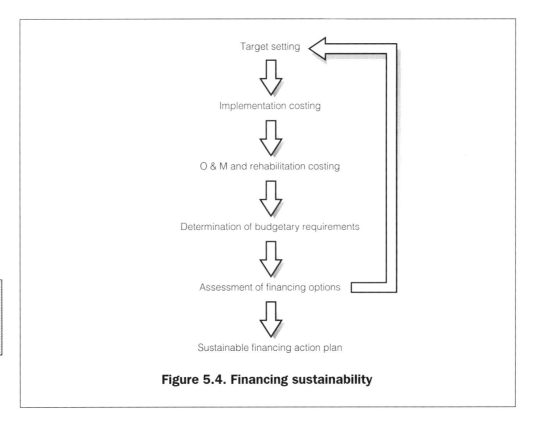

Figure 5.4. Financing sustainability

Step 2. Implementation costing

The second step is to estimate the costs associated with the implementation of new water systems, expansion and upgrading. These are likely to include the cost of:

- Equipment;
- Technical services;
- Community mobilization; and
- Management and regulation.

The total cost per new/upgraded facility can then be calculated for each relevant technology type and the total implementation budget determined.

Step 3. O&M and rehabilitation costing

Detailed O&M costs should then be estimated for all existing and future water systems (see Section 5.2). These should include:

- Repair costs;

- Replacement costs;

- Rehabilitation costs; and

- Cost of institutional support (capacity building, M&E etc.).

It is important that costs which are often hidden, such as transportation, storage and administration costs, are included in these estimates so that a true total budget for O&M and rehabilitation can be determined.

Step 4. Determination of budgetary requirements

Once a detailed estimate of ALL costs associated with a water supply programme has been reached, the total annual budget can be determined. The overall budget will include all implementation and O&M costs which are broken down into specific sections and matched to potential funding sources. Table 5.5 shows a hypothetical example:

5

Table 5.5. Example of budgetary requirements and allocations

Activity	Annual cost (US$)	Financial responsibility
Implementation of 100 new water systems		
Technical services and equipment	500,000	Government/NGO
Community mobilization	50,000	Government/NGO
Management and regulation	20,000	Government/NGO
O&M, repair and/or rehabilitation of 500 systems		
Routine repair and maintenance	17,500	Communities
Replacement of 50 (10% of) systems	16,800	Communities
Rehabilitation of 10 (2% of) systems	10,000	Communities/Government
Institutional support for O&M	50,000	Local government
Total annual budget	**$664,300**	

Step 5. Assessment of financing options

Once the total budget and breakdown have been determined and potential funding sources identified it is necessary to assess the different mechanisms by which these funds can be generated and managed. For example, if communities are to finance all repair, replacement and rehabilitation costs how much is needed from each community or household and how will these funds be collected, stored and managed? Government strategy documents are likely to influence this but rarely dictate inflexible practice. If the financing or management option selected will itself affect the estimated costs then this must be worked into the budgetary calculations.

If after an assessment of the financing options it becomes clear that it will not be possible to achieve the initial targets, it will be necessary to refine these accordingly by returning to Step 1 and repeating the cycle until an affordable solution is found.

Step 6. Sustainable financing action plan

The final step in the process is to draw up an action plan which details how programme activities will be financed and how funds will be managed. This should include year-on-year financial requirements and how these will be met. Ideally, this should include projected finances from:

- Communities;

- Government taxes (central and local); and

- External support agencies.

Figure 5.5 presents an example of a financing action plan whereby a water supply programme is subdivided into phases of five-years' length. After each phase external support is reduced until finally it reaches zero. This may be possible once 100 per cent rural water coverage is reached, providing that adequate provision is made for ongoing O&M of existing systems. Government support can also be reduced further in this way but some level of financing will always be required for M&E and regulation.

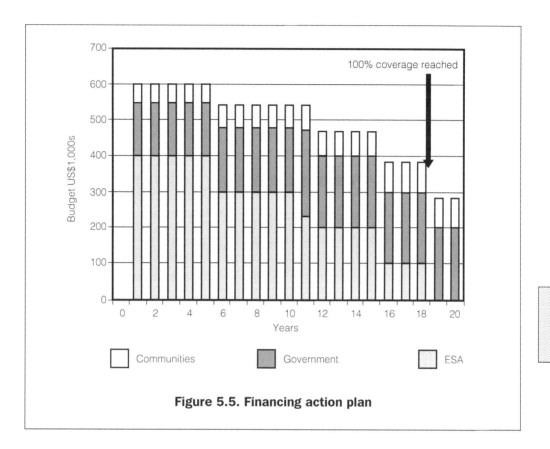

Figure 5.5. Financing action plan

Further reading

Deverill, P, Bibby, S., Wedgwood, A. and Smout, I. (2002) *Designing Water Supply and Sanitation Projects to Meet Demand in Rural and Peri-Urban Communities: Books 1-3.* WEDC, Loughborough University: UK.
http://wedc.lboro.ac.uk/projects/new_projects3.php?id=36

UNCHS (2004) *The Maintenance of Infrastructure and its Financing and Cost Recovery.* United Nations Centre for Human Settlements (Habitat).
http://www.unchs.org/unchs/english/mainten/contents.htm

5

Chapter 6

Technology and the environment

Despite increased emphasis on social and community aspects of water supply, technology does still matter. Technology options which are low-cost, easy to understand and easy to maintain and repair are likely to be more sustainable than those that require specialist skills or equipment. Where feasible, household water supply options remove many of the obstacles to sustainability created by community ownership. Wherever possible, a range of options should be presented to potential users. Local innovation that brings the technology closer to the people should also be encouraged in the interests of sustainability. This chapter highlights the importance of technology choice and its relationship with the environment and sustainability, while paying particular attention to the handpump and groundwater.

6

6.1   The role of technology

While technology alone does not determine sustainability it can have a major impact, especially on ongoing operation and maintenance needs. WaterAid Mozambique has found that technology choice does matter and that O&M has greatly improved when communities have been allowed to select a technology which they believe it is within their financial, managerial and technical capacity to sustain (Breslin, 2003). Technical options should be seen as part of the management solution, however, not as goals in themselves (Lammerick et al., 2002).

6.1.1   Technology choice

The selection of a range of technology for a rural water supply will vary according to environmental conditions, affordability and social acceptance. Although the primary technology addressed in this book is the handpump, it is essential that this is seen as an option in rural water supply programmes, not an exclusive choice. Technology should not be predetermined in any programme and should only be decided upon after a systematic assessment and community consultation process.

According to Skinner (2003) a water supply scheme should be:

- **Acceptable** to the community (e.g. in relation to convenience and traditional beliefs and practices) and also acceptable from environmental and health perspectives;

- **Feasible** (i.e. suiting the relevant local social, financial, technological and institutional factors); and

- **Sustainable** (i.e. possible to reliably operate and maintain in the future with the available financial, human, institutional and material resources).

Once a community has been identified as needing an improved water supply, it is necessary, primarily through community consultation, to assess:

- Existing water supplies;

- Community demand, capabilities and priorities; and

- Potential water sources.

Existing water supplies

Wherever there are people, they must rely on a source of water, no matter how distant this may be from the community. The first important step related to technology selection is to determine from where the population currently collects water and what the possible limitations of this water source are (quality, quantity, accessibility etc.).

Rural water development projects over the past few decades have resulted in the installation of a wide range of different technologies and systems across sub-Saharan Africa. All too often, new water supplies are installed adjacent to existing systems which are no longer operational, and for which no efforts are made to rehabilitate. A common example of this is to drill a new borehole close by an older borehole which is not equipped with an operational water lifting device (see Box 6.1).

There are several reasons for such practices, including unclear ownership of existing systems and hence unclear responsibility for rehabilitation; restrictive project funding mechanisms and implementation approaches which specify

---

Box 6.1. Using what is already there[1]

An NGO recently drilled a new borehole and installed an India Mark II handpump on the edge of the village of Kpasenkpe in West Mamprusi, Ghana. In the centre of the village there are two existing boreholes which are not currently used. One of these has an old Mono handpump which is no longer functioning and for which there are no spare parts available in the country; it has been out of operation for several years. The second borehole is reported to have been drilled by another NGO, to have been successful in terms of yield, but to have never had a handpump installed on it despite that being the original intention. In addition to these, there is a third borehole in the village with an existing India Mark II handpump installed fifteen years ago. This pump is heavily rusted and barely operating (requiring more than 40 strokes to deliver the first water). This begs the question: 'why was a new borehole drilled?'

---

1. World Vision, Ghana, 2003

complete systems; and the simple desire for the neatness and 'donor-appeal' of providing new facilities. Also, where several agencies operate in one area, a new agency may want to ensure that credit for rehabilitation works is not given to the original implementing agency, and rather than run that risk decide to install a completely new system.

6

The tendency for repetition rather than rehabilitation is widespread, but there are several measures which can be undertaken to deter implementers from adopting this approach:

- Effective government monitoring and regulation to identify 'failed' systems and to control approval for new systems. This will prevent independent agencies implementing new supplies on an ad-hoc basis without consideration of existing systems (whether failed or not).

- Integrated approaches, such as SWAp (see Section 2.1.4), whereby there is a co-ordinated approach involving all donors and implementing agencies working in a given area.

- Strategies for establishing clear **legal** ownership of facilities and land to reduce the perception that systems or boreholes 'belong' to a particular implementer or the government rather than the community.

- Government strategies to award contracts that address rehabilitation needs as well as new systems.

Community demand, capabilities and priorities

It is then important to estimate the level of demand from the community. This should incorporate volume and usage requirements (which allow for population increase), individual priorities, willingness to pay, and any preconceived ideas or preferences regarding technology choice (see Section 4.3.3). Economic activities within a community also need to be assessed, as these will have a bearing on the type of technology required (e.g. does it need to cater for water for economic activities in addition to water for drinking?) as well as the affordability of this.

Potential water sources

The third step is to conduct an assessment of all possible water sources in the area including surface water, groundwater and rainwater. This is likely to involve an assessment of available hydrogeological and rainfall data and indicators. It is often the case that a community will combine the use of different sources for different uses and/or seasons, and allowance for this should be made in community-based planning exercises.

In general, the following four essential or 'golden' rules should be applied in selecting appropriate technology:

- **Use what's already there and improve on it.**

- **Opt for low-cost rather than high-cost solutions.**

- **Where possible, opt for household solutions rather than community solutions.**

- **If you can dig don't drill.**

Rural African populations tend to consist of fairly small concentrations of relatively poor people in villages or scattered settlements. Appropriate water supply options therefore tend to be small-scale and low-cost, though this is not always the case, particularly with some piped gravity-fed schemes. As well as systems to cater for the entire community, smaller groupings and household-centred options should also be considered. The number of users per facility should always be assessed taking into account projected population growth during the life of the facility. Possible options will depend on the potential water sources identified and may include:

- Upgrading/protecting existing sources;

- Spring protection;

- Gravity-fed systems;

- Rainwater harvesting;

- Open hand-dug well;

- Handpump-equipped well;

- Handpump-equipped borehole;

- Wind-powered borehole pumps;

- Solar-powered borehole pumps;

- Motorized borehole pumps;

- Surface water treatment and distribution.

It is beyond the scope of this book to address each of these technologies in detail; for further introductory information to these technologies refer to Skinner (2003). It is important that rural water supply projects and programmes present communities with a true technology choice and that they are made aware of the financial and managerial implications of each possible option. Water users need to have the freedom to choose what type and level of water services they are capable of managing without any undue external pressure (van Miert & Binamungu, 2002). Ease of operation and maintenance, user acceptability and cost must be considered jointly. If a water supply system is not maintained it is because it is too complicated, not 'attractive' or too expensive (Holtslag, 2002).

6

6.1.2   Low-cost and household technologies

It is sometimes suggested that communities should not move from an existing level of service to one that is lower (Schouten, 2004). This should not mean that communities cannot move from one technology choice to a lower-cost technology choice. Experiences in Mozambique and South Africa indicate that sometimes communities with failed water systems (including handpumps) have opted for simpler cheaper technologies, such as bucket pumps and protected wells, which they are more confident that they can sustain (Breslin, 2003; Harvey & Kayaga, 2003). Household solutions and small user group options should also be explored (see Section 4.1).

6.1.3   Assessing technical options

Once a number of potential technical options are identified, it is then necessary to assess each of these in terms of:

- Benefits;

- Limitations;

- Costs;

- Maintenance needs; and

- Management needs.

Benefits
What are the potential benefits of the selected technology choice with respect to the current water supply?

These might include reduced distance, shorter waiting times, easier operation and improved water quantity or quality. As a result of such direct benefits there may also be related benefits such as improved health and income generation.

Limitations
What limitations are likely to arise from the selected water supply technology?

Limitations might include variable distances to water point, limited flow rate, the need for human effort to deliver water, or a change in water hardness affecting taste and usage (e.g. to produce adequate lather for laundry purposes).

Costs
How much will it cost to acquire, operate and maintain the technology?

Detailed cost estimates must be produced for construction, operation and maintenance, and this information relayed to potential users and any supporting institutions, as described in Chapter 5. Where possible replacement and rehabilitation costs should be worked into such estimates.

Maintenance needs
What are the recurrent and long-term maintenance needs of the technology?

An estimated maintenance schedule should be produced for each technology option, incorporating both preventive and corrective maintenance. This is needed to inform users of the likely requirements and to assess whether these are within the means of the community or would require outside technical assistance. This presupposes that institutional support levels for maintenance have already been determined. Where this is the case, a range of scenarios based on available knowledge should be presented to the community.

Management needs

What level of management and commitment will be required from the community and other involved institutions in order to sustain O&M?

Communities need to know whether they will be responsible for the management of the improved water supply and if so, what management functions will be expected of the community. These might require a water committee or CBO, tariff recovery and financial management, contract management, or human resource development and management. Institutions that may need to provide support or M&E also need to understand the management implications. **Population density** should also be considered when assessing management needs, since some management systems may require a minimum density of systems to be economically viable.

It is essential that each of these factors be thoroughly assessed in determining an appropriate technology choice for a given community, and that the final decision lies with the user community (see Section 4.3.5).

6

6.2   Groundwater

Groundwater has proved the most reliable resource for meeting rural water demand in sub-Saharan Africa (MacDonald & Davies, 2000) due to its widespread availability beneath much of the continent, generally good water quality, and relative ease and low-cost of access and extraction. Since this book has a particular focus on the handpump, which is the predominant means of groundwater extraction for rural water supplies, some key issues relating to groundwater resource use are addressed below.

6.2.1   Hydrogeology

The hydrogeology of sub-Saharan Africa (SSA) can be divided into four broad groups or domains: basement, sedimentary, volcanic and unconsolidated aquifers. Crystalline basement rocks form the most widespread hydrogeological group and occupy 40 per cent of the land area of SSA. Consolidated sedimentary rocks account for 32 per cent, volcanic rocks 6 per cent, and unconsolidated sediments 22 per cent (MacDonald & Davies, 2000). In all cases, it is essential that local maps, data and expertise are sought out and used in determining local conditions. Government geological survey departments often provide useful sources of such information. Even within a given area and domain there can be significant variation, and there is no substitute for local knowledge. Figure 6.1 indicates the approximate distribution of rural population in SSA by hydrogeological domain (after MacDonald & Davies, 2000).

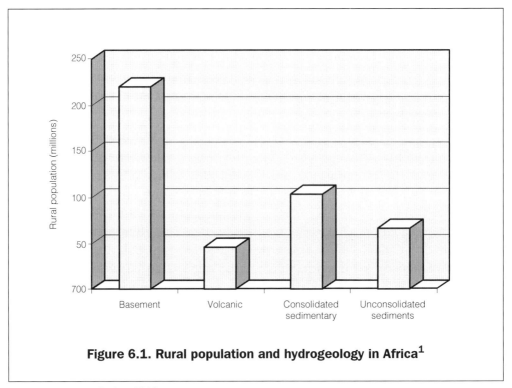

Figure 6.1. Rural population and hydrogeology in Africa[1]

1. MacDonald and Davies, 2000

It is estimated that 220 million people, making more than half the rural population in sub-Saharan Africa, live in areas underlain by ancient crystalline basement rocks. These rocks form low yielding, though widespread, aquifers, and form the most significant hydrogeological group in terms of rural water supply. They tend to have low permeability, so that transmissivity (the rate at which water is transmitted through the aquifer) is also low, and, where unaltered, have low potential for water supply. Fortunately, much of the crystalline basement in Africa has been weathered over time, leaving a mantle commonly 10 to 30 metres thick of more permeable material (Calow et al., 1999). However, the degree of weathering and aquifer properties vary greatly, and in many areas of Africa the weathered zone is insignificant or is unsaturated. In such cases the only easily accessible aquifer is constituted by the underlying unweathered fractured crystalline rocks. Basement aquifers therefore occur within the weathered mantle (sometimes referred to as the regolith) and the fractured bedrock. This means that within basement areas there can be significant local variation in groundwater conditions.

The next most significant group in terms of population is consolidated sedimentary rocks, on which an estimated 110 million people live in SSA. Sandstone, limestone, siltstone and mudstone are all sedimentary rocks, of which sandstone has the highest roundwater potential because of its ability to store water in pore spaces. Fractured and karstic (where water is held in channels rather than pores) limestone can also produce high yields but groundwater can be difficult to find in siltstone and mudstone. Some 60 million people live on unconsolidated sediments which form river basins throughout Africa and store large volumes of groundwater. Such groundwater is often, though not always, shallow and hence can be accessed by hand-dug wells or hand-augered boreholes. Around 45 million people live on volcanic rocks, the hydrogeological potential of which varies greatly. In general, groundwater is found in deep fractures and can only be accessed by boreholes, although shallow groundwater is found in some volcanic areas.

This brief summary of hydrogeological domains indicates the complexity and variability of groundwater conditions throughout the sub-continent. Hydrogeology has a significant impact on the feasibility and sustainability of water supplies and must be investigated thoroughly at local level. Although crystalline basement rocks form the most commonly encountered aquifers for rural water supplies, it is difficult to generalize, even about these. For more information on the hydrogeology of sub-Saharan Africa refer to MacDonald & Davies (2000).

6

6.2.2 Groundwater levels and yields

The single most important factor in determining whether groundwater can be used for water supplies is normally the groundwater level. Most rural water supplies in Africa that rely on groundwater extract water from a depth of less than 100 metres. In some cases, hand-dug wells exploit shallow groundwater sources at just a few metres depth, while in others, drilled boreholes tap into fractures 80 or 90 metres deep. Where groundwater is only available at depths greater than 100 metres it is normally an inappropriate source for water supply, since drilling costs are too expensive to access it and extraction costs also too high. Most deepwell handpumps operate efficiently to a depth of about 40 metres while even the most robust rarely exceed 80 metres. The operation of handpumps becomes more difficult with increasing depth, and where they operate at extreme depth (e.g. 90 to -100m) their operation becomes extremely difficult and beyond the capability of many users, especially the very young and very old, unless the pump is operated by two or more people.

The sustainability of water supplies is intrinsically linked to the water source that they use. A water supply will only be sustained if the extraction rate does not exceed the replenishment rate of the resource over the lifetime of the system. For this reason, it is essential that groundwater sources are assessed and the yield of wells and boreholes estimated (see 6.2.6). Ongoing monitoring is also important to assess changes in the resource and to identify any threats to sustainability.

6.2.3   Water quality

In addition to groundwater levels and yields, water quality is of key importance for sustainable rural water supplies. If the consumption of water from an improved source has adverse health effects it can hardly be said to meet our definition of sustainable water supply in terms of benefits (see Section 1.3). Groundwater is usually safe in terms of bacteriological parameters since only 2 metres of unsaturated fine soil will remove virtually all pathogenic organisms, and even where water passes into coarser soils or fractures, many pathogens die after a few weeks due to the low temperature and absence of nutrients. It is important, however, that groundwater sources are located appropriately with respect to potential sources of contamination, are adequately protected, and use appropriate extraction methods. It is also important that the local hydrogeological environment is adequately assessed. While most hydrogeological zones will prevent rapid movement of bacteriological contaminants through the ground, some fractured conditions can facilitate very rapid transmission from point sources such as pit latrines to wells or boreholes. Such issues need to be addressed locally and expertise sought where necessary. Enforcing a fixed radius between the water source and sources of potential pollution is an important measure, but this may not be effective in all environments.

The primary area of concern regarding groundwater quality usually involves inorganic parameters resulting from natural (and occasionally human-modified) geological conditions. Where possible a thorough analysis of water quality parameters of principal public health concern should be conducted for boreholes, prior to commissioning associated water supplies. This is especially important in areas where there are known water quality problems regarding high concentrations of health-related parameters such as arsenic, fluoride or lead, and particularly where mining activities are commonplace. If borehole water samples are found with concentrations outside those recommended by WHO guidelines for drinking water quality (WHO, 2003) or local standards, the borehole may have to be abandoned or appropriate treatment systems installed, which may be expensive.

Aesthetic parameters such as iron and manganese, which affect colour and taste, do not have any adverse health effects but, where present, may make it difficult to persuade users to accept a new water supply. Where there is community dissatisfaction this is likely to have a direct impact on their willingness to pay for and maintain their water supply. Remedial measures may therefore be necessary, such as iron-removal plants using aeration and filtration, to correct high concentrations. This adds another O&M responsibility, however, which communities may be reluctant or unable to fulfil.

A basic inorganic parameter which can have a major influence on technology choice and sustainability is pH or acidity. Groundwater with low pH is acidic and is therefore aggressive. This will result in the corrosion of any submerged iron-based components, such as galvanized iron riser pipes and rods used for handpumps. Since these components are constantly submerged in or in contact with water, it will not take long before the galvanization is broken down and the parts begin to rust. This can rapidly result in leakage and breakage. Repairs, for example fishing out and replacing fallen pipes, can be difficult and expensive. Groundwater with high pH or alkalinity is also aggressive but its occurrence is rare unless there are high levels of manmade pollution.

6

The pH of groundwater can be measured easily using a pH meter, indicator strips or soluble tablets, and must be considered early on in project design (see Box 6.2). Where there is a high incidence of aggressive groundwater a high level of investment may be required to modify existing handpump technologies (e.g. using stainless steel or plastic components) and this cost should be considered from project inception. Cheaper options such as plastic rising mains should also be investigated in such circumstances.

6.2.4 Wells or boreholes?

Where groundwater is to be used for water supply it is important to determine whether a hand-dug well, hand-augered borehole, jetted or driven tubewell or machine-drilled borehole is the most appropriate water source.

The option selected should not be predetermined but should be decided upon following an objective assessment. Hydrogeological factors will have a significant impact on the options available, but where these are not overly restrictive there are a number of other issues which should be considered.

Photograph 6.1. Testing water quality using a pH meter

Box 6.2. Testing groundwater pH

The simple act of testing groundwater pH before handpump installation can make the difference between success and failure. Where pH values are low (i.e. below pH 6.5) the downhole components should be made of corrosion-resistant material such as plastic or stainless steel.

Table 6.1 summarizes the comparative advantages and disadvantages of each of these three categories.

Each of the three groundwater options in Table 6.1 has specific advantages and disadvantages. The primary constraints are: limited depth and potential for pollution for a hand-dug well; limited depth and suitable environmental conditions for a hand-augered borehole; and high cost and limited access for a machine-drilled borehole. Where hand-dug wells are fully protected this has

Table 6.1. Comparison of wells and boreholes[1]

Issue	Hand-dug well	Hand-augered borehole	Machine-drilled borehole
Geological formation	✓ Flexible procedure in variety of soil conditions x Cannot easily penetrate hard rock	x Not usually suitable in large stones or hard rock	✓ Equipment is available for all types of ground to great depths
Safe depth	x < 20m	x < 30m	✓ > 100m
Water level	x Hand-digging below the water table is not easy	✓ Can penetrate below water table even in loose sand soils	✓Can penetrate well below water table even in loose sand soils
Ease of construction	✓ Equipment, labour and lining materials usually available locally x Time-consuming process	✓Relatively fast ✓Little equipment needed x Needs casing x Limited depth (<30m)	✓ Very fast ✓ Access for heavy rigs difficult x Needs casing (except in some hard rock)
Social issues	✓ Community involved in construction, enhancing 'ownership'	x Fewer people involved, so less community 'buy-in'	x Fewer people involved, so less community 'buy-in'
Financial aspects	✓ Much cheaper than drilled borehole x More expensive than hand-augered well to same depth	✓ Much cheaper than drilled borehole ✓ Usually cheaper than well	x Much more expensive than well or tubewell
Health and safety	x Open wells have associated pollution risks x Some hazards to diggers (and users)	✓ Less risk of pollution of groundwater by users ✓ Negligible safety hazards	✓ Less risk of pollution of groundwater by users ✓ Minimal safety hazards if drilling managed well
Versatility	✓ Handpump-equipped well can still be accessed if pump breaks down	x Needs a sustainable water-lifting device	x Needs a sustainable water-lifting device
Key: ✓ Advantage, x Disadvantage			

1. adapted from Skinner, 2003

been shown to lead to major improvements in water quality, resulting in faecal coliform levels comparable to those for drilled boreholes (Sutton, 2002). The majority of handpumps are installed on drilled boreholes, but where groundwater conditions are favourable protected wells, tubewells or hand-augered boreholes provide effective alternatives, especially in terms of cost. Cost is arguably the most important aspect, and in general, where you can dig don't drill!

6.2.5 Borehole siting

The location of the well, tubewell or borehole can have a significant impact on the sustainability of the water supply. Where possible, boreholes should be sited in a central position in the community, and on community-owned land. This encourages equity, accessibility and communal ownership, and may have other positive knock-on benefits (see Box 6.3). In all cases, siting should be conducted through consultation with the community.

Boreholes must be sited appropriately in relation to environmental and hydrogeological conditions, on-site sanitation, community preferences and land ownership. Poor siting of boreholes impacts negatively on sustainability since this may lead to:

• Insufficient yield;

• Pollution;

• Abandoned boreholes;

• Subsequent re-drilling; and

• Increased cost.

Box 6.3. Unforeseen benefits of optimum borehole siting[1]

Kwaseakane in Ashanti Region, Ghana, is a small village with a population of about 300. The handpump is sited precisely in the middle of the village and acts as a centrepiece for the community; the pump is maintained in immaculate condition and the concrete apron is kept spotlessly clean. During the last dry season a bush fire broke out and threatened to destroy the village. Due to the close proximity of the pump the community was able to collect water quickly and managed to douse the flames before the fire raged out of control. The village was therefore saved from destruction!

---

1. World Vision, 2003

Hydrogeological conditions

The ease of siting successful boreholes depends primarily on the hydrogeology of the project area. It is far easier to site a borehole in a shallow unconsolidated alluvial aquifer than in a fractured basement aquifer, for example. The unequal distribution of fractures in basement rocks and some sedimentary rocks leads to the presence of productive and barren adjacent areas with significantly different drilling success rates. Since drillers are often unable to locate fractures, overall success rates in fractured aquifers tend to be low; for example, in the fractured basement of eastern Chad, Gombert (1999) reports that only 42 per cent of all boreholes drilled contained water. In fractured aquifers it is not even safe to assume that drilling beside an existing wet borehole will result in a second successful borehole. This is illustrated by the case of the village of Kadia, Ghana, which lies on a fractured sedimentary aquifer, where a new borehole was drilled to the same depth as an existing wet borehole only 8 metres away and yet proved to be dry (World Vision, 2003).

Dry boreholes are regularly drilled by contractors due to inadequate or inappropriate siting. Depending on contractual arrangements, the cost of such failures is met by either the implementing agency or the contractor. High failure rates have a significant impact on efficiency, and hence sustainability. This makes careful siting and design of boreholes and wells important, especially in drought-prone areas. Some contractors use geophysics to site boreholes while others rely on environmental indicators, or simply trial-and-error. There are a number of technical options which can be applied for siting, including the following:

6

Remote sensing comprises the study and interpretation of satellite imagery, aerial photography and airborne geophysics. It has been used to site boreholes for rural water supplies in Africa (Teeuw, 1995; Sander et al., 1996) but its application and effectiveness are generally quite limited.

Terrain and vegetation evaluation is essential and requires local knowledge and experience to identify and interpret geographical and biological indicators such as existing water sources, topography, rock outcrops, termite mounds, and vegetation types and patterns. This is should be the first technical step in the siting process immediately after community consultation.

Geophysical survey methods are used by many siting teams and the selected technique depends on the local hydrogeology. The most common method adopted to detect the depth of basement weathering or the water table is resistivity surveying which can also be applied (usually with less effectiveness) to locate water-bearing fractures. Electromagnetic survey methods are used less widely than resistivity in Africa (due to cost and availability) but can be highly effective in locating water bearing fractures and layers. Magnetic surveys are sometimes used to detect water-bearing features such as weathered dolerite intrusions. Seismic survey methods are occasionally used to detect fractures in volcanic rocks. More important than the technique used is the competency and experience of the user, particularly with regard to interpreting results.

Indigenous knowledge is an important resource which is often overlooked. Local people may have knowledge concerning where shallow groundwater used to be exploited by the community or where particular trees or vegetation used to grow. This information may be of great use in detecting current resources. There may also be individuals with particular skills concerning vegetation interpretation or water dowsing.

Photograph 6.2. Electromagnetic survey to locate water-bearing fractures

Water dowsing is an unexplained phenomenon which appears to be successful in some cases. It is widely believed that the earliest evidence of dowsing or 'water divining' worldwide dates back to Africa at least 8000 years ago. Wall murals in the Tassili Caves of North Africa depict tribesmen surrounding a man with a forked stick, possibly dowsing for water (Lyke, 2000). Recent extensive field studies in several African countries including Kenya, Namibia, Niger, and the Congo have shown that a few carefully selected dowsers are able to detect faults, fissures and fractures with relative frequency and surprising accuracy in areas of crystalline bedrock (Betz, 1995). However, a lack of reliable data on un-divined drilling success rates in the study areas means that such findings have to be viewed with care.

On-site sanitation

It is important that boreholes are sited appropriately in relation to sources of potential contamination. In rural communities the most common sources are pit latrines or livestock pens. Some implementing agencies stipulate a fixed minimum radius of 30 metres around the well or borehole within which no pollution sources should be located, and stress the importance of locating latrines downhill of groundwater abstraction points (Médecins Sans Frontières, 1994; World Vision, 2003). Therefore, new boreholes should be sited at least this distance uphill of existing facilities. This is a useful guideline but boreholes are often located downhill of communities because of hydrogeological necessity and there is a danger that implementers will assume that if the 30-metre distance is adhered to there will be a guarantee of no pollution. It is important that local hydrogeological conditions are assessed thoroughly, especially where aquifers are fractured, and where there is doubt bacteriological water quality analyses should be conducted. (For more information refer to BGS, 2001.)

6

Social issues

Of at least equal importance to hydrogeological conditions are social issues. A water supply will only be sustainable if its location is acceptable to the community of users. It is, therefore, essential that community preferences form the starting point of the siting process rather than environmental conditions. Issues of equity of distance, land ownership and priority needs (e.g. for income generation) must be considered in detail. The perfect hydrogeological location might be on land owned by a private individual at a considerable distance from most of the community, and if this is not accepted by the majority of users the sustainability of a point water supply here will be immediately threatened.

Siting process

A generic process for borehole siting is presented below (stages 5 and 6 may only be needed in geologically complex areas).

1. ***Consult the community members*** on their priority needs related to the improved water supply (e.g. distance, water quality, income generation etc.).

2. ***Determine who owns the land*** in and around the community and what implications this is likely to have on site selection and ownership of the borehole and facility.

3. ***Ask the community*** to select three possible borehole locations in order of preference, informing them that their first choice will be considered but cannot be guaranteed.

4. ***Conduct a terrain evaluation*** of the three sites, observing existing water sources, topography, accessibility, geology and vegetation, and seek out indigenous knowledge and expertise.

5. *Where the optimum location remains uncertain select an appropriate geophysical survey method, depending on local hydrogeology and availability of equipment and skilled personnel.*

6. *Conduct a geophysical survey at each location. If using resistivity, for example, carry out constant separation traverses/transects through each of the three sites followed by at least three depth profiles (vertical electrical soundings) along each transect.*

7. ***Feed back results*** of evaluations and surveys to the community members and inform them of the likely drilling success rate at each of the three locations. Inform them of the consequences of drilling a dry bore (cost, time-lag before second attempt etc.) but do not use scare tactics to ensure they choose the easiest site.

8. ***Ask the community*** to make the final decision as to where to drill.

6.2.6 Borehole assessment, design and construction

The siting of a borehole or well is obviously important, but so too is its design. In ensuring water supply sustainability, the source (e.g. borehole) should not be ignored by focusing only on the means of extraction (e.g. handpump). It is essential that both are given equal importance and emphasis.

The primary factor that determines the sustainability of a borehole is its yield, i.e. the rate at which water can be withdrawn from the borehole without producing an undesired result such as depletion of groundwater reserves, intrusion of water of undesirable quality, excessive depletion of streamflow by induced infiltration, or land subsidence (Hyperdictionary, 2003). The maximum yield measured during pumping tests is the maximum pumping (flow) rate at which the water level does not drop below the level of the pump intake. This is not to say that such a yield is 'safe' or 'sustainable'. The term 'yield' is largely subjective and is normally related simply to the drawdown (i.e. how far the water level drops during pumping) that is deemed acceptable for a particular borehole. The drilled diameter of most handpump boreholes is 15cm (6 inches) or 20cm (8 inches), if artificially gravel-packed. The yield of a borehole is usually measured in litres per minute (l/min) or cubic metres per day (m3/d) and is primarily influenced by its depth and screen length, as well as the transmissivity and specific yield of the contiguous aquifer.

The maximum limit of a handpump's delivery ability is estimated to be 25 l/min (a generous figure) and Wurzel (2001) suggests that best practice is to drill until a yield of 25 l/min is obtained and then to drill a further 10 metres to allow for seasonal water table fluctuations and drawdown levels. If one is drilling at the end of the dry season, however, this may be unnecessary and quite costly, depending on the aquifer. It may be better, therefore, to drill several metres further dependent on the season of drilling and aquifer conditions. Local expertise should always be sought.

In many cases, the estimated yield of a borehole is considerably below the optimum 25 l/min, but this does not mean that it will not be able to sustain a handpump. Consequently, some agencies stipulate a minimum yield required to support a handpump, which is normally of the order of **10 l/min** (World Vision, 2003).

6

Yield can be estimated using a variety of pumping tests which usually require a generator, submersible pump, and discharge measuring device (e.g. v-notch weir, flow meter) and take several hours to undertake. A simplified technique which is appropriate for handpump-equipped boreholes is the bailer test (see Annex C). This can usually be carried out during drilling (e.g. after every 3m drilled in water) and after completion. However, where temporary casing is installed while drilling (e.g. in unconsolidated sediments) or where drilling with mud this may not be possible until after drilling has stopped.

When estimating yield, by whatever method, it is essential to consider the time of year at which that assessment takes place. Most yield assessments are conducted immediately after drilling which usually takes place during the dry season. The end of the dry season is the optimum time for yield assessment, since this is when groundwater levels and yields are lowest. If the yield is adequate at the end of the dry season it should remain adequate throughout the year. Where yields are measured during the wet season or early on in the dry season it is important that compensation is made for reduced yields later in the dry season. This can be based on other boreholes in the area.

Borehole design and construction

Even where a borehole is appropriately sited and has sufficient yield its sustainability can be threatened by poor design. A balance must always be struck between reducing costs and maintaining quality. The key aspects of borehole design are:

- Casing and screens;

- Borehole development;

- Gravel packs or other filters; and

- Protection.

Low-cost PVC casing and screening is normally used for handpump boreholes. The screen size is not critical for low yields, unless in very fine-grained aquifer material, and slots with a total opening of 5 per cent and width of 0.5 to 1mm are commonly used (Wurzel, 2001). It is important that drillers have a good understanding of the lithology in order to determine appropriate screening intervals. For example, the greatest yield from a weathered basement aquifer is often at the base of the weathered zone and yet some boreholes are only screened above this.

Appropriate development of the borehole by pumping and surging is crucial for borehole longevity. The purpose of this is to draw out fine material from the aquifer, leaving behind a stable envelope of coarser, more permeable material. The simplest development method is to pump the borehole at high flow rate for several hours or until the water becomes clear.

From a hydraulic perspective an artificial gravel pack is rarely needed for a low-yielding borehole but is frequently used in practice due to national standard procedures or guidelines. Where gravel is available locally and cheaply this should be used but where specialist gravel must be brought in from a long distance it is an unnecessary expense.

Some practitioners argue strongly that gravel pack, casing and screening should be avoided in general when drilling into hard rock since they are an unnecessary expense and block water from freely flowing into the hole (Ball, 2003, Wurzel, 2001). While this is generally true, it is important that practitioners have guidance regarding when and when not to apply these measures, and that this is built into private sector contracts. For further information on drilling and borehole design refer to Wurzel (2001) and Ball (2001).

Photograph 6.3. Installing uPVC casing and screening in a newly drilled borehole

6

Whether casing is used or not, what is essential is that the water source is adequately protected and that the borehole headworks prevent any contamination entering the well. This means that holes must be adequately sealed (grouted) using cement or clay-based grout and that the pump apron is regularly inspected, particularly where the pump pedestal is fixed to the concrete. Adequate drainage from the apron is also important, especially for shallow aquifers which are more susceptible to surface pollution.

Where drilling contracts are awarded at national level the control of district councils over the standard of borehole provision and development is diminished (Harvey & Skinner, 2002). One key advantage of decentralized control of contracts is that it makes effective monitoring of drillers by district-level government staff easier and can ensure that appropriate standards and quality of work are achieved. This should improve borehole yield reliability and also ensure that borehole records are available at district centres. However, district staff may need appropriate training to monitor the contractors at work. Appropriate health and safety procedures should also be specified in contracts and enforced through appropriate regulation.

Another key issue regarding wells and boreholes is that water levels, water quality and yields are recorded after initial construction and monitored over time (see Chapter 9).

6.3 Handpumps

The term 'handpump' is used within this book to describe any water lifting device which is operated by human power (usually using the hands, arms or feet). The handpump remains a major method of delivery of rural water supplies in Africa, due to the ease and low-cost of O&M in relation to many other technologies, ability to pump groundwater from depth and widespread user acceptability. The huge range of different handpump models and designs makes it beyond the scope of this book to assess the relative merits of each, although such exercises have been conducted in the past (Arlosoroff, 1987). It is important, however, to address generic technical issues related to handpumps which affect sustainability.

The focus of handpump development in the past was to develop durable pumps which rarely broke down. There must, however, be a balance between durability and ease of maintenance, since all handpumps, no matter how good, will eventually require maintenance and repair. The search for the 'holy grail' of handpumps which never breaks down is unrealistic and inappropriate. A reliable pump which breaks down but is easy to fix is much more important.

In selecting any handpump there are three crucial aspects that must be considered if sustainability is to be ensured:

• **The operating conditions of the pump (depth of operation, level of usage [number of users/litres to be pumped], groundwater pH etc.)**;

• Ease and cost of maintenance;

• Availability and affordability of spare parts.

The first of these criteria is the most crucial. Many handpumps only operate at shallow depth which immediately limits the range of options for deep groundwater. Suction pumps will only operate to 7 metres (less at altitude), and direct action pumps to about 15 metres. The standard Afridev, a deepwell pump, operates at lifts up to 45 metres, and the India Mark II, another deepwell pump, is available in a version that can pump from up to 80 metres. Some pumps such as the Afridev and Consallen which normally operate at medium lifts can be adapted to operate in deeper conditions. The level of usage in terms of water pumped and hours used per day is also important in the selection of a suitably durable and capable pump.

Village Level Operation and Maintenance (VLOM) pumps can be operated and maintained using community management structures. They are typified by ease of maintenance and repair, i.e. maintenance which can be undertaken without the need for heavy equipment. The majority of handpumps currently in operation in Africa are classed as VLOM pumps, but the level of technical difficulty involved in their upkeep varies greatly. Models which require a range of specialist or heavy lifting tools to repair, such as the India Mark II, also present additional maintenance problems in that access to these tools must be assured.

The cost of spare parts for different handpumps varies considerably and can have a major impact on sustainability. It is important that these costs are estimated as accurately as possible when presenting technical options to communities. The availability of spare parts also varies considerably. Handpump standardization policies were introduced, at least in part, to promote the availability of spare parts in country, but have had only limited success to date (see Chapter 8).

6.3.1   Types of handpump

Handpumps generally fall into one of five categories:

- Suction pumps;

- Direct action pumps;

- Deepwell reciprocating pumps;

- Progressive cavity rotary pumps; and

- Displacement pumps.

6

Figure 6.2 illustrates each of the five generic types of pump. The deepwell reciprocating pump is the most widespread in Africa, although direct action pumps are common in areas with higher water tables (many direct action pumps are also reciprocating but are considered a separate pump type here). Suction pumps are relatively rare and are more widespread in shallow groundwater areas of Asia than in Africa. Diaphragm pumps are relatively widespread, especially in Francophone Africa, while progressive cavity pumps are the predominant handpumps in South Africa but rare elsewhere in the continent.

6.3.2   Handpump standardization

The term 'standardization' as applied to handpumps is used in two different ways which can cause confusion, i.e. it can be:

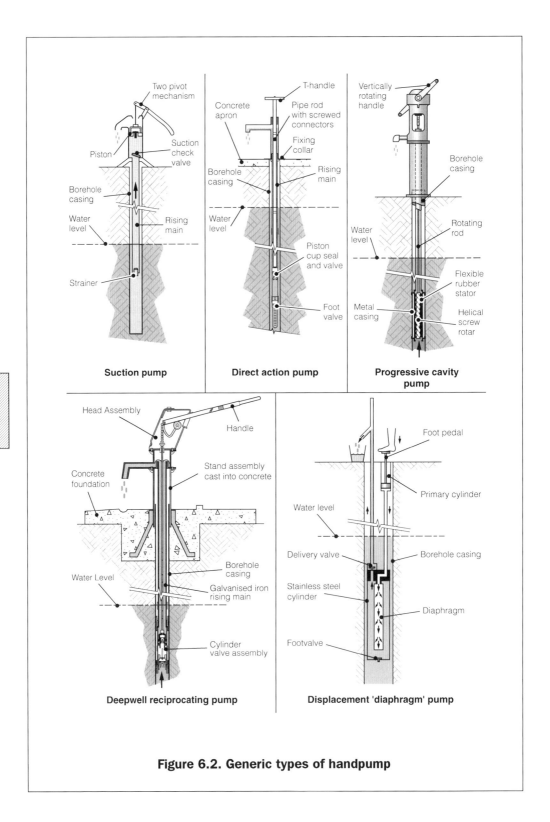

Figure 6.2. Generic types of handpump

- A policy which limits the range of handpumps that can be used within a particular country; or

- The development of fixed standards and specifications for public domain pumps (see Section 6.3.3).

The first definition is the one used in this book. Many national standardization policies were influenced by international agencies such as UNICEF and consequently many of the pumps on which countries have standardized are public domain pumps, such as the India Mark II and III and Afridev pumps. There is no reason, however, why a proprietary pump cannot be selected as a standard pump for a particular country, although this has happened rarely to date due to reluctance among governments to favour a sole manufacturer. The relative advantages and disadvantages of standardization are listed below.

Advantages

- Number of models in use in a country will be less and hence a smaller range of spare parts will be required.

- Technical skills and training needs can be focused on just a few pumps.

- Increased potential for effective quality control of pumps and parts.

- There is potential for local pump manufacture where demand is sufficiently high.

6

Disadvantages

- Lack of competition in manufacturing can occur if it is not a public domain pump, leading to the cost being higher than necessary.

- Lack of incentives to improve quality of pumps and components.

- Rigid policies can stifle local innovation and alternative technologies.

Standardization has obvious pros and cons and there are strongly held conflicting views on the subject among sector professionals. Field research undertaken by the authors indicates that countries which do not currently have handpump standardization polices in place, such as Kenya and South Africa, do not demonstrate significantly lower levels of handpump sustainability than those that do, such as Ghana and Zambia. The primary difference is that Kenya and South Africa have a larger range of pumps in country (most but not all with available spares) and there is a greater level of local innovation.

6.3.3   Public domain pumps

Public domain pumps are handpumps for which the designs are available in the public domain. This means that, in theory, any company or individual can choose to manufacture them, and this is seen as a way of encouraging in-country manufacture of high quality pumps and/or to promote competition between international manufacturers. Local manufacture of public domain pumps in Africa, however, has been much less successful than originally hoped for due to cheaper imports from Asia. SKAT/HTN has prepared and published international handpump specifications covering most field-proven handpump designs in the public domain. These are readily available from SKAT/HTN (Erpf, 2002). Public domain pumps include the following:

- India Mark II and III (reciprocating);

- Afridev (reciprocating);

- Tara (direct action);

- Malda (direct action);

- Jibon (reciprocating);

- Yaku-Maya-Tara (direct action);

- Bush pump (reciprocating); and

- Rope pump.

6.3.4   Proprietary pumps

Proprietary pumps are simply handpumps for which the designs are not kept in the public domain but remain the patented property of private manufacturers. The number of models of proprietary pump found in the field has decreased significantly with the widespread adoption of standardization policies focusing on public-domain pumps. However, a limited number of proprietary pumps remain widespread and have a major impact in the field. These are generally of good quality and include:

- Mono (progressive cavity);

- Orbit (progressive cavity);

- Nira (direct action);

Photograph 6.4. Afridev handpump on hand-dug well

- Consallen (reciprocating);

- Volanta* (flywheel-operated reciprocating);

- Wilimi/SWN* (reciprocating); and

- Vergnet (diaphragm).

6

* Soon to become public domain

With the exception of South Africa where Mono and Orbit pumps are manufactured in-county and dominate the market, much of sub-Saharan Africa is dominated by the India Mark II and III pumps and the Afridev. The Vergnet remains widespread, especially in Francophone Africa, and pumps such as the Volanta and Nira have been selected for inclusion in a range of standardized pumps in countries such as Mozambique and Ghana. It is true to say, though, that most manufacturers of proprietary pumps now struggle to compete because of an uneven playing field. As a result, some such as the Volanta and Wilimi are likely to become public domain pumps in the near future.

Public domain pumps have now become widespread but there is still a role for proprietary pumps. Where manufacturers can demonstrate a willingness to support in-country manufacture and supply chains for their products they may be able to offer more sustainable solutions than existing structures. Maintenance arrangements such as the Total Warranty Scheme (see Chapter 7) are based on a manufacturer's commitment to sustaining water services and promoting future sales of pumps and parts. Governments are right to resist the introduction of a huge range of different models which may not be sustained, but since current levels of sustainability are generally low they should remain flexible and open to new approaches, including those linked to proprietary pumps. For detailed technical issues regarding different handpump models refer to Baumann (2000).

6.3.5 Locally developed pumps

As the 21st century gets under way it may be time to accept that reliance on imported pumps, whether public domain or not, is not delivering acceptable levels of sustainability. While there are many factors that contribute to this situation, it is undoubtedly true that the majority of handpumps remain 'outsider' technologies which presents one specific O&M challenge: they rely on imported specialist components which are not available within existing markets and are often expensive. This means that supply chains must be set up to ensure that specialist spare parts are made available to rural populations. Technology can make a huge contribution to sustainability if pumps use simple components which are already available in country for other purposes, are easily understood, and easy to repair and maintain. The working principles behind most handpumps (whether reciprocating, displacement or direct action pumps) are very simple and there is considerable potential for these to be taken and developed locally, to produce truly local pumps.

A surprising number of locally developed and manufactured VLOM pumps can be found throughout Africa. The DIT Wonder pump in Ghana, the Barry pump in South Africa, the Kiare pump in Kenya, the Mark Vpump in Malawi, the Zimbabwe Bush pump, and the AFRI-pump are just a few. The majority of these were developed exclusively by local people, with little or no outside support, and use non-specialized low-cost components available in existing markets. Many of them are also designed so that they can be repaired using standard tools and equipment.

The Zimbabwe Bush pump is an example of a local success story. Originally designed in 1933 and later modernized, the Bush pump is the National Standard Handpump of Zimbabwe. In 1998 it was manufactured by 12 different companies in the country and around 3000 pumps were installed per annum (Erpf, 1998). Preventive maintenance can be easily carried out by communities and most repairs are within the means of area pump mechanics. Its success is due to a sturdy and reliable design, and government endorsement and support.

Photograph 6.5. Afri-pump, Kenya

6

Many other locally developed pumps have been greeted with less enthusiasm by government staff, and consequently are represented by just a few prototypes. This is a great shame and there remains a need for governments to develop strategies to support and promote local initiatives. Some new developments such as the AFRI-pump in Kenya have relied on the support of local NGOs, but without government endorsement have limited application.

6.3.6   Rope pump

The Rope pump, or Rope and Washer pump, is a simple technology developed in Nicaragua, based on a pumping principle first used by the Chinese at least one or two thousand years ago (Alberts, 2000; Pump Aid, 2004). The Rope pump has now been transferred to several African countries including Kenya and Ghana. A variation on the design known as the Elephant Pump has also been used in Zimbabwe. The beauty of the pump is its simplicity. It consists of a rope, rubber washers (which at their most basic can be made from discs cut from old car tyres but are best made from moulded plastic), a pulley wheel (which at its most basic can be made from an old bicycle wheel) and a rising main (usually consisting of uPVC pipe but which can even be made using bamboo).

The Rope pump (Figure 6.3) is viewed by many as a technological breakthrough, when compared to conventional handpumps. Here is a technology which is easy to understand, easy to reproduce and easy to maintain. The only recurrent maintenance needs are repairing or replacing the rope and washers. It is also

Photograph 6.6. Rope pump on hand-dug well

6

highly versatile. It can be manufactured locally from a variety of different materials, including wood, bamboo or iron. While most models are best suited to hand-dug wells (at depths of 5 to 30m), versions can be manufactured for use in boreholes and can operate at up to depths of 60 metres. Critics argue that the pump cannot withstand heavy use but stronger more durable versions can be produced at much lower cost than most handpumps. There is also concern that the Rope pump has greater potential for pollution than a conventional handpump. While this may be theoretically true, so far there are no published data that support this assertion. A study of water quality in Nicaragua showed 60 per cent lower coliform concentration with Rope pumps than with traditional Bucket wells (Gorter et al., 1993). For further details on the Rope pump refer to van Hemert et al. (1992).

6.3.7 Bucket pump

The Bucket pump (Figure 6.3) is another level down from the Rope pump in terms of simplicity, but perhaps another step up in terms of sustainability. The Bucket pump is operated by a chain (or rope) and windlass in any borehole or

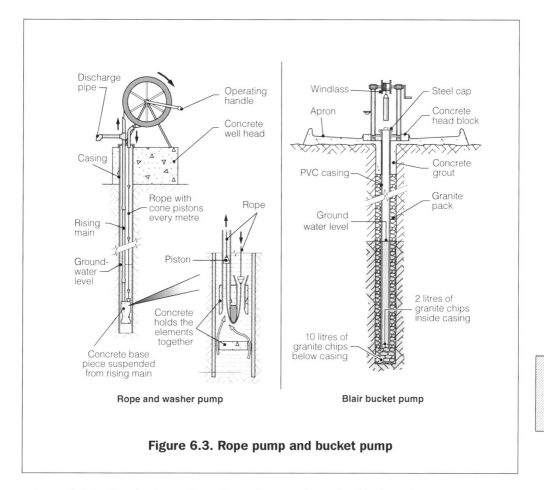

Figure 6.3. Rope pump and bucket pump

tubewell. The 'bucket' consists of a galvanized steel cylinder with a simple valve in the base which allows the cylinder to fill when it is lowered into the water and which closes when the bucket is lifted to the surface. The bucket holds about five litres of water and must be lowered and raised three times to fill the average household bucket or jerrycan. This technology is so simple that it can be manufactured in any small town and it can be easily repaired at community or household level without specialized equipment.

While it has limited application in terms of depth and number of users, the Bucket pump is an ideal solution in areas of shallow groundwater and soft ground conditions, and is best suited to use by households, though it is sometimes adopted by communities. Although it may be seen by some as a regressive step in technology terms, there have been cases in South Africa where communities have rejected or vandalized conventional handpumps in favour of Bucket pumps (Harvey & Kayaga, 2003).

Photograph 6.7. Bucket pump on tubewell, and undergoing repair

6.3.8 Pump selection process

The selection of the most appropriate handpump for a given situation is often a difficult task. Figure 6.4 summarizes a generic selection process that can be used.

1. A thorough assessment of the groundwater conditions is the most logical starting point for the process. This should include measurement of groundwater levels and seasonal variations, so that the maximum lift required of the pump is estimated. The maximum lift should be measured from at least 2 metres below the lowest recorded water level to ground level. The number of users and corresponding flow rate required should be estimated and the yield of the borehole and groundwater pH should be measured. Where pH values are below 6.5 or above 8, corrosion-resistant materials should be used for all down-hole components.

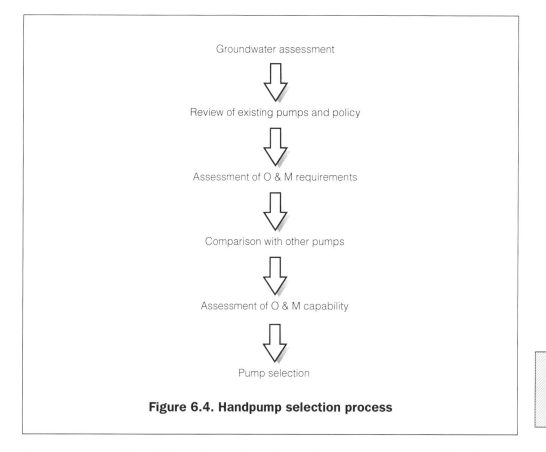

Groundwater assessment

Review of existing pumps and policy

Assessment of O & M requirements

Comparison with other pumps

Assessment of O & M capability

Pump selection

Figure 6.4. Handpump selection process

6

2.   A review should then be conducted of all existing pumps used in the area or country and of any policies affecting choice, such as standardization. The following points should be noted for each pump:

- Maximum lift;

- Materials from which components are made; and

- Maximum pumping rate at required lift (i.e. depth from which water must be pumped).

These data should then be matched to the groundwater conditions to see which pumps, if any, are capable of meeting the pumping requirements. If government policy limits the range of pumps which can be used, these pumps should be assessed first, but where these are deemed inappropriate other options should be considered.

3.   The next step is to conduct a thorough assessment of the O&M requirements for each of the pumps identified. This should consider:

- Spare parts, skills and tools required;

- Estimated costs of maintenance, repair and replacement over time; and

- Projected maintenance and management requirements over time.

4. If the pump choice remains uncertain, this information may then be compared to that for other pumps which are not used locally. These may include handpumps used in other countries, including proprietary and public domain pumps, or simplified pumping technologies such as the rope pump. The performance data and O&M requirements for each should be compared to determine if there is a more appropriate option which is not currently used locally. Where handpump standardization policies exist, however, attempts should be made to keep to these wherever possible.

5. At this stage it is likely that the most suitable pump has been selected or that only two or three options remain. However many options remain, the O&M requirements for each must be matched against local O&M capability. It is therefore necessary to assess whether appropriate skills, tools, spare parts and finances are available for each remaining pump. This should be done through consultation with local communities and private companies. If specialist tools or spare parts which are not currently available are required for a particular pump this should NOT be selected.

6. The selected pump will be the one that fulfills the necessary pumping requirements and for which there is local capacity for O&M.

6.4 Operating and maintaining technologies

If water services are to be sustainable it is essential that technologies are operated and maintained in an appropriate manner.

6.4.1 Service levels

The first step to encourage appropriate use is to determine appropriate service levels. In general, handpumps are installed on the basis of a fixed number of people per pump. The most widespread standard adopted is 250 people per pump, although there are examples where this is increased to 300 or even interpreted as 250 households per pump. One problem with setting service levels in this way is that the users may not agree with the provider and may decide to determine their own service levels. An example of this is where four pumps are installed in a community of 1000 people and gradually one by one the pumps break down until only one remains functioning. The community then wait until this pump breaks down and then decide to repair it since they have no other option. Their chosen service level is therefore 1000 people per pump, not 250. This will result in heavy usage of the one operating pump but it is difficult to change this without taking away the freedom of choice of the empowered community.

An alternative approach to 'people per pump' is to match water demand to the flow rate of a pump over a given period (Skinner, 2003). This considers the population, the volume of water required per person per day, and the number of hours convenient for pumping. This information can be used in the following equation to calculate the yield (in litres per minute) that must be delivered from the borehole by the pump.

$$\textbf{Required yield, Y} = \frac{1.1 \times P \times g \times W}{60 \times H} \text{(litres/min)}$$

P = population

g = population growth factor (i.e. if the estimated population increase over the life of facility is 20%, g = 1.20)

W = water usage per person per day (l/p/d)

H = preferred number of hours available to collect water (hrs)

(The factor of 1.1 is used to provide a 10% margin of error)

This method is not foolproof, by any means, but allows a consultative approach to determining service levels. An example is presented in Box 6.4.

6.4.2   Appropriate use
Community mobilization activities should include training users how to operate a handpump correctly, i.e. not to bang the handle on the pump head and to pump using long, regular strokes. Where possible, however, pumps should be designed to endure heavy and 'incorrect' usage. It is common practice in some areas for communities to keep handpumps locked for much of the day to prevent children playing on them, but even where this is the case, there can be no guarantee of 'appropriate use'. Perhaps the best approach is to simply inform users of the consequences of poor operation and help ensure that they are able to respond to any resulting problems.

Box 6.4. Service level determination example

A population of 200 people use an average of 18 l of water per person per day and wish to collect this water within a two hour period in the morning and a two hour period in the evening (a total period of four hours). The population is expected to increase by 25 per cent over the next 20 years. The yield required is given by:

$$\textbf{Required yield, Y} = \frac{1.1PgW}{60H} = \frac{1.1 \times 200 \times 1.25 \times 18}{60 \times 4} = 20 \text{ l/min}$$

If a handpump-equipped borehole is to be used, then the handpump needs to be capable of lifting 20 l/min, and the yield of the borehole must be sufficient to support this.If the system is unable to fulfil these requirements (as is likely) the community must decide to either increase the hours of operation or opt for a second pump. The cost implications of opting for second pump must be made clear in order for the users to make an informed decision.

6.4.3 Maintenance requirements

Whatever technology is selected, 'maintenance' is of key importance if systems are to be sustained. Effective maintenance requires appropriate skills, tools, spare parts, finances and institutional frameworks. A recent study of handpump water supplies in Mozambique found confidence in local technical competence to have the strongest relationship with the sustainability of system (Batchelor et al., 2000). That is to say, where users were confident that they had access to technically competent repair personnel, the downtime and frequency of breakdown of pumps were lowest. It is essential that appropriate technical skills are available, since where there is an ability to improvise there will be less reliance on specialist tools and parts. Different technologies have different maintenance requirements and it is important that there is an effective system to ensure that institutional capacity and maintenance systems are matched to technologies for which they can effectively deliver.

Chapter 7 addresses the importance of maintenance in more detail and provides different maintenance options.

6.5   Maintaining the water source

Whether the pump is installed on a hand-dug well or borehole it is important that the water source is maintained as well as the water-lifting device. Even if this is done there may eventually come a time when rehabilitation is required or the source must be abandoned. This may arise because the yield of the source has decreased, the water quality has deteriorated, or the water-lifting device is no longer able to deliver water from the source (e.g. due to depletion of the water table). It is difficult to predict future problems or rehabilitation needs, since there are many variable factors which affect the 'rehabilitation-free' lifespan of water sources and facilities. If rehabilitation needs are to be minimized, however, it is essential that water sources are monitored and maintained.

Monitoring is addressed in more detail in Chapter 9, and in relation to the water source refers to monitoring of groundwater levels, yields and quality. There must also be regular inspection of facilities and systems, since where communities are left alone to manage their own facilities maintenance needs of the water source are often unrecognized or go unreported.

6.5.1   Apron and drainage maintenance

An important aspect of maintaining the water source is to maintain the well or borehole apron and associated drainage system. This is crucial to prevent contamination of the source. Concrete or masonry aprons should be checked regularly as part of routine monitoring activities to ensure that they are in a good state of repair. This should ensure that any cracks or deterioration are detected early, so that repairs can be conducted before contamination occurs. The drainage system to take waste water and storm water away from the water point should also be inspected regularly. Where required, drainage channels should be cleaned and repaired to prevent standing water. This is important, both to prevent pollution of the water source and to reduce breeding grounds for insect vectors such as mosquitoes.

6.5.2   Hand-dug well maintenance

In general, hand-dug wells require minimal maintenance and there are many examples of traditional wells that have been in successful operation for generations. Most problems with hand-dug wells arise from contamination or groundwater depletion.

Deepening

Where groundwater levels have dropped over time, causing once-reliable wells to become ephemeral in nature (i.e. to contain water only during the wet season), it may be necessary to deepen the well by digging. This is a simple operation which is best conducted at the end of the dry season and can be undertaken by community members. Safety issues are of paramount importance to ensure that workers are able to enter and exit the well safely, are protected from falling objects, and are not exposed to hazardous gases. Where concrete well rings are used the well can be deepened by excavating below these. A telescoped design can be used in which rings of smaller diameter are lowered inside the existing well to the additional depth.

Well cleaning

Where wells have become silted or contaminated over time they may need to be cleaned. This can be done by pumping the well until it is completely or almost empty of water. In some cases the well can be de-watered manually using bailers but this may not empty the well sufficiently. One individual should then climb into the base of the well, supported by a rope and pulley system, and wearing a safety helmet. He or she should remove any solid objects and sludge by using a bucket and rope which is pulled to the surface from above. The rate at which water recharges the well should be checked regularly. Once all waste has been removed, the inside walls of the well should be scrubbed using a stiff brush and chlorine solution. This should be carried out along the whole depth of the well if possible. The well should then be left for several hours (or overnight) to give time to recharge and for the water level to rise to normal. Once full, the well should be shock chlorinated, i.e. a bucketful of concentrated HTH (high test hypochlorite) solution or bleach should be thrown into the well, and the water pumped out again several times to purge the well and ensure that the taste or odour of chlorine will not deter people from using the water. Finally, the well should be left to fill up once again. The water quality can be tested after this if appropriate. (See Annex C for more details.)

In general, **ongoing chlorination of wells to maintain water quality is not recommended** due to the need to handle toxic chemicals at community level and the need for effective management to ensure correct and regular dosing, and sufficient contact time. Good source protection and a hygienic method of collecting the water to prevent contamination are more effective.

6.5.3   Borehole maintenance assessment

Boreholes may require maintenance or rehabilitation for a number of reasons and this is generally more technically complex than for hand-dug wells. The first stage in the process is to identify the problem early by regular inspection of the borehole. Monitoring visits should be used to:

1. Check the output from the pump, i.e. number of strokes/revolutions to fill a 20 litre jerrycan. This should be approximately 40 and should not exceed an absolute maximum of 100. If more than 10 strokes are required before the delivery of water there is a significant problem with the pump or footvalve, or there is a leak in the riser pipe.

2. Check the turbidity of the water, which should not exceed 5NTU (WHO, 2003). If it is higher than this there is a problem of siltation in the borehole.

3. Remove the pump, including the down-hole components, and inspect it to ensure that it is working correctly and that no components are in need of replacement. Also examine for signs of incrustation or corrosion.

4. Check the water level in the borehole.

The most common problem encountered is a problem with the pump. Where this is not the case, the most common problem with the borehole is a reduction in borehole output, which may be due to a range of causes (see Annex C for more details). The simplest measure is to try to redevelop the borehole, though this may not always be successful. Whatever situation is encountered there is a need for experienced personnel, patience and realism. Rehabilitation may not be possible or cost-effective in many cases, and hence there may sometimes be a need to abandon the borehole. Where this arises a replacement borehole will need to be drilled. Ideally, appropriate rehabilitation financing strategies should be developed which allow for this.

6

6.5.4   Borehole rehabilitation techniques

The basic principles of the main borehole rehabilitation techniques are described below.

Redevelopment by air lift

Air lift is the most common method of borehole development and can also be used to redevelop boreholes where yields have decreased. An air compressor is used to pump compressed air into the borehole and lift a column of water upwards. The air valve is then closed, and the column of water in the pipe allowed to drop down into the formation. Repeated cycles create a surging affect which draws silt and fine materials into the borehole, removes clogging and recreates a natural filter outside the screen. The fine material can be removed from the borehole by pumping or bailing. Air lift is not always usable, since it depends on having a reasonably deep water column in the borehole in comparison to the required lift to ground level.

Redevelopment by surge block

An alternative to air lift is to use a surge block (swab) which forces water gently into the formation beyond the borehole screening when pushed downwards, and pulls water through the screen on the upstroke. This surging action has the same effect as the air lift method by pulling fines into the well and recreating a natural filter bed around the screened section of the borehole.

Hydrofracturing

Hydrofracturing is used to increase the yields of low-production boreholes in rock where the fracture/joint systems are so poorly developed, or so tight, that little or no water can move through them. Hydrofracturing is accomplished by lowering an inflatable seal or borehole 'packer' into the borehole and expanding it below the static water level and above the fracture/joint system. Water is then pumped down through the water injection pipe at high pressure and high volume simultaneously. The pressure and flow created in the production zone usually cause small, tight fractures/joints in the rock to open up and spread radially. The newly opened and flushed out fractures provide connections between nearby water-bearing fractures and the borehole.

Hydrofracturing has proven highly effective at increasing yields, improving reliability and reducing suspended sediment in boreholes. The cost of equipment may be restrictive, but experience in India suggests that costs can be considerably reduced where the technique is applied to a large number of boreholes, and that the cost per borehole is only a small percentage of the cost of drilling a replacement borehole (Joshi, 1996). Experience suggests that the technique is more effective in fractured igneous basement aquifers than fractured sedimentary aquifers (World Vision, 2003).

Internal gravel packs

Where the yield of the borehole is adequate but the level of turbidity is too high, due to high levels of siltation, a number of simple rehabilitation methods can be used. Godfrey & Ball (2003) suggest the use of internal gravel packs or telescoped design for such boreholes. For the installation of internal gravel packs the borehole is first flushed with compressed air and then a volume of 1-5mm sized gravel is added inside the borehole casing to a depth of about 0.5m above the top of the slotted area of screening. The borehole is then redeveloped using compressed air to develop an internal filter. This method is relatively cheap and simple and has shown positive results in reducing turbidity (Osola, 1998), and for boreholes equipped with handpumps the negative affect on yield is insignificant.

Telescoped design

In areas where there is adequate depth of aquifer, a long, small diameter (50mm or 2") well screen can be inserted inside the existing (100mm or 4") casing of the borehole, to create a telescoped design. The pump cylinder should be placed above the reduction in diameter but low enough to allow for drawdown. This approach makes it possible to create a greater thickness of graded gravel around the centralized well screen to reduce siltation and hence turbidity levels. A high capacity large open area 50mm/2" screen can be selected that will provide the same open area as a conventional 100mm/4" slotted screen, to ensure that there is no reduction in flow. Like the internal gravel pack solution, this technique is relatively easy and low-cost.

6.6   Steps towards technical sustainability

The following process can be used by the implementing agency in conjunction with the community to be served to ensure appropriate technology choice and to maximize sustainability (Figure 6.5).

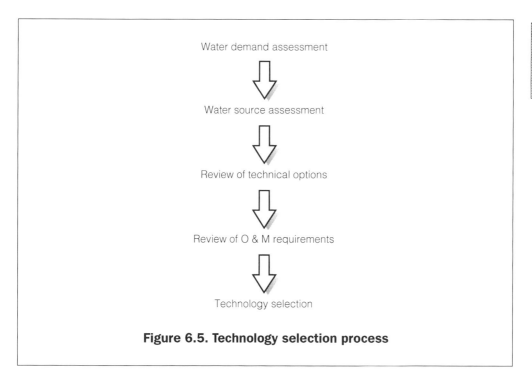

Figure 6.5. Technology selection process

Step 1. Water demand assessment

The first step is to undertake an assessment of the demand for a new water supply among community members. This should measure the:

- Quantity of water required per day or required flow rate;

- Quality of water required (i.e. for drinking, cooking, washing etc.); and

- Acceptable maximum distance from water source required.

This will be achieved through consultation with individual community members and focus groups. Random consultation can be carried out by interviewing an individual from every third house in the village and selecting a male then female in turn. This exercise will provide the ideal characteristics required of the water supply.

Step 2. Water source assessment

An assessment should then be conducted of all possible water sources in the vicinity, including existing or traditional sources used by the community and other potential but untapped resources. The characteristics of these water sources should then be matched to the ideal requirements of the community. A range of sources or a single source may be identified which best meets the community demand.

Step 3. Review of technical options

Based on the water source(s) identified, a range of possible technologies should be investigated. For example, if groundwater is identified as the most appropriate water source, options would include open hand-dug wells, handpump-equipped boreholes, and electrical borehole pumps and distribution systems. All possible options should be listed and presented to the community. Household solutions should be considered as well as community options.

Step 4. Review of O&M requirements

For each technical option identified the O&M requirements must then be assessed. These will include the tools, spare parts, skills, management needs and finances required to sustain operation and maintenance. The requirements should be presented beside the listed options and matched to current capacity to fulfil each of these. A consultative process should be used to establish whether the necessary skills, equipment and finances are available for each option and whether they will continue to be available for the foreseeable future.

Step 5. Technology selection

The final step in the process is to determine which technology option can:

a) Deliver the appropriate quantity and quality of water to an acceptable location;

b) Be operated and maintained by or for the community/households at affordable cost; and

c) Be replaced or upgraded with relative ease.

The final selection should be made by the community of users and where a number of options remain at this stage consensus should be sought by majority preference.

Even where the most appropriate technology choice is selected this is not a guarantee of sustainability, as social, managerial and financial issues will all have an influence. Technical monitoring also has a crucial role in ensuring technical and environmental sustainability. This is addressed in Chapter 9.

Further reading

BGS (2001) *Guidelines for Assessing the Risk to Groundwater from On-site Sanitation.* BGS: Wallingford, UK.
(can be accessed at http://www.bgs.ac.uk/hydrogeology/argoss/home.html)

Macdonald, A.M. and Davies, J. (2000) *A Brief Review of Groundwater for Rural Water Supply in Sub-Saharan Africa.* Technical Report WC/00/33, Overseas Geology Series, British Geological Survey: UK.
(can be accessed at http://www.bgs.ac.uk/hydrogeology/ruralwater/home.html)

Macdonald, A.M., Davies, J. and Dochartaigh, B.E.O. (2002) *Simple Methods for Assessing Groundwater Resources in Low Permeability Areas of Africa.* Commissioned Report CR/01/168N, British Geological Survey: UK.
(can be accessed at http://www.bgs.ac.uk/hydrogeology/ruralwater/home.html)

Erpf, K. (2002) *Technology Selection - and Buyers' Guide for Public Domain Handpumps for Drinking Water.* HTN/SKAT: St. Gallen, Switzerland.
(can be accessed at http://www.skat.ch/htn/publications/specifications.htm)

Rowles, R. (1995) *Drilling for Water: A practical manual.* Avebury, Aldershot, UK.

Skinner, B.H. (2003) *Small-Scale Water Supply: A review of technologies.* ITDG Publishing: London, UK.

6

Sutton, S. (2002) *Community led Improvements of Rural Drinking Water Supplies*. SWL Consultants: Shrewsbury, UK.

Wurzel, P. (2001) *Drilling Boreholes for Handpumps*. Working Papers on Water Supply and Environmental Sanitation, Volume 2, SKAT: St. Gallen, Switzerland.
(can be accessed at http://www.skat.ch/htn/downloads/bh4handpumps.pdf)

Chapter 7

Maintenance systems

Operation and maintenance of systems is of key importance in sustaining water services. Despite its growing prevalence in recent years, community management of O&M has had limited success and is not the only available option. New and innovative maintenance systems require further investigation, especially those that encourage indigenous private sector participation. This chapter looks at different maintenance systems which can be implemented and sustained based on various experiences and case studies. The fact that there is no universal solution to maintenance and repair is emphasized, and the importance of seeking locally appropriate solutions is highlighted.

7.1   Maintenance

Maintenance can be defined as the 'activity involved in maintaining something in good working order' or 'the act of sustaining' (Hyperdictionary, 2003). Maintenance is a prerequisite for sustainable water systems and can be divided into the following categories as defined by UNCHS (2004):

- *Preventive maintenance* refers to systematic pre-scheduled activities or programmes of inspections and maintenance activities aimed at the early detection of defects and implementation of actions to avoid breakdowns or deterioration. Preventive maintenance is 'preactive' since activities are conducted before a defect occurs. Often the cost of preventive maintenance activities is low compared with corrective maintenance or rehabilitation.

- *Corrective maintenance* refers to activities conducted or repairs carried out as a result of breakdowns or noticeable infrastructure deterioration. Corrective maintenance is inherently 'reactive' in that it is carried out after some defect is discerned, often because the system is not operating as intended.

- *Rehabilitation* refers to activities carried out to correct major defects in order to restore a facility to its intended operational status and capacity, without significantly expanding it beyond its originally planned or designed function or extent. Rehabilitation activities are generally more expensive than corrective maintenance activities.

Each of these maintenance aspects is important, although there is a tendency among rural communities to miss out preventive measures and focus on corrective maintenance only. This shortens the lifespan of components and increases pump downtimes. Effective preventive and corrective maintenance should minimize the need for rehabilitation, though this may still be necessary (for example, due to borehole siltation). The term *routine maintenance* may be used to refer to preventive and corrective maintenance activities carried out more often than once a year. Some of these activities can be defined on the basis of operating hours. *Periodic maintenance* refers to preventive maintenance activities carried out less often than once a year, such as once every two or five years. These maintenance tasks are often programmed in predetermined plans or schedules.

7.1.1 Maintenance needs

Maintenance needs vary considerably with the type of technology used. For example, a protected spring may require little maintenance except occasional cleaning of the outlet, while a pumped water system may require regular maintenance of pumps, valves, tanks and pipes. It is therefore important that potential users are provided with comprehensive information regarding likely ongoing maintenance requirements, frequency of activities and associated financial, human and material resources. Box 7.1 shows a typical maintenance schedule for a handpump, though this will vary with different pump types.

Box 7.1. Typical handpump maintenance schedule[1]

Daily checks: Pump operation
Pump and base cleanliness
Wastewater drainage
Comments of users

Weekly: Lubricate moving parts
Check and tighten nuts and bolts
Check security of pump on base

Monthly: Check output (flow) rate
Check condition of concrete
base and apron

Yearly: Remove downhole assembly
Inspect, tighten and replace parts
where necessary

---

1. after Elson et al., 1999

If preventive measures are carried out at appropriate intervals (depending on the chosen model and operating conditions) the handpump should continue operating without breakdown. This requires regular preventive maintenance visits or services to detect minor faults and pre-empt problems that may result in future breakdowns. Such actions might include simple interventions such as tightening nuts, or slightly more intricate measures such as replacing wearing parts, for example seals, prior to complete failure. Table 7.1 gives examples of preventive and corrective maintenance measures for a handpump. It is essential, however, that competent personnel are available to carry out such tasks effectively.

Table 7.1. Preventive and corrective maintenance for a handpump

Maintenance activity	Preventative measure	Corrective measure
Grease chain link	✓	
Tighten base plate nuts	✓	
Tighten and oil handle	✓	
Tighten pipe and rod connectors	✓	
Replace seals	✓	✓
Replace chain link	✓	✓
Replace bearings	✓	✓
Replace connecting rods		✓
Replace riser pipes		✓
Replace foot-valve		✓
Fish out fallen pipes and rods		✓

Many major repairs can be avoided by undertaking thorough preventive maintenance and adopting best practices. A simple example of this is to pull out the rising main of a pump once a year to inspect its condition and tighten rod and pipe joints. Best practice such as using PTFE tape on pipe connections can also increase performance. This type of intervention can avoid the need for difficult and expensive repairs such as fishing out and replacing fallen pipes. The simple act of regularly tightening bolts can also prolong the life of a pump since excessive play encourages wear.

Routine maintenance should also include sanitary measures such as keeping the pump surrounds and drainage channels clean and ensuring that potential contaminant routes, such as cracks in the pump apron, are sealed.

7.1.2 Maintenance objectives

Preventive maintenance may be an unfamiliar concept in some societies or cultures. Indeed, in some African languages there is no word for 'maintenance'. It is therefore important that needs and benefits are clearly conveyed to water users and maintenance providers. It is also necessary to set clear and realistic objectives for both preventive and corrective maintenance, and to ensure that these are budgeted for accordingly. This includes community budgeting for the setting of water tariffs, and institutional budgeting for monitoring, technical support and backstopping (i.e. where specialist technical assistance is required).

Responsibilities for decision-making and implementation should be clearly defined, and detailed maintenance schedules developed. Maintenance contracts between a community or local authority and a private maintenance provider need to set clear objectives with measurable indicators. For example, a contract might stipulate that at least 90 per cent of facilities and systems should be operational at any one time, or that the response time for reported breakdowns should not exceed two days.

7.1.3 Regulation

Whatever maintenance model or system is adopted, regulation of those responsible for maintenance is essential. This includes regulation of the activities of community volunteers, area pump mechanics, private contractors and independent service providers. Regulation by local government authorities (or where this is not possible, a local NGO or faith-based organization) should ensure:

• Value for money for water users;

• Appropriate quality of workmanship;

• Fair remuneration for maintenance provider; and

• Efficient and effective maintenance systems.

Monitoring of maintenance providers and activities is essential to measure indicators and assess these issues (see Chapter 9). This must be backed up by effective legislation and contractual arrangements which allow the regulator to enforce improved performance and impose penalties for failure.

7.1.4   Maintenance models

Whatever technology is selected it is important that an appropriate maintenance system is set up. The currently favoured model of community management (or VLOM), whereby the users are responsible for the management of maintenance of the water supply, has clearly failed to deliver the levels of sustainability initially hoped for (WSSCC, 2002). However, at present there is a lack of incentives for the private sector or others to assist with O&M and the supply of spare parts. There are, however, new emerging models for service delivery and maintenance which move away from the community maintenance model. These approaches merit further investigation and may become more widespread in Africa in the coming years. The different maintenance models can be divided into the following three categories:

- **Village Level Operation and Maintenance (VLOM)** is the predominant approach used at present and refers to maintenance systems which are managed by the user community.

- **Public-Private Operation and Maintenance (PPOM)** refers to situations where a private sector organization is responsible for managing and delivering maintenance services, regulated by the government.

- **Private Ownership, Operation and Maintenance (POOM)** refers to situations where the water supply facility is owned and maintained by a private organization or individual.

7

Each of these categories has two key factors in common: the cost of O&M is financed by the users of the water system or facility, and maintenance is regulated by the government. Table 7.2 summarizes the key advantages and disadvantages of each category of maintenance system, although these may vary slightly with different models under each category.

Examples for each of these categories are described in the following sections of this chapter, with particular reference to handpumps.

7.2   Village Level Operation & Maintenance (VLOM)

The term VLOM is generally used to refer to community management systems where communities have overall responsibility for O&M. Typical stakeholder roles for VLOM are:

Table 7.2. Advantages and disadvantages of different maintenance options

Maintenance option	Advantages	Disadvantages
VLOM	Fast initial response to problems Community in control of own affairs Develop pride in own achievements	Needs motivated people Needs appropriate local skills and tools Difficulty in accessing spare parts
PPOM	Easy access to spare parts Concentration of skills and resources Community choice of freedom	Potentially higher cost Potentially slower response times Needs active government regulation
POOM	Easy access to spare parts Clear ownership and responsibility Concentration of skills and resources Strong incentive for rapid repair	Ownership removed from community Limited application due to high initial cost to owner

- The community is responsible for managing, financing and facilitating O&M;

- The private sector is responsible for the provision of spare parts and technical services (though this is sometimes done by government or NGO); and

- The public sector (or NGO) is responsible for monitoring and regulation.

There are, however, slight variations on the model which have been implemented in different settings. These are described below.

7.2.1 Community volunteers

The traditional VLOM approach is typified by the community maintenance system in which the users are responsible for all maintenance activities including physical repair. In general, members of a community volunteer to act as pump technicians, are approved by the rest of the community, and are trained in preventive and corrective maintenance by the implementing agency. They are usually provided with appropriate tools, or these are shared by more than one community, and they fulfil their role in the spirit of voluntary service, rather than for remuneration or reward.

Although this approach has demonstrated significant success in countries such as Ghana, Kenya and Malawi, it has a number of key limitations. Firstly, the system relies on voluntary commitment, which is difficult to sustain. Since individuals must make a living from other activities, these are bound to take priority and may result in them leaving the community to seek employment. There is also the need for equipment, tools and spare parts, and users may lack easy access to

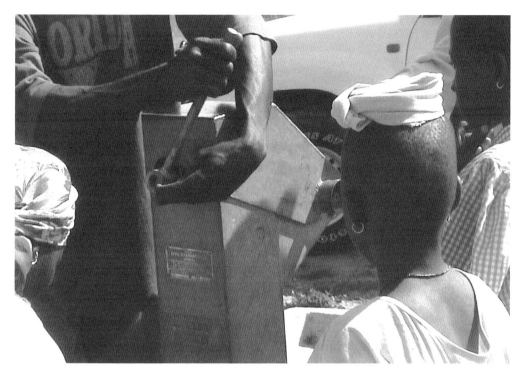

Photograph 7.1. Volunteer removing Afridev pump cover for routine maintenance

7

transportation to obtain these. Even where community volunteers are active, some repairs are beyond their ability. Ongoing technical support is therefore required for difficult technical repairs and refresher training, and ongoing institutional support is required to encourage ongoing social mobilization (Batchelor et al., 2000). The model is only successful, therefore, where there is significant support from NGOs or local government.

7.2.2   Area Pump Mechanics

A decentralized maintenance approach using Area Pump Mechanics (APMs) has been applied in several countries in Africa, including Uganda, Kenya, South Africa, Ghana and Zambia. This approach has replaced village level maintenance volunteers with trained private repairers responsible for a certain number of handpumps in several communities. Each community is still likely to have a pump caretaker but he or she is responsible only for routine chores such as cleaning the pump apron, tightening bolts and greasing the chain. APMs are trained by district institutions or NGOs, and are paid by the communities they serve. In general, they do not carry out preventive maintenance and only attend to a handpump when called upon by the community. Invariably this means the pump has stopped functioning. APMs usually have better back-up from local government and sometimes compete with neighbouring repairers for work. Some institutions set fixed repair rates for above and below ground repairs but APMs may not always adhere to these. Evidence from the Zambia suggests that both men and women make effective APMs, providing that they are selected by the communities that they are to serve (Harvey & Skinner, 2002). These individuals often have another profession such as bicycle repairer or farmer, and may not make enough money from pump maintenance and repair to make it a worthwhile activity.

The APM model has demonstrated significant advantages over the community volunteer approach:

- There is a clear incentive for the APM, i.e. they make money;

- There are fewer APMs to train and monitor/regulate than community volunteers;

- Fewer tools are needed;

- Turnover of APMs is lower than that of volunteers, and replacements easier to find;

- Individuals may fulfill dual roles, such as APM and environmental health assistant or community development officer; and

- Competition between APMs has the potential to improve service standards and lower costs to the community.

It is important that APMs are monitored and regulated by a local (government or NGO) institution to avoid exploitation of, or by, communities (see Box 7.2). Ongoing technical training for pump repairers and access to tools and spare parts may also require appropriate institutional support. In general, the APM does not sell spare parts but may purchase them on behalf of the community.

7.2.3   Circuit Riders

The Circuit Rider model has been implemented in Uganda and is similar to the APM model (Consallen, 2002). A number of handpump mechanics (HPMs) are selected and trained by district-level government, and each is responsible for about 35 handpumps. Each HPM is provided with a bicycle and is required to undertake a preventive maintenance visit (PMV) to each pump on his/her list at four-month intervals. The community pays US$3 for each visit. The HPM checks that the pump is working and the function and condition of the

---

Box 7.2. APM regulation[1]

In Munyumbwe village, Gwembe District, Zambia, the APM was called out to repair the pump, which he did and the community paid him with a bag of maize. However, the pump only worked for three hours and then stopped again. The APM was called back but demanded another bag of maize before he would attend to the pump. The WATSAN committee refused to give him this but did not know who else to approach for assistance and the APM would not lend them his tools. The pump had not worked for more than a year since this happened.

---

1. Harvey and Skinner, 2002

components on each PMV. If a spare is shortly to be required, the community is informed that this is the case. It is their responsibility to buy spares before the next PMV, during which the HPM will fit parts at no extra cost to the committee. In an emergency, the HPM is available just a short bike ride away to do repairs or maintenance between regular scheduled visits. HPMs live in the community which they serve, and have other means of earning their main income. This system can be subsidized, whereby the community and district council pay agreed portions of the maintenance costs. In any case, it requires strong institutional support and regulation if it is to be effective.

The Circuit Rider model is a step up from the APM model in that both preventive and corrective maintenance are incorporated. It relies, however, on understanding among community members of the importance of preventive maintenance. This is a surprisingly difficult concept to get across to people who may subscribe to the 'if it's not broke don't fix it' maxim (Box 7.3).

Box 7.3. Preventive maintenance concept[1]

In Busoga region, Uganda, the preventive maintenance element of the Circuit Rider model is no longer working in many project areas since many communities do not want the HPM to tamper with the pump if it is working. There is a general lack of understanding of need for and purpose of preventive maintenance, and consequently communities only call on the HPM and pay him/her if a fault arises with the pump. In general, the HPM has now adopted the role of the APM.

---

1. Harvey, 2003

The Uganda experience would suggest that the Circuit Rider model has been less successful than the APM model. It provides, however, a worthy goal and there remains a need to investigate alternative approaches which raise awareness and promote the concept of preventive maintenance among communities and service providers.

Photograph 7.2. APM undertaking Vergnet pump repairs

7.3   Public-Private Operation and Maintenance (PPOM)

The Public-Private Operation and Maintenance (PPOM) option is typified by the following stakeholder roles:

- The private sector is responsible for management of maintenance and repair;

- The public sector is responsible for regulation; and

- The community owns the facility and finances maintenance costs.

The chief difference between this and the APM or Circuit Rider model is that it is the private sector, not the community, that is responsible for managing maintenance. Critics argue that PPOM approaches remove power and autonomy from communities and undermine the gains made by the community-centred approaches of the past. In actual fact, the communities still own the facilities and finance O&M, and for those reasons community mobilization remains important.

The key advantage is that the responsibility for management is lifted off the shoulders of the community or CBO. This grants them greater freedom and, where the private sector becomes well established, greater choice. Another advantage of PPOM is that private contractors are responsible for the procurement of spare parts and specialist equipment and skills.

For any PPOM model to be successful the capacity of the local indigenous private sector must be sufficient. It may, therefore, be necessary for governments to help build capacity where the private sector is currently weak or limited. In order to minimize the downtime of systems, private enterprises must be within easy access of communities and accountable to water users and local government. There are several different, but similar, PPOM models which are described below.

7.3.1 Bidding for Least Subsidy approach

The Least Subsidy approach has been developed by the World Bank in Latin America and is sometimes referred to under the umbrella term of 'output-based aid' (Sansom, 2002). This involves a private company or consortium bidding for the minimum or least subsidy to install and maintain water systems to agreed service levels for a fixed period (e.g. 15 years). These private companies need to assess how much revenue they will recover from community contributions in order to determine what level of subsidy they will require from government over this time period. This should be achieved through consultation with the communities involved and willingness-to-pay surveys. The government then pays the minimum subsidy to the company and the communities pay their water tariffs.

7

The Least Subsidy model accepts the need for some subsidization of rural water supply and requires sufficient private sector capacity to promote competition and effectiveness. It also requires effective public sector regulation. This approach has not been tried for rural water supplies in Africa to date, but has significant potential.

7.3.2 Total Warranty Scheme

The Total Warranty Scheme is essentially a partnership between a (foreign) pump manufacturer, local after-sales private enterprises, local governments and users (Parry-Jones et al., 2001a). This places the onus on the manufacturer to support and train the local enterprises, and provide spare parts. The users pay an annual contract fee to the local enterprises which are responsible for all aspects of maintenance and are regulated by local authorities. This model was first used by the French handpump manufacturer Vergnet in Mauritania (see Box 7.4 and has now been applied in other countries.

Since the short pilot study in Mauritania the Total Warranty Scheme has been expanded to other countries in West Africa and has demonstrated high sustainability levels in countries such as Burkina Faso (van Beers, 2003). In order to be successful, the incentives for the manufacturer must be sufficient in terms of future sales of pumps, as well as spares, and strong partnerships must be developed with local enterprises.

Box 7.4. Total Warranty Scheme[1]

In the late 1990s the community maintenance model was deemed to be failing in Mauritania, mainly due to problems with access to spare parts and lack of qualified mechanics. Vergnet therefore decided to pilot the Total Warranty concept on 75 water points. The manufacturer's commitment was to support and train the local enterprises. The users paid an annual contract fee (equivalent to US$1.50 per person per year) to the local enterprises, which were responsible for all aspects of pump maintenance. The government administration role was one of regulation. After the pilot project had been running for two years an evaluation found that 60% of the villages had paid the enterprise, and 20% had paid half. Where the cost recovery rate was low, systems were not operating. Vergnet decided that, based on the pilot results, the Total Warranty concept should be further developed in Mauritania and elsewhere.

---

1. Bernage, 2000

7.3.3 Water Assurance Scheme

The Water Assurance Scheme (WAS) is a new approach similar to the Total Warranty Scheme (see 7.3.2), but with a crucial difference. Instead of the manufacturer providing a warranty on a piece of equipment, WAS places the emphasis on the ongoing provision of safe, adequate and accessible water regardless of the technology involved. Rural communities pay a monthly premium to an indigenous private company, which is regulated by local government. For as long as the premium is paid the company provides an annual maintenance and water monitoring service, and is responsible for any repairs needed to the handpump or alternative water source.

This acts as an insurance scheme or contract between the water users (communities) and the private water service provider. The service provider will be expected to test and ensure water quality, maintain and repair installations, and upgrade services in line with demand. Each service provider will be responsible for a range of water technologies within a given geographical area, dependent on the communities which subscribe to the scheme. The private companies involved are not linked to a particular manufacturer or technology, but require transferable skills, capacity and expertise.

Rural Water Development (RWD) in Kenya has recently successfully trialed a 'membership scheme' similar to the Water Assurance Scheme where communities had the choice of whether or not to join (Harvey et al., 2003). This approach means that communities are empowered to make their own decisions, since if they choose not to enter the scheme they can continue to manage their water facilities themselves. From this perspective, WAS therefore builds upon the past advances made in community management approaches such as VLOM. Like the other PPOM models described, the local private sector must have sufficient capacity if such a scheme is to be successful. At the time of writing, plans are under way to implement pilot studies that will assess the wider potential of WAS in sub-Saharan Africa.

7.3.4 Government maintenance contracts

The most basic public-private maintenance model is one in which local government manages and finances the system and contracts out maintenance to the private sector. Maintenance contracts for point water sources such as handpumps are largely a thing of the past in most of sub-Saharan Africa, but remain the norm in some areas of South Africa. Here, if a problem arises with the handpump, someone from the user community contacts the local council to report the fault or breakdown. The time lag then before the pump is repaired can vary from several weeks to several months or years. The reasons for such lengthy delays include inadequate budgeting, bureaucratic procedures, and the inefficiency of repairing a single pump at a time. This results in councils waiting until there are several pumps in need of repair in a given area before contracting a company to attend to these. Most contracts entail the wholesale replacement of pumps, rather than repair, and consequently the efficiency of such approaches is highly questionable. As a result, some communities bypass such systems and pay for maintenance themselves, and some implementers have promoted the VLOM approach instead (Harvey & Kayaga, 2003).

Such a public-private approach is used only where water is provided by the government free of charge and consequently is no longer appropriate over much of the continent.

Photograph 7.3. Contractor undertaking maintenance on a Mono pump in South Africa

7.4   Private Ownership, Operation and Maintenance (POOM)

7

Private Ownership, Operation and Maintenance (POOM) is distinctly different from VLOM and PPOM in one way in particular. The water supply facility is not owned by the community but by a private individual, institution or organization. Critics of this approach argue that if communities do not own the water supply facility they are in effect 'disempowered'. There is, however, little evidence to suggest that privately owned schemes have any major debilitating effect on the community. It can be argued that this approach perpetuates dependency and inequality, since power over the source remains in the hands of the private owner/operator, but where regulation is effective ultimate control remains with the water users as paying customers. The term POOM is used broadly to refer to any system where the water facility is owned by a private entity which derives revenue from its operation. The following stakeholder roles apply:

• The private sector owns the water system and is responsible for management and implementation of maintenance and repair;

- the community pays the private sector to collect water from the system; and

- The public sector is responsible for regulation.

7.4.1   Individual ownership

Due to the emphasis placed on the perceived link between user 'ownership' and 'sustainability' there has been little attention given to options where water supply facilities are owned by individuals or households rather than communities. There are, however, many examples of privately owned handpumps throughout Africa, where users pay the owner to collect water from the pump (see Box 7.5).

Box 7.5. Privately-owned handpump[1]

In Bugiri, Uganda, there is an ancient handpump which was fitted to a privately drilled borehole in the 1950s. According to the many people who collect water there every day, it has broken down several times but the owner has always repaired it within a day of it breaking down. The main reason for this is because he is making an income when the pump is working but he is not getting anything when it's broken down. For this service, local households are willing to pay 50 Uganda shillings (US$0.03), per 22 litre jerrycan and there is a line of yellow jerrycans every morning put there by their owners. The jerrycans are filled by the caretaker and his helper who are paid by the owner. People then come and collect their full jerrycans and pay the caretaker.

---

1. Wood, 2001

7

Although the private ownership model may not work in every situation, particularly where there are no individuals with sufficient wealth, where it does work, it often demonstrates very high levels of sustainability. There is a huge incentive for the owner to repair the pump rapidly since he or she is potentially losing money for every minute that the pump is out of operation. This approach has been particularly successful where the local shopkeeper owns the pump and can easily access spare parts when travelling to replenish stock for the store.

A similar approach can be used for alternative water supply technologies such as Bucket pumps on family tubewells. In Maputaland, Kwazulu-Natal, South Africa, some families which own tubewells have been reported to charge their neighbours a nominal amount to come and collect water (Harvey & Kayaga, 2003). Even where there is a limited cash economy variations on the model can be successful, whereby users pay in agricultural produce rather than cash.

This approach could also be used where individuals obtain pumps on hire purchase and use the revenue raised to pay off the loan. In order for the approach to be successful ownership of the land and facility must be clear to all involved. Where individuals have unsecured tenure on land or property this is likely to threaten the security, and hence sustainability, of such a system.

7.4.2   Handpump Lease concept

The Handpump Lease concept is where a local company (normally the local water authority) owns a number of handpumps and provides operation and maintenance services under a contract signed with the communities. This is similar to the Total Warranty Scheme, except handpumps remain the property of the water company. Maintenance contracts are provided for existing handpumps and lease contracts for new or replacement handpumps, which include borehole regeneration. The annual cost per family is set at the beginning of the contract and responsibility for collection of fees lies with pump caretakers. The caretaker is responsible for routine maintenance of his/her pump and the water company is responsible for more complex maintenance and repair for all handpumps. An example of the application of the lease concept in Angola is summarized in Box 7.6.

Box 7.6. Handpump Lease concept[1]

In Lubango, Angola, the local water company owns several hundred handpumps, while the communities they serve own the boreholes or wells on which they are installed. Each family pays an equivalent of US$0.40 to the pump caretaker each month, which is within their financial means and for which they receive an 'official invoice'. Half the revenue raised pays the pump caretaker's salary and half goes to the water company. Some handpumps serve over 50 families and raise $240 per year, $120 of which goes to the water company. Meanwhile the water company estimates an average maintenance cost of only US$30 per handpump per year, resulting in a healthy profit.

---

1. Van Beers, 2001a

Van Beers (2001a) argues that the Handpump Lease concept can be integrated with the management of small piped water systems to enhance efficiency and sustainability of both. The concept has been implemented only on a relatively small-scale to date but has significant potential for expansion. If it is to be successful, however, it is important that it has the approval and support of local government. There is also scope for a lease to buy model or hire-purchase, as has been suggested in Kenya (Sarkinnen, 1994).

7.5   Steps towards sustainable maintenance

As demonstrated above, a range of different maintenance systems can be adopted in the field. In order to select the most appropriate system or model the following process can be applied (Figure 7.1). This is a dynamic process which should ideally be conducted by local and regional government agencies in partnership with relevant NGOs, private sector organizations and communities. Even where a single ideal maintenance system is selected by government, communities should retain the power to decide on the system that best matches their needs. For this reason, a certain degree of flexibility may be required to facilitate choice.

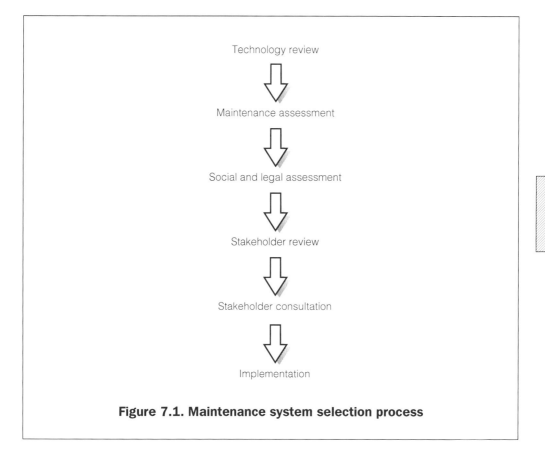

Technology review

Maintenance assessment

Social and legal assessment

Stakeholder review

Stakeholder consultation

Implementation

Figure 7.1. Maintenance system selection process

This process can be conducted at a regional or district level, and should be co-ordinated by a planning committee comprising representatives of relevant government ministries and departments, and external support agencies involved in water supply.

Step 1. Technology review

The first step in the process is to review the existing water supply technologies in the area under consideration. This will help to determine whether the maintenance system should apply to one type of technology only or to a range of options. It should also identify how many different models of pumps there are. A thorough survey of the area should be conducted and a list produced of all communities which specifies what technologies exist in each.

Step 2. Maintenance assessment

Once the range of applicable technologies has been identified an assessment of the maintenance needs for each should be conducted. This will take each technology type and identify the skills, spare parts, tools and equipment that are required to maintain and repair it, and the relative ease of the required maintenance activities. It should also try to determine the expected frequency of breakdown for each technology and estimate the number of maintenance visits required within a year. The following information can be collected and used to assess maintenance needs and determine appropriate budgetary requirements:

- Total population served by technology type;

- Difficulty of maintenance - cost, skills, tools and equipment needed (ranked 1 to 10); and

- Frequency of maintenance (number of visits per year).

Step 3. Social and legal assessment

Following the review of technologies and associated maintenance needs a range of social and legal issues should be assessed. The following questions should be addressed:

- Who owns the water supply systems?

- Who owns the land on which water systems are installed?

- Are communities homogeneous (in terms of tribes, religion, clans etc.)?

- What evidence is there of existing community-based organizations or co-operatives?

The answers to these questions will be useful in setting the social and legal context in which the selected maintenance system will be required to operate.

Step 4. Stakeholder review

Having identified the relative maintenance needs and socio-legal context it is then necessary to review all potential stakeholders in the area which could potentially be involved in the rural water supply maintenance system. These will include private sector organizations and individuals, community-based organizations, local government and NGOs. For each stakeholder their incentives and capacity to be involved should be assessed, and their track record reviewed for similar ventures. Table 7.3 presents an example of how this might be done and what issues should be considered.

Table 7.3. Stakeholder review

Stakeholder	Incentive	Capacity	Track record
e.g. Community Private sector Private individual government NGO	Humanitarian motivation Profit Political goodwill	Mobility Access to spare parts Technical skills Equipment and tools Managerial skills Community liaison skills	Performance elsewhere Management record Transparency Value for money

The stakeholder review is used to identify which stakeholders have the potential to participate and their relative strengths and weaknesses. No decision regarding the most appropriate maintenance system is made at this stage.

Step 5. Stakeholder consultation

This step is the decision-making stage in which all interested parties are involved. This is a consultation exercise in which each party is given the opportunity to express their views and put forward their case for involvement. The information gathered during the stakeholder review can be used to compare the relative advantages of different stakeholders' involvement but does not consider different maintenance models. Table 7.4 summarizes the different requirements and consequences which need to be considered in reaching a final decision. Cost implications should be estimated for each model so that users have an indication of the likely cost per household per month. Again, this should be done in consultation to avoid distortion of figures by one particular party or individual.

The stakeholder consultation process may result in the selection of a predominant maintenance model for a particular area. The final decision as to which maintenance system is adopted, however, will depend on the user

Table 7.4. Selecting maintenance options

Maintenance option	Requirements	Consequences/limitations
VLOM		
Community volunteers	Motivated people within community Appropriate local skills and tools Community cohesion/accountability Active NGO/government support	Cost implications Migration/Follow-up training required Difficulty in accessing spare parts
APMs	Trained pump repairers Sufficient motivation Respect of communities Active NGO/government support	Cost implications Migration Difficulty in accessing spare parts
Circuit Riders	Trained pump repairers Sufficient motivation Respect/awareness of communities Active NGO/government support	Cost implications Migration Difficulty in accessing spare parts
PPOM		
Least Subsidy model	Established private sector Adequate density of systems* Active NGO/government regulation	Cost implications Management responsibility removed from community
Total Warranty Scheme	Established private sector Adequate density of systems* Active NGO/government regulation	Cost implications Management responsibility removed from community
Water Assurance Scheme	Established private sector Interested manufacturer Adequate density of systems* Active NGO/government regulation	Cost implications Management responsibility removed from community
POOM		
Individual ownership	Privately owned land/systems Interested individuals Active NGO/government regulation	Cost implications Limited application due to owner affordability Ownership removed from community
Lease concept	Established private sector Adequate density of systems* Active NGO/government regulation	Cost implications Ownership removed from community
* Density of systems refers to the number of water systems within a given geographical area		

community. Therefore, if a PPOM water assurance scheme was selected and is operating in a particular area, each community is given the opportunity to join but some may decide to maintain their systems themselves. Where maintenance systems depend on a certain density of water facilities the number of communities that 'opt in' will affect the ultimate viability of the system. If a selected system is supported by local government and operates successfully for the first few months/years this should encourage communities to opt in and promote the sustainability of the maintenance system itself. If the system is not supported or is not made sufficiently attractive to water users it may fail from the beginning.

Step 6. Implementation

Once the maintenance system has been selected through consultation for a given area it can then be implemented. It is essential, however, that an appropriate regulatory and legislative framework is in place first, and that contractual arrangements are well designed and clearly defined. If it is the first time that such a maintenance system is to be implemented it may be appropriate to conduct a pilot study whereby the system is given a trial run for a smaller number of communities and if successful this is expanded for the entire programme area. If the chosen model has already been implemented successfully in the area or region it may be implemented immediately.

Further reading

Bernage, F. (2000) 'Local private sector involvement: the Mauritania experience'. Paper presented at SKAT HTN workshop on Civil Society and Government Partnerships in RWS, Hyderabad, India, March 2000, published by SKAT: Switzerland.

Elson, B., Franceys, R, and Shaw, R. (1999) 'Maintaining Handpumps' in Shaw, R.J. (ed.) *Running Water*. IT Publications: UK.

UNCHS (2004) *The Maintenance of Infrastructure and its Financing and Cost Recovery*. United Nations Centre for Human Settlements (Habitat). http://www.unchs.org/unchs/english/mainten/contents.htm

van Beers, P. (2001) 'Leasing, a new Handpump O&M concept.' in Scott, R. (ed.) *People and Systems for Water, Sanitation and Health, Proceedings of 27th WEDC Conference, Lusaka, Zambia, August 2001*. WEDC, Loughborough University: UK.

7

7

Chapter 8

Spare parts supply

The problem of supplying spare parts for rural water supply facilities such as handpumps has often been highlighted in the past. Private sector provision of spares is not, in general, a viable option on the basis of profit alone. Where spares supply is linked to other private sector activities such as technical services for construction, operation and maintenance, and the provision of pumps and equipment, it is much more likely to be sustained. Alternative approaches include links with advertising or the involvement of not-for-profit organizations. The spares supply problem can be reduced to an even greater extent through the use of local technical solutions which do not require imported components, whether from overseas or from the national capital. This chapter outlines the requirements for sustainable spare parts supply and obstacles to successful supply chains.

8.1   The supply chain challenge

Spare parts supply for pumps (specifically handpumps) in rural water supply is one of the weak links in the quest for sustainability. Hardly anywhere has satisfactory spare parts distribution been achieved (Baumann, 2000). This problem has been widely recognized for several years now, and has led to a number of key developments, such as the Supply Chains Initiative led by the Water and Sanitation Program (WSP), to promote sustainable supply chains for rural water supplies.

8

Despite much focus on spares supply and distribution, a successful supply chain is not a guarantee of sustainability. It is only part of the solution. Even where it is achieved, there must still be sustainable management and financing structures in place if water services are to be sustained. Locally appropriate technologies that avoid specialist spares, or alternative maintenance models to community management, can also make the supply chain goal much easier to achieve.

8.1.1 Defining the goal

What constitutes an effective and sustainable supply chain? The overall goal is to ensure that spare parts are:

- Available - i.e. the required components are in stock or can be rapidly delivered;

- Accessible - i.e. customers are aware of where to find spares outlets and the nearest of these is within easy travelling distance;

- Affordable - i.e. priced within the means of the target customers; and

- Appropriate - i.e. of correct specification and good quality.

In order to ensure that these requirements are met, there must be a sustainable chain of incentives from the manufacturer to the eventual customer. Most handpumps installed in Africa are imported or manufactured in the major cities, while most customers are community-based organizations or pump mechanics in rural areas. This means that there must be a supply and distribution network for the recurrent delivery of spares from the point of manufacture to the points of use, at an acceptable price and quality. Ideally, handpump users should be able to obtain spares the same day as a fault arises in order to facilitate rapid and effective repair or people may be left with no alternative than to return to using contaminated water sources with the associated health risks.

To review our sustainability criteria, the supply chain needs to be:

- Effective - i.e. adequate quality parts are supplied from manufacturer to outlets;

- Efficient - i.e. the delivery process is rapid and cost-effective;

- Equitable - i.e. parts are accessible to all users at a price they can afford; and

- Replicable - i.e. the supply process can be repeated on an ongoing basis.

The predominant approach to spares supply in the past was for implementing agencies, i.e. government or NGOs, to maintain stocks of spare parts and provide these to users at nominal cost or free of charge. In recent years, responsibility for the provision and distribution of spare parts has increasingly been given to the private sector in order to increase sustainability levels (Oyo, 2002; Baumann, 2000). This model relies on a 'business approach' whereby private sector actors have sufficient incentive to become involved and to maintain their involvement.

The primary incentive for the private sector is profit, whether generated directly or indirectly.

8.1.2   Identifying barriers

What factors obstruct successful supply chains for rural water supplies? Currently, there are very few examples of sustainable private sector supply chains for handpump spare parts. There are a number of fundamental reasons for this.

Profit

Selling spare parts is generally not a profitable business and therefore the willingness of the private sector to take on this commercially uninteresting activity is minimal (Baumann, 2000). The reasons for low profitability are simple. The density of handpumps in most rural areas is low, and since most pumps are reasonably reliable, the demand for spare parts is low. Individual profit margins for most 'consumable' components are very small (e.g. an O-ring for an Afridev pump might generate a profit of less than $1 for the retailer). Consequently, capital turnover is very low and yet retailers must keep many components in stock. This ties up capital which could be used to invest in more profitable products. This simple chain reaction is summarized below:

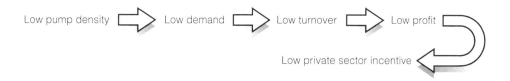

Procurement

The procurement of spare parts is often separated from the procurement of pumps. Most implementing agencies buy pumps in bulk, especially where the 'project' approach is used. This means that manufacturers and suppliers are selected primarily on the basis of cost and consequently many agencies order pumps directly from manufacturers overseas. The private sector is keen to compete for such contracts since the profit margins on pumps are attractive. This practice means that an isolated supply chain must be set up for the ongoing supply of spare parts, for which there are few incentives for the private sector.

Poverty

Most users of rural water supplies are relatively poor. This means that they are relatively immobile and do not have easy access to transportation to travel long distances to purchase spare parts. Consequently, spares outlets must either be relatively close to rural communities or there must be clear information provided as to where spares can be found and how they can be accessed relatively cheaply.

Another knock-on effect of poverty is limited economic development, which means that the level of commercial activity in most rural areas is limited. This makes it difficult to add handpump spares to the existing product lists of retailers. Where retailers have large turnovers they may be able to afford to lock capital in spare parts even though they make very little profit from this new product line.

Policy

Government policies and strategies may also act as indirect barriers to sustainable supply chains. Relaxation of import duties on handpumps may favour agencies importing pumps, but does little to encourage local procurement which is likely to help stimulate local spares supply.

Where private sector supply chains are inefficient, some agencies may provide subsidized spare parts, or even provide these free of charge. This distorts the market and may prevent the lower links of the supply chains from working. Where subsidy is necessary this must be regulated by government to ensure a uniform approach is adopted by all implementers. This will allow phased-in private sector participation and help to determine the lowest feasible level of the chain.

Maintenance systems

Reliance on the community management model of maintenance also creates additional demands on the supply chain which make it unsustainable. Since community management decentralizes control to scattered communities this means that spare parts must be available local to rural populations, which is often not commercially viable. Alternative centralized maintenance systems which cover many communities mean that spares do not need to be available at as many levels, and put less stress on the supply chain. Those responsible for such systems tend to be based in larger settlements and have their own means of transportation, and hence can access spares at national or regional level more easily.

Technology

Reliance on imported technologies using specialized components is the primary cause of the supply chain challenge. Where pumps can be manufactured, maintained and repaired using resources and equipment that are already available locally there is no need to set up a new supply chain specifically for a rural water supply technology. If pumps use components already available in plumbing stores or vehicle spares retailers, the need for sector-specific strategies disappears.

8.1.3 Evaluating needs

What are the ingredients of a successful supply chain? Having identified some of the barriers to effective and sustainable spare parts supply chains, it is necessary to identify and evaluate the factors required to make them successful. According to Oyo (2002) there are five key factors for successful and sustainable private sector supply chains:

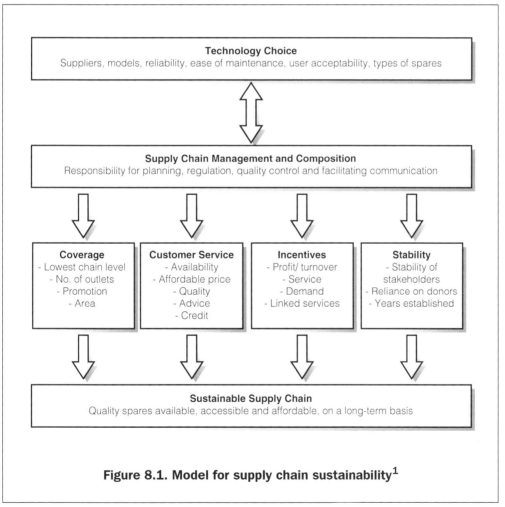

Figure 8.1. Model for supply chain sustainability[1]

1. Adapted from Alexander, 2003

- Adequate demand for the goods and services provided through the supply chain.

- Sufficient stakeholder incentives (i.e. profit) to motivate private sector involvement.

- Effective information flow between stakeholders to create and maintain the supply chain.

- Effective supply chain management to build effective stakeholder partnerships and create a collaborative environment for planning.

- An enabling environment resulting from the policies and strategies of governments and NGOs which does not inhibit the market.

Alexander (2003) also stresses the importance of supply chain management, but identifies technology choice as the overall determining factor (see Figure 8.1).

The emphasis given to effective supply chain management is important since it recognizes the need for an overview to ensure that the four sustainability criteria are met. Ideally, the supply chain should be managed by the private sector, but where it is accepted that spare parts supply is not a stand-alone commercially viable activity, external (government or NGO) facilitation, monitoring and regulation are essential. Effective supply chain management must address adequate coverage, customer service levels, stakeholder incentives and stability.

Coverage

First, it is important to determine the lowest level in the chain (regional, district, village etc.), and hence the number of spares outlets required. This should be based on the area covered by each outlet (to ensure accessibility), and the number of pumps catered for. Appropriate promotional activities will then be required to raise awareness among customers, so that they know where to go for spares. Such activities include advertising, visits to communities and liaison with community health assistants and volunteers.

Customer service

Second, the appropriate level of customer service for each outlet must be determined. This may vary depending on the level of the supplier; for example, whether at national, regional or district level. Customer service should include the range of components made available, the price and quality of these, technical advice and services on offer, and appropriate credit facilities.

Stakeholder incentives

The incentives for different stakeholders in the chain must then be identified. This is most likely to be profit for the private sector, whether directly through sales of spares, or through linked services and sales. Incentives may also include advertising opportunities and the kudos or 'feel-good factor' from providing a community service. It is also important to assess whether these incentives are likely to be sustained.

Stakeholder stability

Finally, the stability of all stakeholders in the chain must be considered, whether private sector, non-profit, NGO or governmental. Where the chain relies on external support from donors, this is likely to result in a considerable degree of insecurity and instability. The number of years that private companies have been established should also be considered, as well as the range of products and services that they offer, which is likely to influence their long-term stability and sustainability.

8.2   The profit incentive

Since the private sector 'business approach' must be driven fundamentally by profit it is important to examine this issue in more detail.

8.2.1   Lessons from the past

Many donors have promoted private sector participation in spares supply by providing a 'seed fund' to private enterprises to stimulate commercial involvement and viability. The principle behind this approach is to provide a private company (often an existing hardware store) with a stock of spare parts (at nominal cost or free of charge), to set fixed retail prices for parts, and to instigate an advertising and marketing campaign. The company is then expected to use the profits generated from sales to replenish stocks from a central supplier and hence sustain the supply of spare parts. Such initiatives have been implemented in many African countries, including Ghana, Malawi and Zambia. In general, this approach has not proved successful to date due to low turnover and low profits, meaning the retailer has little ongoing incentive to invest profits in new spares. This is particularly the case for small businesses where cash flow is critical to survival (see Box 8.1).

Such examples are commonplace, and sustainability often relies on the goodwill of the retailer rather than sound commercial sense. For example, a recent study in Malawi and Mozambique indicated that private suppliers did not make

8

Box 8.1. Commercial viability[1]

In Kalomo, Zambia, the District WASHE committee helped establish a private spare parts supplier by providing spares to an existing hardware store in the town to act as a seed fund. This venture failed because the owner did not use the money from sales to replenish the stock of spares, due to low turnover and profitability. Consequently, the District committee itself now stocks and supplies spares to communities.

---

1. Harvey and Skinner, 2002

sufficient profit from the provision of spares to motivate them and only sold spares as a community service (Batchelor et al., 2000).

There is also evidence to suggest that the privatization of existing supply chains can sometimes hinder sustainability. An example of this can be seen in Malawi where a government-owned chain of hardware shops once provided spare parts in almost every district and sub-district centre in the country, but was subsequently privatized. This resulted in the selling-off of individual shops to several bidders, thus breaking the supply chain and reducing the availability of spares (Kandulu, 2004).

Some donors have attempted an alternative approach where spares provision is linked with the provision of technical services such as pump installation, borehole drilling and community mobilization. Here, the supporting agency assists in building the capacity of indigenous private sector companies by providing staff with a range of skills and equipment, so that they are able to provide a range of services. This approach tends to be more successful than the simple 'seeding spares' approach but requires considerable investment and has limited application. For example, limited demand for services is likely to limit such enterprises to the larger towns which may still mean that community members have considerable distances to travel.

The following national framework for spares supply, as suggested by Baumann (2000), has also been implemented in some countries:

Photograph 8.1. Typical spare parts shop

- National supplier keeps sufficient fully comprehensive stocks of spares centrally.

- In each region, regional dealer keeps adequate stocks to cover at least 80 per cent of breakdowns. Regional dealer sells parts either directly to communities or through an area mechanic.

- Area mechanic is the principal outlet for spares to communities and sells these with a small profit margin.

- Government prepares a list of recommended spare parts retail prices for all standardized pumps.

8

Baumann recognizes that such a system might not be sustainable in many rural areas of Africa, since after-sales structures tend to break up soon after sales of pumps drop. The distances that area mechanics must travel to access spares are often significant, and present another obstacle to an effective supply chain.

As a result of the widespread lack of sustainable private sector spare parts supply, many external supply agencies (ESAs) continue to subsidize supply chains without well planned phasing-out strategies. This might take the form of direct subsidy of retail costs or indirect subsidy of storage and transportation costs. Such approaches have, unfortunately, simply promoted, rather than relieved, the dependency culture.

8.2.2 Handpump density

In order to test the commercial viability of spare parts supply at the user level, one approach is to establish the density of pumps required to produce enough demand to generate sufficient turnover of spares and sufficient profit for the retailer. The minimum density required to fulfil this is defined as the Handpump Density Breakpoint (HDB). We can estimate the HDB by using a very crude method, as follows:

1. There are N pumps in a given area, and t is the average time period between subsequent spare parts required for any given pump; which will depend on selected technology, quality of components, groundwater conditions etc. The number of parts, n, required from the retailer per year is therefore given by:

    $$\mathbf{n} = N/t \text{ (years)}$$

2. If the average profit per spare part sold is p_a, the annual profit, P, generated from the sale of spare parts will be given by:

    $$\mathbf{P} = p_a \times n$$

    Approximation 1: Based on all parts weighted for frequency of breakdown the average profit per part is approximately one dollar: $p_a = US\$1$.

    $$\mathbf{P} = 1 \times n = \mathbf{N/t} \rightarrow \mathbf{N} = P \times t$$

3. If Pmin is the minimum annual profit (in US$) required by the retailer for commercial viability, then the minimum number of pumps, Nmin, required within a given radius of access, will be:

$$N_{min} = P_{min} \times t$$

Approximation 2: P_{min} is likely to vary from retailer to retailer but an average value based on stakeholder interviews can be used.

4. Radius of access, R_a, is defined as the average of the maximum distances from the retailer to potential customers in all directions, and determines the area realistically served. This will be heavily influenced by transportation links, topography, geographical and political boundaries etc.

5. The Handpump Density Breakpoint (pumps/km^2) is given by:

$$\textbf{HDB} = P_{min} \times t / \pi R_a^2$$

Alternatively, for a given area of access:

Min no. of pumps = Min yearly profit (US$) x average time between breakdowns (years)

This is a very crude method of estimation, since the average profit and the average time between breakdowns (which generally decreases with the age of the pump) are difficult to assess. It is purely intended as an approximation to test commercial viability. Box 8.2 presents a worked example for an India Mark II handpump in Ghana.

Box 8.2. Calculating Handpump Density Breakpoint

For an India Mark II pump, average time between the spare parts required **t** = 2 years, and for study area in Ghana radius of access, $\textbf{R}_a$ = 20km

Based on interviews with retailers, an annual profit of at least $100 is required to make spares supply commercially worthwhile. This is a conservative figure, based on minimum figures quoted and P_{min} is likely to be higher in most cases.

$$\textbf{HDB} = 100 \times 2 / \pi 20^2 = 0.159 \text{ pumps/km}^2$$

$$\textbf{N}_{min} = P_{min} \times t = 100 \times 2 = 200$$

i.e. 200 pumps within 20km of outlet

The above example illustrates the relatively high density required, still assuming that the retailer expects only a nominal annual profit of $100 and that all pump users visit the same outlet to buy spare parts. This is backed up by the findings of Vergnet in West Africa which has established an optimum ratio of 200-300 Vergnet handpumps per spare parts shop (Oyo, 2002). Although 200 pumps

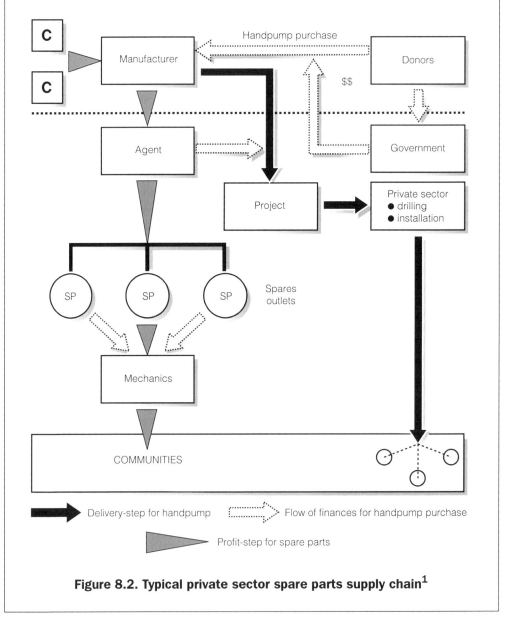

Figure 8.2. Typical private sector spare parts supply chain[1]

1. Adapted from van Beers, 2001b

within a radius of 20km does not sound a huge number, 0.159 pumps/km2 is a far higher density than is usually found in sub-Saharan Africa. The density of rural populations in SSA is generally quite low, and consequently so too is the density of handpumps. A study of eight districts in central Ghana indicated a **maximum** density of 0.070 pumps/km2 (only 40 per cent of the required density) and an average of only 0.052 pumps/km2, even in more populous areas where there had been intensive handpump installation programmes for more than a decade (data from World Vision, 2003). This demonstrates that spare parts supply for handpumps is **not a stand alone profit-generating exercise** in the rural African context.

8.2.3   Linking pumps and parts

Figure 8.2 illustrates the contrast between the typical route for the provision of spares and that for the provision of pumps.

The diagram represents the typical scenario where handpumps are manufactured outside of the country of use, as indicated by the dotted black line. The step from the suppliers of key components and raw materials (C) to the manufacturer is the same for pumps and spares, but after that the routes diverge completely. The handpump is usually purchased directly from the manufacturer by the donor or government, though a few donors may purchase from an in-country agent. It is then delivered to the project and finally installed by the private sector. In contrast, the spare parts are purchased from the manufacturer by an agent, and then pass down the supply chain to spares outlets (SP) distributed around the country, from where they are purchased by area mechanics and finally by the users.

The large number of necessary 'profit steps' that exist between the user and the manufacturer are indicated in the diagram. This inevitably leads to higher prices for the user while minimizing profits for each step in the supply chain. Reducing the number of steps can help to increase the efficiency and effectiveness of the supply chain (Box 8.3). Promoting local production and local agents selling

---

Box 8.3. Minimising private sector involvement[1]

'Minimal involvement of the private sector in spares supply means more benefit to the consumer.'

---

1.   Mr S. Ram Mirpuri, Handpump and spares supplier, Tema, Ghana

directly to users, and linking parts with pumps, can help to reduce the number of steps.

Figure 8.3 presents an alternative model for spare parts supply which minimizes the number of private sector stakeholders by streamlining pumps, spares and technical services together. By purchasing pumps at the lowest level possible, i.e. as close to the community as possible, this ensures that spare parts are also available at this level. Where possible, the private enterprise (PST) can also provide technical services such as drilling and pump installation to diversify profit-making activities. The advantage of such a programmatic approach is that pumps are purchased routinely from the local suppliers on a continual basis, rather than by occasional bulk order, meaning that they generate continuous revenue. The cost of this to the implementing agency may be slightly higher, but this should be a price worth paying to promote sustainability. Promoting local (in-country) manufacture, using local resources where possible, also reduces the number of profit steps and can help to ensure appropriate quality control mechanisms are put in place, as well as to increase local economic activity.

The linking of pumps, technical services and spare parts can go a long way to increasing supply chain effectiveness but there remains the barrier of the lowest appropriate level. Making pumps available at regional or district level may be achievable, but to go beyond this is likely to be problematic. Where community management is the norm, this may mean that customers still have to travel considerable distances to access spares.

8

The level of commercial activity within a country can have a big impact on the level of coverage that such an approach can achieve. Where commercial activity is already relatively high, handpump spares can be added to the existing product lists of retailers which can afford to sustain involvement even where they make negligible profit from such a venture (see Box 8.4).

The profit incentive alone is not sufficient to make handpump spare parts supply a stand-alone commercial activity. Experience would suggest that virtually nowhere in SSA are handpump densities sufficient to generate adequate demand for spares and sufficient turnover and profit for the private sector. Linking products and services can increase the viability of supply chains, and provide considerably improved access for rural communities, but this requires considerable change in the priorities and practices of donors and implementers. What is undeniable is that there is no universal, proven solution.

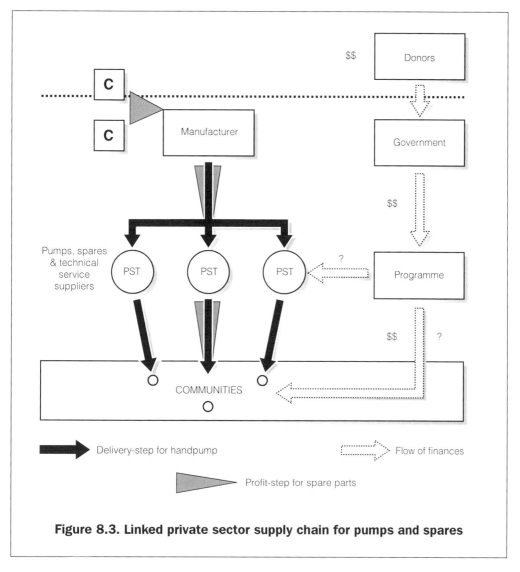

Figure 8.3. Linked private sector supply chain for pumps and spares

8

8.3 The need for realism

It is the firm conviction of the authors, based on recent field research, that while the density of handpumps in rural areas remains relatively low, **private sector** supply chains for spare parts will **not be sustainable** unless at least one of the following three criteria is met:

• Spares supply is strongly linked to the supply of pumps and related services;

• Community management of maintenance is replaced with more centralized public-private systems; or

---

Box 8.4. Partial private sector success[1]

Davis and Shirtliff (Dayliff) is a private company in Kenya which specializes in water pumps, borehole services, swimming pools and water treatment equipment. There are over 50 Dayliff pump centres and stockists nationwide, and at each of these any spare part for the Afridev, India Mark II or 'Popular' (GangaSagar) handpumps can be requested and delivered within 24 hours. Negligible profit is made from handpump spare parts, but since the necessary infrastructure and systems are already in place for the provision and distribution of other pumps and related spares, it is a relatively easy option to add handpump spares to their product list. The company recognizes the importance of promoting a supply chain network, both as a service and to promote future sales of handpumps. Despite the large number of stockists, many communities have to travel more than 100km to the nearest outlet and many are not even aware that spares are available. Access therefore still remains a constraining factor, especially for the more remote communities.

---

1. Harvey et al., 2003

- Technologies are installed which use 'standard' spares that are already available.

Even where one these criteria is met, however, this should not be taken as a guarantee of sustainability, since further implementation studies are required. If none of these criteria are fulfilled then alternative strategies for spares supply, such as subsidy and non-profit approaches, must be adopted.

Procurement and service linkages

It is clear that strengthening links between pumps, services and parts can increase the viability of supply chains. Procurement practices of donors can have a major influence on this and can stipulate roles and responsibilities of manufacturers within contracts. **This requires a shift from selecting pump suppliers by lowest price internationally, to selecting local suppliers who can also provide spares and related services.** This may result in slightly higher cost to the donor in the short term but is a more sustainable long-term option. government decentralization policies can also contribute by encouraging the procurement of pumps and services at district or local level. Where successful, this approach can stimulate supply chains down to district level, which may or may not provide sufficient coverage. Its sustainability remains dependent on adequate ongoing demand for pumps. The viability of this approach will be limited in any given

Photograph 8.2. Pump and spares supplier, Kenya

situation and may do little to increase accessibility to spares in sparsely populated areas with poor transport routes.

Public-private maintenance systems

8

It can be argued that the community management of maintenance option creates unreasonable demand on spares supply chains. Where VLOM is replaced by PPOM, the needs of the supply chain are considerably reduced. Instead of needing spares outlets in most rural towns, these will be needed only in the larger regional settlements where private companies can access them. PPOM and POOM models such as the Total Warranty Scheme, Handpump Lease Concept and Water Assurance Scheme (see Chapter 7) place the responsibility for spares procurement with private service providers who have greater mobility than rural communities. The application of this approach may be limited by the density of communities served, the willingness of community members to pay for services, and the capacity of the private sector.

Appropriate technology

The simplest solution to the spare parts conundrum is to use only simple technologies which do not require specialist spare parts and components. Invariably, the more complex the technology used, the longer (and hence more complex) the supply chain needed to support it (Oyo, 2002). Technologies such as the Rope pump, Bucket pump and locally developed pumps such as the Bush pump or AFRI-pump remove the need for complex technology-specific supply chains. While some pumps use standard factory components it is more important that they use spares which can be found in the average rural hardware store (or be fabricated in a local workshop). Likewise, it is important that tools for repair are widely available. A study by International Development Enterprises in Bangladesh showed that the rural poor often prefer cheaper, shorter-life technologies in spite of the need to repair or replace them more frequently (Oyo, 2002). This suggests that the argument for high quality technology and parts may be externally driven rather than demand responsive.

Supply chains in inaccessible areas with low population density are especially problematic. For this reason many implementing agencies working in such environments opt for simple technology solutions such as hand-dug wells equipped with bucket-and-windlass or the Rope pump. Conventional handpumps are likely to be inappropriate in such areas unless there is ongoing subsidized provision of spares by the implementing agency.

If the predominant procurement practices, maintenance systems and technologies remain as they are, alternatives to the traditional private sector 'business approach' must be developed.

8.3.1 Subsidies and 'boosters'

Many supply chains are currently subsidized by governments or donors. This may involve direct subsidy of retail prices to reduce costs to users or, more commonly, subsidized storage, transportation or promotion. In investigating subsidy options it is important to assess their sustainability. Subsidies from external donors or support agencies are likely to be unsustainable by definition and appropriate phasing out or transfer strategies should be implemented. Subsidies from government or the indigenous private or non-profit sector may, however, be the most sustainable option where a pure business approach is not possible. Instead of subsidizing the cost of spare parts, however, an alternative approach is to provide financial grants to poor communities for them to purchase spare parts. This will enable communities to appreciate the full cost of spares and inform them of where they are available.

Lemine and Münger (2003) introduce the concept of a private sector 'booster'. This is, in effect, a private sector organization contracted out by government to manage the supply chain for water system delivery and O&M (incorporating spare parts). The booster organization is responsible for sub-contracting private enterprises for installation, O&M and spares supply, regulation of water tariffs, and technical and financial monitoring. This is a public-private model which combines service delivery and maintenance, and recognizes the need for ongoing government support and subsidy.

8.3.2   Sponsorship and advertising

A non-traditional approach to private sector participation in supply chains is to seek subsidies from the private sector, in the form of sponsorship. Baumann (2000) suggests that sponsorship of spare parts supplies for rural water could be attractive to big companies for advertising purposes. There are several ways in which this could be implemented. One approach is for the company to pay advertising fees directly to the spares retailers to display sponsorship slogans and logos on signs used to promote spares outlets. Alternatively, a large company with widespread visibility could add spare parts to the products it distributes and advertise the fact that it is supporting rural water supply. The sponsorship approach has not been tried on a large scale to date, but can make effective use of the social incentive of helping ensure clean water is available to poor rural communities, and the good opinion gained from this.

A sponsorship approach to rural water supply has been attempted in South Africa where the cost of maintenance and repair (including spares) for the Play pump, a children's roundabout which pumps water as it turns, is met by the advertising fee paid by the sponsor to display their advertisement on the elevated tank to which the pump lifts water before it is distributed to taps. This is a new approach which appears to work best beside roads where the advertisements will be seen by many (Harvey & Kayaga, 2003).

8.3.3   Non-profit options

The use of non-profit-making organizations (such as churches) in spares provision has been suggested as a more viable alternative to the private sector approach for many situations (DeGabriele, 2002). Recent research in Malawi has indicated that indigenous religious organizations provide a viable long-term option, so long as they have a reliable funding base, and examples are given of supply chains that have been in operation for 10 to 20 years (Alexander, 2003). Although the number of such organizations with adequate capacity, stability and motivation may limit coverage, they have proven to provide an effective alternative where the private sector approach is unsuccessful. They should not, therefore, be automatically dismissed as unsustainable.

8.4   Steps towards sustainable spares supply

A range of constraints to sustainable spare parts supply are outlined above and a number of different options are discussed. In order to select the most sustainable spares supply option for a particular context the process in Figure 8.4 can be used. This is a lengthy process that requires considerable consultation and a detailed survey of communities. It is important, however, that this is conducted fully if spares supply chains are to be sustainable, especially where community management is the preferred O&M model. This is not a rigid process but should be used to guide appropriate decision-making and planning.

The process can be conducted at a national or regional level, and should be co-ordinated by a planning committee comprising representatives of relevant government ministries and departments, private sector organizations, and external support agencies involved in water supply.

Step 1. Technology review

The first step in the process is to review the existing water supply technologies in the area under consideration. This will help to determine which items of equipment and which components the supply chain must deliver, whether this applies to one type of technology or to a range of options. A thorough survey of the area should be conducted and a list produced of all communities which specifies the technologies that exist in each, and the range of spare parts and equipment that is required for the operation and maintenance of each technology type.

Step 2. Demand assessment

Following on from the technology review a demand assessment exercise must be conducted. The aim of this is to assess the respective demands for different components and related tools and equipment. This can be conducted by combining a series of visits to user communities and interviews with existing distributors and suppliers. Table 8.1 shows an example of how this assessment can be carried out. Each component or equipment item should be listed for each relevant technology and the frequency with which it is required (F) should be recorded. Respective values of F can be estimated by reviewing community records if they exist. The annual demand (D) for each component can then be estimated by calculating the total number of a particular technology in the study

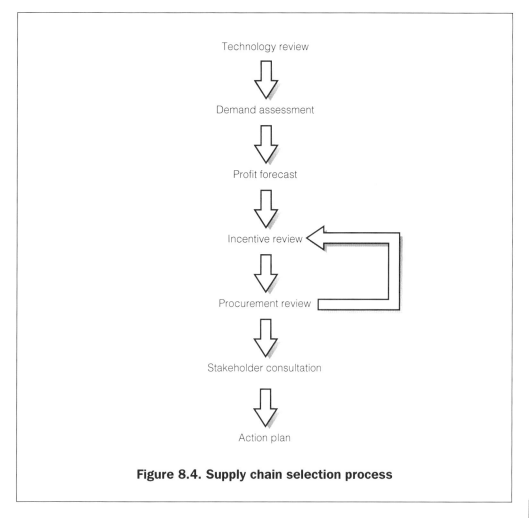

Figure 8.4. Supply chain selection process

area (N) by F. The chosen study area should be small enough to be served by a single retail outlet and may be defined by a radius of access (see Section 8.2.2).

This exercise estimates the annual demand, i.e. the number of components required per year, for each 'consumable' component for each relevant technology.

Step 3. Profit forecast

Once the demand has been estimated the annual profit that is likely to be generated through stocking and selling each component can be forecast. In order to do this the average profit for each component, p, must be calculated. This can be achieved through consultation with existing retailers. If there are no local retailers, figures for the nearest retailer (for example in the capital city) will need

Table 8.1. Demand assessment example

Technology type	Number in study area, N	Component	Frequency required, F (years)	Annual demand, D (N/F)
India Mark II handpump	72	O-ring seal	2	**36**
		Cup leather	2	**36**
		Chain	3	**24**
		Handle axle	3	**24**
		...etc.		
Afridev handpump	45	...etc.		
Electrical submersible pump	3	...etc.		

to be adjusted for local application, and transportation and storage costs should be taken into account. The total profit, P, for each component in the study area can then be estimated by multiplying the profit per component, p, by the respective annual demand, D. The total potential profit, T, can then be found from the sum of all component profits.

It is recognized that not all communities in the study area will visit the retailer and that not all components will be replaced. Therefore, the total estimated annual profit is given by multiplying the total potential profit by a percentage factor (e.g. 75 per cent in Table 8.2). This percentage factor is the percentage of communities that will visit the outlet. This can be determined through interviews with all communities in the area but it is important that this is not overestimated. Community members may say that they would visit the outlet but may not actually do this in practice. Evidence of existing practice will help to support reported behaviour.

Table 8.2. Profit forecast example

Technology type	Component	Profit per component, p (US$)	Annual demand, D	Total profit, P (US$) (pxD)
India Mark II handpump	O-ring seal	0.5	36	**18**
	Cup leather	0.6	36	**22**
	Chain	2.5	24	**60**
	Handle axle	1.0	24	**24**
	...etc.			**..**
Afridev handpump	...etc.			**..**
				..
		Total potential profits, T		**432**
				(for 75%)
		Expected TOTAL Annual Profit = %T		**$324**

Step 4. Incentive review

Once the annual profit for a given area has been estimated it is necessary to evaluate whether this profit would provide sufficient incentive for private sector (commercial) participation. This can be achieved through consultation with existing retailers and potential retailers. Where profits are deemed to be insufficient to guarantee sustained involvement, alternative incentives must be assessed. The flow diagram in Figure 8.5 can be used to guide this process.

If the profit incentive is insufficient the next step is to determine whether the provision of spares and equipment can be combined with private sector provision of technical services. Again, consultation is necessary to establish whether there will be sufficient incentive for the private sector to take on this activity. If this is not the case then advertising and sponsorship options should be investigated and it should be established whether there are sufficient incentives to sustain such private sector involvement. If there are not, then non-profit supply chain options will provide the only solution.

Step 5. Procurement practice review

Following the incentive review it is necessary to undertake a review of how equipment and pumps are currently procured and what procurement measures could be undertaken to increase incentives and strengthen the supply chain. By

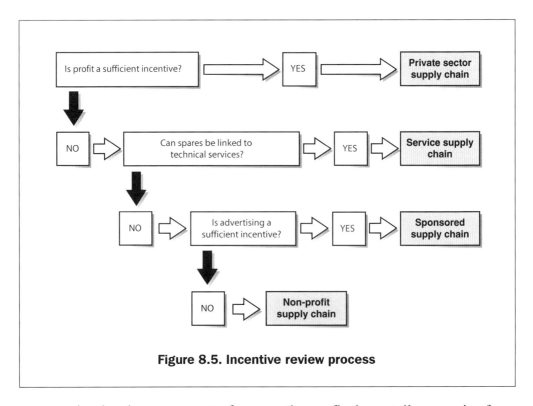

Figure 8.5. Incentive review process

encouraging local procurement of pumps the profit that retailers require from spare parts may become lower and less crucial as an incentive. After conducting a review of procurement practices it may therefore be necessary to repeat the incentive review.

Step 6. Stakeholder consultation

The penultimate step in the process is to conduct a consultation exercise involving all relevant stakeholders. This will establish firmly the supply chain option that should be adopted based on incentive levels, stakeholder capacity and stability. The way in which the supply chain will be managed must be determined, as well as how it will be monitored and regulated. The roles and responsibilities of all stakeholders involved in the chain must also be clearly defined.

Step 7. Action plan

Once agreement has been reached about the supply chain to be set up and the respective roles and responsibilities for each stakeholder, an action plan should be formulated which defines how and when the supply chain will be set up and the stages involved in this.

It is important to note that where O&M is not dependent on community management but is managed by a private (or public) sector organization it may not be necessary to establish a supply chain to reach rural areas since private sector service providers can more easily access spares and equipment in national and regional centres.

Further reading

Baumann, E. (2000) *Water Lifting*. Series of Manuals on Drinking Water Supply, Volume 7, SKAT: St. Gallen, Switzerland.

Brocklehurst, C. (2001) *Promoting Robust Supply Chains for Rual Water and Sanitation Goods and Services*. Phase 1 Synthesis Paper, Water and Sanitation Program: Washington D.C.
(can be accessed at http://www.wsp.org/publications/global_sc_synthesis.pdf)

Oyo, A. (2002) *Creating Successful Private Sector Supply Chains: A resource guide for rural water supply and sanitation practitioners*. WSP: Washington D.C.
(can be accessed at http://www.wsp.org/publications/global_scrg.pdf)

WSP (2000) *Supply Chains: A global initiative*. Water and Sanitation Program: Washington D.C.
(can be accessed at http://www.wsp.org/publications/global_supplyupdate.pdf)

8

8

Chapter 9

Monitoring

Monitoring, evaluation and review are the mortar that holds the building blocks for sustainability together and ensure the integration of the different sustainability factors. Monitoring is an ongoing process that should cover all levels of operation (from national governments to communities) and all aspects of rural water supply programmes (e.g. policy, institutions, finances, technology and O&M). This chapter addresses the important need for monitoring of rural water systems and services, to ensure sustainability. It identifies different aspects that need to be monitored and presents possible frameworks and tools that can be used for this. It also emphasizes the importance of evaluation and review to inform decision-makers and to improve performance.

9.1　The importance of monitoring

Many of the other chapters of this book have emphasized the need for assessment and planning. Monitoring is essential for this and acts as the mortar that joins the building blocks for sustainability. There are many reasons why monitoring is so important for rural water supply sustainability, and why many government strategies stress this. Unless activities and outcomes are monitored it is impossible to determine whether or not strategies and approaches have been successful and achieved the desired goals. Monitoring is also necessary to measure the sustainability success criteria: effectiveness; efficiency; equity and replicability.

9.1.1　Monitoring objectives

In developing appropriate monitoring frameworks and activities it is necessary to set objectives. One of the main objectives of monitoring is simply to:

- **Determine whether communities have access to adequate quantities of safe drinking water** (i.e. is enough water of acceptable quality coming out of the spout/tap?).

Other broad monitoring objectives are to:

- Assess performance of different stakeholders and strategies;

- Determine overall success rates for a given programme, area or technology;

- Determine water service coverage figures;

- Identify problems early in order to find timely solutions and pre-empt failures;

- Identify community needs for technical and financial support;

- Measure service effectiveness, efficiency and equity; and

- Inform decision-makers to improve performance.

9.1.2   Monitoring needs and constraints

One of the main reasons that rural water supplies are not sustained is that planning and implementation agencies are often unaware of how bad problems are with existing systems. Decentralization offers an opportunity to change this, through effective planning based on monitoring by local government (e.g. district water offices). This can then create demand for effective maintenance, rehabilitation, upgrade and expansion. There are instances, of course, when poor monitoring is due partly to the desire to suppress bad news. Implementers may not want to know whether services are sustainable for fear of the worst, i.e. that systems are no longer working. Such bad news may be perceived to threaten job security, morale or future financial resources. Financial monitoring may also touch upon issues of corruption, since this inevitably effects efficiency and effectiveness. Care needs to be taken, however, that this does not lead to strong resistance to monitoring in general because it is seen as a checking-up exercise or 'witch-hunt'. There may, therefore, be a need to adopt measures to remove the perceived threats posed by monitoring, and to highlight the benefits.

Poor existing levels of sustainability may provide a strong argument for increased financing for institutional support to communities, where this is currently low. Evidence of high levels of sustainability may lead to opportunities to share successes with other stakeholders locally, nationally and internationally. Incentives for individuals and institutions need to be identified and highlighted to develop a monitoring mindset.

Monitoring costs money. Quarterly monitoring of all water supplies within a district takes considerable staff time, resources and effort, and consequently it must be budgeted for accordingly. This is a recurrent cost and should be viewed in the same way as recurrent staff salary costs.

9.2   Performance measurement

The term 'performance measurement' is being used increasingly to describe the process of collecting and analysing monitoring data to obtain relative measures of performance in different areas. Performance measurement can be expanded to include monitoring (regular measurement of performance), evaluation (periodic measurement of performance) and review (periodic assessment of what has been learned) as summarized in Table 9.1 (Thomson, 2003).

In order to monitor and measure performance it is necessary to consider performance indicators against which progress is measured. Monitoring for rural water supplies can be based on the following broad performance themes:

- Management performance;

- Operational performance;

- Maintenance performance; and

- Environmental performance.

Table 9.1. Performance measurement mechanisms[1]

Monitoring	Evaluation	Review
• Regular measurement of performance - annually or more frequently • Focuses on the review of inputs and intermediate outputs • Aims to identify operational problems that can be rectified and operational successes that can be replicated • Common techniques include field inspections, quarterly District reporting, technical audits, financial tracking studies	• Periodic measurement of performance - annually or less frequently • Focuses on the review of outputs and outcomes • Aims to identify the reasons for good or poor performance • Common techniques include participatory user assessments, analysis of household survey data, value for money studies, one-off studies to review a particular policy or issue	• Periodic assessment of what has been learned - during the course of the year and at the end • Focuses on the identification of implications of the monitoring and evaluation analysis • Aims to develop mechanisms for disseminating learning, influencing policy and affecting resourcing • Common techniques include policy forums, joint sector reviews

1. After Thomson, 2003

9.2.1 Management performance

Management performance addresses the capacity and effectiveness of the management structure and stakeholders, whether CBO, NGO or private sector. This should consider revenue collection efficiency, financial management and accounting, and transparency issues. It should also evaluate the competency of the management framework in place, with respect to efficiency and effectiveness, and the relationship between managers, workers and users. Management issues can make the difference between sustainable and unsustainable services, and it is therefore important to determine whether or not management performance is satisfactory.

9.2.2 Operational performance

Operational performance considers how the system is actually functioning and being operated. For example, is the quantity and quality of water sufficient and acceptable? Are users satisfied with walking distances and waiting times to collect water? Are community members using alternative water sources, and if so why, and for what purposes? It is important to obtain an overview of how a water system is operating, whether it is being used appropriately, and what the benefits and impacts of the water supply are. If such information is collected for all water systems in a given area, or installed under a given programme, such data can be used to determine the rate of failure of systems and why or why not facilities are operational.

9.2.3 Maintenance performance

Maintenance performance is linked to functionality and applies to how well the system is actually maintained. This considers the quality of workmanship, response time, average downtime of the system, and relationship between maintenance provider and users. This applies to observed physical characteristics and customer views and perceptions.

9.2.4 Environmental performance

Environmental performance is related to operational performance but specifically concerns environmental issues that influence or are influenced by the operation of the system. In particular, groundwater issues such as well yields, water levels and water quality can have a major impact on the operation and sustainability of a handpump water supply. By regularly monitoring such environmental indicators, problems such as falling water tables can be recognized in good time and appropriate remedial action, such as lowering the handpump cylinder, undertaken. It is therefore **essential that boreholes and pumps are designed in such a way that groundwater levels can be routinely**

recorded without the need to dismantle or remove the pump. Where such information is collected for a large number of point sources, regional trends can also be identified to help improve efficiency and sustainability of future supplies. The effect of water systems or industrial activity on the environment can also be assessed.

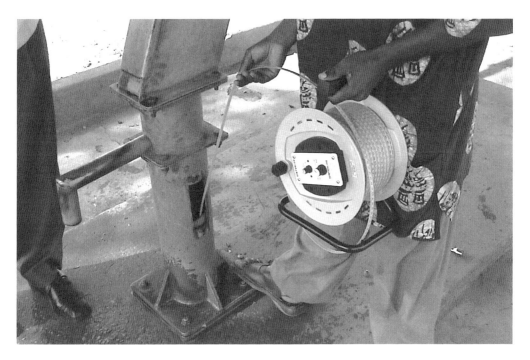

Photograph 9.1. Monitoring groundwater levels in Ghana

9.2.5   Performance indicators

Each of the four broad performance themes (management, operational, maintenance and environmental) can be broken down into a number of specific indicators. According to WHO (2000) these should:

- Be truly representative of the quantities and characteristics they are intended to represent;

- Be verifiable, i.e. it should be possible to check the accuracy of the values of indicators;

- Provide information which can be used by decision-makers;

- Provide information in time to influence decisions; and

9

- Be linked into the system to allow feedback of information for the decision-making process.

Examples of specific measurable performance indicators are given below, based on the four performance themes. The majority of indicators can be measured at community level and the data then analysed to determine measured indicators for the overall programme.

- **Management performance**

  - % of staff positions filled

  - % of staff satisfied with working conditions

  - average price of an improved water supply per person

  - % of users paying for water

  - % of household income spent on water

  - average price per jerrycan

- **Operational performance**

  - average daily water consumption

  - % of total estimated needs that are met

  - % of consumers that are satisfied with the quantity of water provided

  - % of consumers satisfied with quality of water provided

  - % of population with access to improved (safe) water supplies

  - % usage of improved water supplies

  - average time taken to collect water

  - average distance to water source

  - average water use per capita per day

- **Maintenance performance**

  - % of water facilities operational at a given time

  - average number of days per year that water systems are in operation

- average response time to facility breakdown

- % of users satisfied with maintenance service

• **Environmental performance**

- % of change in groundwater and surface water levels over a given time

- % of improved water sources that comply with national water quality standards.

Performance indicators may also be expanded to consider issues of key importance in the local context, such as water provision for people living with HIV/AIDS, or exclusion of particular social groups from water services.

9.3   Monitoring frameworks

In order for monitoring to be effective it is essential that a practicable and sustainable framework be set up. This should include stakeholder responsibilities, monitoring schedules and data requirements.

9.3.1   Stakeholder responsibilities

Local government provides the optimum institution to assume overall responsibility for monitoring of rural water supplies, since it is usually the most stable long-term stakeholder in rural areas. Government institutions such as District water offices are normally responsible for managing monitoring activities, but rather than setting up completely new systems, existing networks can often be used to conduct monitoring. These may include environmental health assistants, clinical officers or community development officers who visit communities regularly and can gather additional information related to water supply. Participatory monitoring which actively involves the community can also be adopted, though this may require more time to set up and regulate. Stakeholders who can undertake monitoring include:

• District water offices/teams;

• Environmental health assistants;

• Community development officers;

• Community based organizations; and

• Community members.

9.3.2 Monitoring schedules

Monitoring is by definition an ongoing process and is most effective when information is collected at regular intervals. Ideally, quarterly monitoring should take place to allow for seasonal variations in rainfall, water levels, community activities, income and expenditure. Rather than collect all information every quarter, however, certain activities such as user surveys can be conducted every six months, and information such as water quality data can be collected even less often. Table 9.2 presents an example of a quarterly monitoring schedule for community managed O&M.

Table 9.2. Monitoring schedule example

Activity	1st Quarter	2nd Quarter	3rd Quarter	4th Quarter
Observe facility status	✓	✓	✓	✓
Sustainability snapshot (see Table 9.4)	✓	✓	✓	✓
User satisfaction survey		✓		✓
Interview water committee		✓		✓
Interview private mechanic		✓		✓
Record groundwater levels	✓	✓	✓	✓
Measure water quality		✓		
O&M Audit				✓

The data collected may vary depending on the type of technology used and monitoring equipment available. For example, a well-dipper is needed to measure groundwater levels and laboratory equipment is required to assess water quality parameters. It will also depend on the type of management system adopted. For example, a public-private management model will require regulatory monitoring of private sector organizations, as well as visits to communities.

It is better to start simple than not at all. It may, therefore, be best to adopt a staged approach to monitoring which starts by using a simple tool such as the 'sustainability snapshot' of 'facility datasheet' (see Section 9.4). Once this monitoring system is established it can be expanded to include other issues and indicators using other monitoring tools.

9.3.3 Data processing

Monitoring is only useful if the data collected is managed and used effectively. Performance indicators can be given different weights depending on perceived importance in order to analyze collected data and draw conclusions. Computer databases can be used to compare communities, technologies and areas, and present this information graphically (Soley & Thogerson, 2003).

One of the primary purposes of monitoring is to inform decision-making. It is therefore useful to obtain a relative measure of performance indicators against each of the four performance areas for which sustainability is important (see Table 9.2) to determine where changes need to be made. Data should be shared between stakeholders and should feed into planning processes. User communities should not be excluded from this process. Monitoring can be used to identify specific problems or successes related to individual communities and systems should aim to feed back this information to users to enable them to identify short-comings, learn from mistakes and implement measures to increase sustainability. Monitoring is also essential for programme planners to obtain an overview of programme effectiveness, efficiency, equity and replicability.

Developing a system of monitoring, evaluation and review is one way to ensure that monitoring data is analyzed and used to its maximum potential. This means that periodic evaluation and review exercises should be scheduled alongside monitoring activities to ensure that the process of performance measurement is ongoing and dynamic.

9.4   Monitoring tools

9

There is a large range of different monitoring tools that can be used and many agencies have developed their own. Most monitoring tools are user-focused while some are facility-focused. Monitoring is most effective where a balance of 'hardware' and 'software' issues is achieved. Monitoring also needs to occur at different levels and from different perspectives. Participatory monitoring should involve not just user communities, but also Government institutions, NGOs, the private sector and policy-makers. Table 9.3 presents a monitoring matrix which addresses key issues related to sustainability for each performance theme.

Table 9.3. Monitoring matrix

Performance theme	Sustainability indicator			
	Effectiveness	**Efficiency**	**Equity**	**Replicability**
Management	Record keeping Relationship with users	Financial and resource management	Pro-poor strategies Gender equity	Management capacity & commitment
Operation	Flow rates Water quality	Ease of operation Waiting times	Use of alternative sources	User acceptability
Maintenance	Workmanship Frequency of breakdown	Average downtime of facility	Cost to communities	Ease of maintenance Affordability
Environment	Water quality	Well yields	Effect on all other water sources	Water levels

9.4.1 Participatory tools for communities

Much of the information required during monitoring is best provided by the community of users of the water service. A number of participatory tools can be used to collect this information.

Methodology for Participatory Assessment

Methodology for Participatory Assessment (MPA) is a qualitative and quantitative method that provides an ideal monitoring framework at policy institutional and community levels. It also provides indicators, means of verification and participatory tools that can facilitate flexible monitoring processes. MPA uses the following sustainability indicators and sub-indicators (Dayal, et al., 2000):

- System quality

  - construction matches design, quality of materials and workmanship

- Effective functioning

  - service operation in terms of water quantity, quality, reliability and predictability

- Effective financing

- coverage of investment and/or recurrent costs

- universality and timeliness of payments

• Effective management

- level and timeliness of repairs

- budgeting and keeping accounts

• Hygienic and environmental use

- proportion and nature of population using service

- degree of improvement of water use habits

MPA uses a range of participatory tools, including:

• Community mapping - to visually represent community situation in relation to water supply;

• Transect walks - to review construction quality and functionality of water service;

• Pocket voting - to detect patterns and changes in behaviour and decision-making by different categories of users and at different points in time;

• Ladders - to assess whether water service meets users' demands;

• Card sorting - to assess contributions, capacities and responsibilities;

• Matrix voting - to assess divisions within communities in relation to a water service;

• Hundred seeds - to obtain percentage distributions.

For more information on MPA tools for monitoring refer to Mukherjee & van Wijk (2002). Some participatory methods are described in more detail below.

Transect walk

This is simply an informal walk through the village to identify key features, and to visit and inspect all the handpumps and other sources that the villagers are using. The monitoring team should be accompanied by local residents so that questions can be asked and issues clarified as they arise. Much of the data for the handpump data sheet (see Annex E) can be obtained during the transect walk.

Focus group discussion

A small group (say, maximum 15) of representatives from the village is asked to attend a closed meeting to discuss certain issues. It is normally useful to get a representative cross-section of water users and managers to attend a focus group discussion to address key issues covered by the monitoring exercise. This can be used to form the basis of a user satisfaction survey and/or sustainability snapshot. The facilitation of this type of group is important since it needs to be well-managed and controlled without directing or manipulating the responses from the group. Separate groups for men and women may be necessary in some cultures.

User satisfaction surveys

User satisfaction surveys are fundamental to capture the perceptions and views of the users (WHO, 2000). Such a survey can be in the form of a simple questionnaire which is completed through informal discussions and interviews. User satisfaction surveys can be used for qualitative classification, for example into 'very satisfied', 'satisfied', … 'poor' etc., and also to explore issues about which users express particular concern or dissatisfaction.

Sustainability snapshot

The sustainability snapshot is a simple and rapid monitoring method which can be conducted in collaboration with community members using focus group discussions. The snapshot, as developed by Sugden (2001) identifies three aspects crucial to sustainability: financial issues, technical skills and spares/equipment. For each aspect there are three options, one of which should be selected for each community visited. A numerical value is assigned to each statement, 1 being the least sustainable, and 3 the most sustainable (see Table 9.4). The sum of all values awarded gives an overall sustainability score.

This is a very rapid method which can be used with communities to obtain a 'snapshot' of the current situation with respect to sustainability. This is useful in identifying which of the three factors is strongest and which is weakest. Some completed examples of the sustainability snapshot are presented in Annex D, where there is also an expanded version which addresses other issues affecting sustainability such as the project process, institutional issues and community issues.

9

Table 9.4. Sustainability snapshot[1]

Factor	Statement
Financial	1. No funds available for maintenance when needed. 2. Funds available but not sufficient for the most expensive maintenance process. 3. Funds available and sufficient for the most expensive maintenance process.
Technical skills	1. Technical skills not available for maintenance when needed. 2. Some technical skills for maintenance but not for all. 3. Technical skills for all maintenance processes available.
Spares and equipment	1. Spares and equipment not available when needed. 2. Spares and equipment available but not for all repairs. 3. Spares and equipment available for all repairs when needed.

1. After Sugden, 2001

9.4.2 Technical monitoring

In addition to participatory approaches, monitoring data can be collected related to technology and the environment based largely on observation and measurement.

Facility data sheets

Table 9.5 presents a simple format that can be used to record operational data for a range of communities. This can be used for routine quarterly monitoring and the user requires little specialist or technical knowledge. In this case, the numbers of handpumps, water committees and pump mechanics are noted, and it is indicated whether or not they are functioning. 'Functionality' must therefore be defined for each.

Table 9.5. Monitoring data sheet

Zone, ward or community	No of handpumps		Water committee		Pump mechanic	
	Fu[1]	**NF**	**Fu**	**NF**	**Fu**	**NF**
XX	3	0	1	1	1	0
YY	2	2	2	0	2	0
ZZ	1	2	1	0	0	2
Total	**6**	**4**	**4**	**1**	**3**	**2**
Operational rate	60%		80%		60&	

1. Fu - Functioning, NF - Not functioning

The terms 'functioning' and 'non-functioning' need to be defined clearly for each group to ensure consistency.

This approach is easy to implement and can be conducted alongside the sustainability snapshot. It provides a good overview of communities and easy identification of problems. Such an exercise might then be followed by more detailed monitoring of selected communities. For example, a handpump data sheet can be used to collect greater information on pump performance and maintenance (an example of this is reproduced in Annex E).

Groundwater monitoring

Borehole data collected during drilling should be stored on a database which is, ideally, compatible with a national database. Continued groundwater monitoring is of key importance to assess and ensure environmental sustainability. Borehole yields, groundwater levels and water quality data should be collected as part of routine monitoring where possible. Groundwater levels are of particular importance in assessing seasonal fluctuations as well as longer-term trends and for this reason should be recorded quarterly. Water quality parameters may be limited to those of particular concern for given water sources. For example, where there is potential for contamination from on-site sanitation, bacteriological testing should be conducted, but where there are known cases of arsenic, samples should be tested for this parameter. Full routine analysis of all chemical and bacteriological parameters is expensive and unnecessary in most cases. The use of Geographical Information Systems (GIS) can provide excellent opportunities for data management and mapping performance.

9.4.3   Participatory tools for institutions

Just as participatory tools can be used with communities to monitor performance, they can also be used with institutions and policy-makers. Stakeholders' meetings can be used to assess performance indicators for institutional support and management. These can use open discussions and ranking exercises, like those used with communities. Structured interviews can also be conducted with selected policy officials and policy dialogue workshops can be held. These can be used to assess the enabling organizational climate, discuss the results of monitoring at community level, and score relevant policies and strategies accordingly (Mukherjee & van Wijk, 2002).

9.5   Evaluation and review

Evaluation is an extension of monitoring but is a periodic measurement of performance - annually or less frequently. This is usually a more in-depth assessment of all issues affecting programme sustainability, which focuses on the review of outputs and outcomes, and aims to identify the reasons for good or poor performance. Evaluation should assess the results of monitoring, otherwise there is a risk that monitoring is done 'for its own sake' and is never synthesized or acted upon. The traditional project approach to rural water supply has one distinct advantage over the programmatic approach in that it provides convenient intervals at which to conduct evaluations, i.e. at the end of each project or phase. Where a programme approach is taken it is important to identify fixed time periods when evaluations should be conducted to obtain a holistic picture of the current status of the programme. Evaluations can take the form of participatory user assessments, analysis of household survey data, value for money studies, or one-off studies to review a particular policy or issue

9.5.1   O&M Audit

An O&M audit is an independent assessment of O&M functions, objectives, organization and practices, designed to complement routine monitoring. This is, in effect, an evaluation of O&M and is particularly useful to establish its status and effectiveness prior to implementing institutional or policy changes, and for comparative purposes to set performance targets, operational plans and guidelines.

An O&M audit is a valuable management tool for assessing the way that O&M is working. The results of the audit should feed directly into the development of action plans to improve both the function and structure of the management processes for O&M. Ideally, an O&M audit should be a participatory process which involves whole communities. WHO (2000) outlines the following process for its implementation.

- *Background information* - obtain basic information on the organization and systems being audited.

- *The culture of the organization* - understand the culture and fundamental operating principles within the organization responsible for O&M.

- *Responsibilities within the organization* - develop a clear understanding of all O&M responsibilities and their relation to the overall management of the water system.

- *Setting O&M objectives* - find out if there are clear management objectives set for O&M.

- *Planning structures for O&M* - find out if there is a clear planning structure for O&M.

- *Resource management* - find out the procedures that are in place for managing different resources.

- *Personnel management* - find out the extent to which personnel management skills exist and are used.

- *Action* - prepare a report from this audit procedure in order to assess the effectiveness of the O&M management system and develop action plans for improving the system.

O&M audits are useful to acquire an overview of operation and maintenance issues, and to identify constraints to sustainability. For example, an O&M audit in Volta Region, Ghana indicated that over 80 per cent of all O&M problems where managerial or financial in nature (Soley & Thogerson, 2002).

9.5.2　Programme evaluation

There are many different formats for project and programme evaluation, depending on the donor or institution concerned. Ideally, any evaluation should build upon the monitoring process and should provide an overview of the achievements, impact, constraints and failings of a given programme. This can be used to guide future programmes and approaches. An evaluation should address the following aspects:

- Programme setting - institutional framework, policy, socio-economic climate, environment etc.

- Programme preparation - objectives, strategy financing, activities, partnerships etc.

- Programme implementation - implementation procedures, activities, plans, time frames etc.

- Programme impact and achievement of objectives - effect on institutions and communities, performance, effectiveness, efficiency, equity etc.

- Lessons learned - programme design, implementation, sustainability, O&M, affordability, replicability etc.

9.5.3　Programme review

Programme review is a periodic assessment of what has been learned, both during the course of the year and at the end. A review process focuses on the identification of implications of the monitoring and evaluation analysis, and aims to develop mechanisms for disseminating learning, influencing policy and affecting resourcing. Review activities include policy forums and joint sector reviews; they are key events that contribute to policy development and programme planning.

9.6 Steps towards sustainable monitoring

The steps outlined in Figure 9.1 should be followed in order to set up an appropriate monitoring system and strategy.

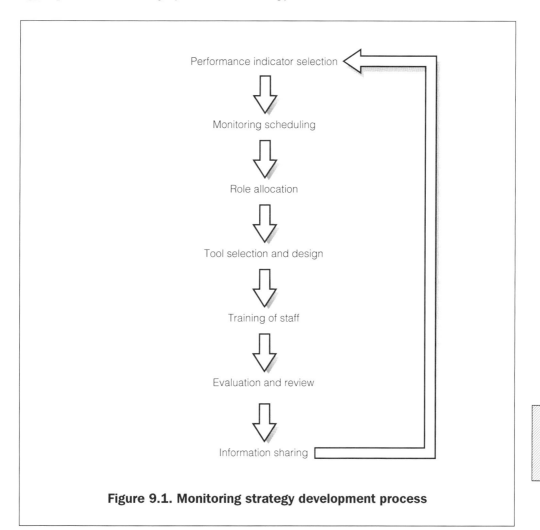

Figure 9.1. Monitoring strategy development process

This process is best conducted at a national level to ensure replicability and compatibility of data from different regions and districts. The process should be co-ordinated by a national planning committee comprising representatives of relevant government ministries and departments, and external support agencies involved in water supply.

Step 1. Performance indicator selection

The first step in developing an appropriate monitoring strategy is to select appropriate performance indicators which can be used to monitor rural water supply issues. These will include indicators (see Table 9.3) for:

• Management - effectiveness of management system (organizational and financial) related to overall programme and individual water supplies;

• Operation - user satisfaction with service and technical or social problems/ impacts;

• Maintenance - effectiveness and efficiency of maintenance activities; and

• Environmental - water quantity and quality and unintended environmental effects.

These broad issues can be broken down into more specific indicators, some of which can be measured through observation or measurement, and some of which require consultation with different stakeholders. Indicators should be selected based on the following two questions:

• What do we want to know about the water supply now and in the future? and

• What are we going to do with this information?

A focused and balanced set of 'core' indicators (those of most importance) need to be agreed upon. There should then be a range of secondary indicators, which are important but less crucial. The purpose of collecting certain information and how this will be used must be established clearly from the onset of the planning process. It is a waste of time and money to collect information that is not really needed.

Step 2. Monitoring scheduling

Once it has been decided what information the monitoring system should be collecting, the next step is to determine how often this information should be collected. Quarterly intervals are ideal for most monitoring issues, since this allows for most seasonal variations. Monthly monitoring is normally too time consuming and is simply unrealistic in most situations. Table 9.6 shows a simplified monitoring schedule for addressing different issues relating to rural water supplies. This will depend on how often changes are likely to occur for different issues, but may also be influenced by the monitoring tools selected in Step 4.

Table 9.6. Monitoring schedule example

Issues to be monitored	1st Quarter	2nd Quarter	3rd Quarter	4th Quarter
Management issues		✓		✓
Operational issues	✓	✓	✓	✓
Maintenance issues		✓		✓
Environmental issues	✓	✓	✓	✓

Rather than implementing a full-scale monitoring schedule immediately it may be more appropriate to develop a phased approach in which the core indicators are monitored in the first instance, and the secondary indicators subsequently.

Step 3. Role allocation

Monitoring activities do not all have to be conducted by the same individual or even the same organization. For example, water levels and water quality may be monitored by a different individual to the one who monitors community and management issues. In most cases, however, monitoring systems are more efficient where all activities are undertaken by one individual or group. Local government staff most commonly fulfil this role although community volunteers with specific roles such as environmental health assistant or community development officer may be just as effective. Roles and responsibilities must be clearly defined, both in terms of who collects the information and also who collates, analyses and uses this information for programme activities. Responsibilities for training and supervising monitoring staff should also be clearly defined.

Step 4. Tool selection and design

It is then necessary to select the particular monitoring tools to be used and to refine these or to design alternatives. A range of methods and tools are available as described earlier in this chapter. The key is to select the minimum number of tools that can be used to collect all the information required and to match these to the individuals or groups responsible for monitoring.

9

Step 5. Training of staff

Having established the monitoring goals, schedule, tools and roles it is then necessary to ensure that the organizations and individuals given responsibility for monitoring activities are trained effectively. If government staff and key community members are to use selected monitoring tools they should receive training in their use. This may consist of a one-week training programme initially but is likely to involve follow-up training every six months or so. It is especially important that non-technical staff are made aware of the reasons for recording technical data such as water levels and that they are trained in identifying technical problems. Similarly, staff with less experience of community liaison should be trained in effective communication and consultation techniques.

Step 6. Evaluation and review

Once staff are adequately trained they should be provided with an appropriate means of transport to visit communities (if they do not already have this) and the monitoring system can be implemented. It is then essential for the system to be reviewed regularly and for the information recorded to be used effectively. Monitoring is pointless unless the information collected is used to inform decision-making, improve effectiveness and efficiency, and contribute to the sustainability of water supplies. Evaluation of the data collected provides the means to inform decision-making and improve effectiveness. A local government or NGO unit should be charged with the task of managing the monitoring system and setting times for periodic evaluation and review. This should ensure that the information collected has maximum benefit.

Step 7. Information sharing

The final step once the monitoring system is set up is to share information collected with stakeholders through the monitoring, evaluation and review process. This will facilitate the identification of information gaps or information overload, and on the basis of this the performance indicators can be adjusted and the overall monitoring framework refined over time.

Further reading

Dayal, R., van Wijk, C. and Mukherjee, N. (2000) *Methodology for Participatory Assessments: With communities, institutions and policy makers.* Water and sanitation Program, The World Bank: Washington D.C. (can be accessed at http://www.wsp.org/pdfs/global_metguideall.pdf)

Mukherjee, N. and van Wijk, C. (2002) *Sustainability Planning and Monitoring in Community Water Supply and Sanitation: A guide to the methodology for participatory assessment (MPA) for community-driven development programs.* Water and Sanitation Program, The World Bank: Washington D.C. (can be accessed at http://www.wsp.org/publications/mpa%202003.pdf)

UNDP (1997) *Results-oriented Monitoring and Evaluation: A Handbook for Programme Managers* UNDP, Office of Evaluations and Strategic Planning: New York.

9

9

References

Abrams, L. (1996) *Capacity Building for water supply and sanitation development at local level: The Threshold Concept.* A paper delivered at the 2nd UNDP Symposium on Water Sector Capacity Building, Delft, Netherlands, 4-6 December 1996. http://www.thewaterpage.com/threshld.htm

Abrams, L. (1998) *Understanding sustainability of local water services*, March 1998, http://www.africanwater.org/sustainability.htm

Alberts, H. (2000) 'Community rope pumps in Nicaragua; a private sector approach', paper presented at *Clean water delivery, Village Power 2000*, December 2000.

Alexander, Z.J. (2003) *Non-Profit Sector Supply of Handpump Spares - Lessons from Malawi.* Unpublished MSc Dissertation, WEDC, Loughborough University: UK.

Allen, V. (1996) *Clean Water = Primary Health.* Consallen: UK. (http://www.consallen.com)

Annan, K.A. (2000) *'We the Peoples' The role of the United Nations in the 21st Century.* United Nations: New York.

Arlosoroff, S., Tschannerl, G., Grey, D., Journey, W., Karp, A., Langenegger, O. and Roche, R. (1987) *Community Water Supply: the handpump option.* The World Bank: Washington D.C.

Ball, P. (2001) *Drilled Wells.* Series of Manuals on Drinking Water Supply, Volume 6, SKAT: St. Gallen, Switzerland.

Ball, P. (2003) *Drilled Water Supply Holes in Africa - Why do they cost so much? Do they need to cost so much?.* Overview presentation at the 4th HTN Forum, 2-5 June 2003, Durban, South Africa.

Batchelor, S., McKemey, K. and Scott, N. (2000) *Exit Strategies for Resettlement of Drought Prone Populations (Project Technical Report)*. Gamos Ltd: Reading, UK.

Baumann, E. (2000) *Water Lifting*. Series of Manuals on Drinking Water Supply, Volume 7, SKAT: St. Gallen, Switzerland.

Bernage, F. (2000) 'Local private sector involvement: the Mauritania experience'. Paper presented at SKAT HTN workshop on Civil Society and Government Partnerships in RWS, Hyderabad, India, March 2000, published by SKAT: Switzerland.

Betz, H.D. (1995) 'Unconventional Water Detection: Field Test of the Dowsing Technique in Dry Zones,' *Journal of Scientific Exploration*, 9:1 and 9;159. Stanford University: CA.

BGS (2001) *Guidelines for Assessing the Risk to Groundwater from On-site Sanitation*. BGS: Wallingford, UK. (can be accessed at http://www.bgs.ac.uk/hydrogeology/argoss/home.html)

Breslin, E. D. (2003) 'The Demand-Responsive Approach in Mozambique: Why choice of technology matters.' *Waterfront*, Issue 16, Fall 2003, UNICEF: New York.

Calow, R.C., Robins, N.S., MacDonald, A.M., Nicol, A.L. and Orpen W.R.G. (1999) *Planning for Groundwater Drought in Africa*. Proceedings of the International Conference on Integrated Drought Management - Lessons for Sub-Saharan Africa. Pretoria, South Africa, 20-22 September, 1999.

Cambridge Dictionary (2003) *Cambridge Advanced Learner's Dictionary Online*. Cambridge University Press: UK. (http://dictionary.cambridge.org)

Cannock, G. (2001) 'Expanding Rural telephony: Output-based contracts for pay phones in Peru', in: Brook, P.J. and Smith, S.M. *Contracting for Public Services: Output-based aid and its applications*. The World Bank: Washington D.C.

Carter, R. (2002) *Issue of Government and other agencies support*. [Cmup3-11] Contribution to 'Beyond the Community' E-conference on Scaling up of Community Management of Rural Water Supplies: http://www.jiscmail.ac.uk/lists/WSSCMANP.html

Carter, R.C., Tyrrel, S.F. and Howsam, P. (1999) Impact and Sustainability of Community Water Supply and Sanitation Programmes in Developing Countries. *Journal of the Chartered Institute of Water and Environmental Management*, Vol. 13, pp 292-296, August 1999.

Chambers, R. (1983) *Rural Development: Putting the last first.* Longman: Harlow, UK.

Chambers, R. (1997) *Whose Reality Counts? Putting the first last.* Intermediate Technology Publications: London.

CIDA (2000) *Planning and Implementation of SWAps: An Overview.* Issues Paper prepared as a background document for CIDA President's Forum on Sector-Wide Approaches (SWAps) October 10, 2000

Coates, S., Sansom, K and Kayaga, S. (2001) 'PREPP - improving utility watsan services to low income consumers.' in Scott, R. (ed.) *Proceedings of 27th WEDC Conference, Lusaka, Zambia, 2001.* WEDC, Loughborough University: UK. (can be accessed at http://wedc.lboro.ac.uk/conferences/conference.php)

Colin, J. (1999) *Lessons learned from village level operation and maintenance.* WELL Study Task 162, WELL, WEDC, Loughborough University: UK.

Consallen (2002) http://www.consallen.com. October 2002.

Cummings, R.G., Brookshire, D.S. and Schulze, W.D. (1986) *Valuing Environmental Goods: An Assessment of the Contingent Valuation Method*, Rowman & Allanheld: Totowa, NJ.

Danert, K., Carter, R.C., Rwamwanja, R., Ssebalu, J., Carr, G., and Kane, D. (2003) 'The Private Sector in Water and Sanitation Services in Uganda: Understanding the context and developing support strategies.' *Journal of International Development*, 15 (8) 1099-1114.

Davis, J. and Brikké, F.T. (1995) *Making Your Water Supply Work: Operation and maintenance of small water supplies.* IRC: Delft, The Netherlands.

Dayal, R., van Wijk, C. and Mukherjee, N. (2000) *Methodology for Participatory Assessments: With communities, institutions and policy makers.* Water and sanitation Program, The World Bank: Washington D.C.

DeGabriele, J. (2002) *Improving Community Based Management of Boreholes; A case study from Malawi*. BASIS, University of Wisconsin-Madison: USA.

Deverill, P., Bibby, S., Wedgwood, A. and Smout, I. (2002) *Designing Water Supply and Sanitation Projects to Meet Demand in Rural and Peri-Urban Communities: Book 1. Concept, principles and practice*. WEDC, Loughborough University: UK.
(can be accessed at http://wedc.lboro.ac.uk/projects/new_projects3.php?id=36)

Diwi Consult and Bureau d'Ingénierie pour le Développement Rural (BIDR) (1994) *Etudes d' Réhabilitation des Points d' Eau Existants*.

DFID (2001) *Addressing the Water Crisis: Healthier and more productive lives for poor people, Strategies for achieving the international development targets*. Department for International Development: UK.

Duncker, L.C. (2001) *The KAP Tool for Hygiene: A manual on knowledge, attitude and practices study for hygiene awareness in rural areas of South Africa*. WRC Report No. TT 144/00, Water Research Commission: Pretoria, South Africa.

DWD (2002a) *Issue Paper 1: Overview of the Water Sector, Reform, SWAP and Financial Issues*. Directorate of Water Development, Ministry of Water, Lands and Environment, The Republic of Uganda.

DWD (2002b) *Rural Water and Sanitation Operation Plan: 2002-2007*. Version 1, September 2002, Directorate of Water Development, Ministry of Water, Lands and Environment, The Republic of Uganda.

Erpf, K. (1998) *The Bush Pump: The National Standard Handpump of Zimbabwe*. HTN Case Study, HTN/SKAT: St. Gallen, Switzerland.

Erpf, K. (2002) *Technology Selection - and Buyers Guide for Public Domain Handpumps for Drinking Water*. HTN/SKAT: St. Gallen, Switzerland.

Elson, B., Franceys, R, and Shaw, R. (1999) 'Maintaining Handpumps' in Shaw, R.J. (ed.) *Running Water*. IT Publications: UK.

Evans, P. (1992) Paying the Piper: an overview of community financing of water and sanitation IRC: Delft, The Netherlands.

Godfrey, S. and Ball, P. (2003) 'Making Boreholes Work: Rehabilitation strategies from Angola' in Harvey, P.A. (ed.) *Proceedings of 29th WEDC Conference, Abuja, Nigeria, 2003*. WEDC, Loughborough University: UK. (can be accessed at http://wedc.lboro.ac.uk/conferences/conference.php)

Gombert, P. (1999). Strategy of hydrogeological prospection in the eastern Chad basement by optimization of the number and depth of investigation boreholes. *Rev. Sci. Eau* 12 (3) : 597-608 [article in French].

Gómez-Lobo, A. (2001) 'Making Water Affordable: Output-based consumption subsidies in Chile', in: Brook, P.J. and Smith, S.M. *Contracting for Public Services: Output-based aid and its applications*. The World Bank: Washington D.C.

Gorter A.C., Alberts J.H., Gago J.F. and Sandiford P. (1993) A randomised trial of the impact of rope-pumps on water quality, *Journal of Tropical Medicine and Hygiene*, 98: 247 - 255.

Gosling, L. and Edwards, M. (1995) *Toolkits: A practical guide to assessment, monitoring, review and evaluation*. Save the Children: London.

Gross, B., van Wijk, C. and Mukherjee, N. (2001) *Linking Sustainability with Demand,*

Gender and Poverty: A study in community-managed water supply projects in 15 countries. IRC: Delft, The Netherlands.

Harvey, P.A. (2003) *Sustainable Handpump Projects in Africa: Report on Fieldwork in Uganda*. WEDC, Loughborough University: UK. (can be accessed at http://www.lboro.ac.uk/wedc/projects/shp)

Harvey, P.A., Ikumi, P.N. and Mutethia, D.K. (2003) *Sustainable Handpump Projects in Africa: Report on Fieldwork in Kenya*. WEDC, Loughborough University: UK. (can be accessed at http://www.lboro.ac.uk/wedc/projects/shp)

Harvey, P.A., Jawara, D. and Reed, R.A. (2002a) *Sustainable Handpump Projects in Africa: Report on Fieldwork in Ghana*. WEDC, Loughborough University: UK. (can be accessed at http://www.lboro.ac.uk/wedc/projects/shp)

References

Harvey, P.A., and Kayaga, S.M. (2003) *Sustainable Handpump Projects in Africa: Report on Fieldwork in South Africa*. WEDC, Loughborough University: UK. (can be accessed at http://www.lboro.ac.uk/wedc/projects/shp)

Harvey, P.A., Reed, R.A. and Skinner, B.H. (2002b) *Sustainable Handpump Projects in Africa: Interim report*. WEDC, Loughborough University: UK. (can be accessed at http://www.lboro.ac.uk/wedc/projects/shp)

Harvey, P.A. and Reed, R.A. (2003) 'Sustainable Rural Water Supply in Africa; Rhetoric and reality', in Harvey, P.A. (ed.) *Proceedings of 29th WEDC Conference, Abuja, Nigeria, 2003*. WEDC, Loughborough University: UK. (can be accessed at http://wedc.lboro.ac.uk/conferences/conference.php)

Harvey, P.A., and Skinner, B.H. (2002) *Sustainable Handpump Projects in Africa: Report on Fieldwork in Zambia*. WEDC, Loughborough University: UK. (can be accessed at http://www.lboro.ac.uk/wedc/projects/shp)

Hazelton, D. (2000) *The development of community water supply systems using deep and shallow well handpumps*. WRC Report No, TT132/00, Water Research Centre, South Africa.

Holtslag, H. (2002) *Importance of Technology, Bold Ideas*. [Cmup2-32] Contribution to 'Beyond the Community' E-conference on Scaling up of Community Management of Rural Water Supplies: http://www.jiscmail.ac.uk/lists/WSSCMANP.html

Hyperdictionary (2003) http://www.hyperdictionary.com (accessed 05/11/03).

IRC (2002) *Participatory Learning and Action Initiative*. IRC: Delft, The Netherlands. http://www.irc.nl/projects/genini/plaresults.html

Jones, D. (2001) *Conceiving and Managing Partnerships: A guiding framework*. Practitioner Note Series, Business Partners for Development, Water and Sanitation Cluster: London.

Joshi, B. (1996) 'Borewell Rejuvenation for Sustainability', in Pickford, J. (ed.) *Proceedings of 22nd WEDC Conference, New Delhi, India 1996*. WEDC, Loughborough University: UK.
(can be accessed at http://wedc.lboro.ac.uk/conferences/conference.php)

References

Joshi, D. and Fawcett, B. (2001) *Water Projects and Women's Empowerment.* People and Systems for Water, Sanitation and Health, Proceedings of the 27th WEDC Conference, WEDC, Loughborough University: UK.

Kandulu, J. (2004) Personal communication with the author, March 2004.

Karasoff, P. (1998) *Collaborative Partnerships: A Review of the Literature.*San Francisco State University.

Kjellerup, B. (2004) Personal communication with the author, February 2004.

Lammerick, M.P., Bolt, E., de Jong, D. and Schouten, T. (2002) *Strengthening Community Water Management.* IRC: Delft, The Netherlands.

Lemine, H.O.M. and Münger, F. (2003) *Water Solar System Supply Chain, a Sustainable Approach - ANEPA: An example of booster.* Supply Chain theme presentation at the 4th HTN Forum, 2-5 June 2003, Durban, South Africa.

Lockwood, H. (2004) *Scaling Up Community Management of Rural Water Supply.* Thematic Overview Paper, IRC: Delft, The Netherlands.
(can be accessed at http://www.irc.nl/content/view/full/8857)

Lyke, M.L. (2000) 'Ancient Art of Water Witching Survives the Centuries'. *Seattle Post*, March 28, 2000.

Macdonald, A.M. and Davies, J. (2000) *A Brief Review of Groundwater for Rural Water Supply in Sub-Saharan Africa.* Technical Report WC/00/33, Overseas Geology Series, British Geological Survey: UK.

Macdonald, A.M., Davies, J. and Dochartaigh, B.E.O. (2002) *Simple Methods for Assessing Groundwater Resources in Low Permeability Areas of Africa.* Commissioned Report CR/01/168N, British Geological Survey: UK.

MacDonald, D.A. and Pape, J. (2002) *Cost Recovery and the Crisis of Service Delivery in South Africa.* Human Science Research Council: Cape town, South Africa.

Mawunganidze, S. (2002) *Sustainability and Alternative Water Sources - Mozambique* [Cmup1-64] Contribution to 'Beyond the Community' E-conference on Scaling up of Community Management of Rural Water Supplies: http://www.jiscmail.ac.uk/lists/WSSCMANP.html

References

Médecins Sans Frontières (1994) Public Health Engineering in Emergency Situation. Médecins Sans Frontières: Paris.

Mukherjee, N. and van Wijk, C. (2002) *Sustainability Planning and Monitoring in Community Water Supply and Sanitation: A guide to the methodology for participatory assessment (MPA) for community-driven development programs.* Water and Sanitation Program, The World Bank: Washington D.C.

Mumbo, G. (2001) *Literacy and numeracy.* Contribution to 'E-conference on Handpump Sustainability' http://www.jiscmail.ac.uk/lists/htn.html (November, 2001).

MWR (1999) *Sessional Paper No. 1 of 1999 on National Policy on Water Resources Management and Development, April 29, 1999.* Ministry of Water Resources, Republic of Kenya.

Narayan, D. (1995) *The Contribution of People's Participation: Evidence from 121 rural water supply projects.* Environmentally Sustainable Development Occasional Paper Series 1, The World Bank: Washington D.C.

Nedjoh, J., Thogersen, J. and Kjellerup, B. (2003) 'Challenges of O&M in the Sustainability of Rural Water Facilities', in Harvey, P.A. (ed.) *Proceedings of 29th WEDC Conference, Abuja, Nigeria, 2003.* WEDC, Loughborough University: UK.
(can be accessed at http://wedc.lboro.ac.uk/conferences/conference.php)

Ockelford, J. (2002) *Lack of understanding of the need for support systems.* [Cmup2-07] Contribution to 'Beyond the Community' E-conference on Scaling up of Community Management of Rural Water Supplies:
http://www.jiscmail.ac.uk/lists/WSSCMANP.html

Ockelford, J. and Reed, R.A. (2002) *Participatory Planning for Integrated Rural Water Supply and Sanitation Programmes: Guidelines and Manual.* WEDC, Loughborough University: UK.

Ogus, A.L. (1994) *Regulation: Legal forum and economic theory.* Oxford University Press.

Osola, M., (1998) 'A Few Buckets More: reducing sand-invasion and siltation in Angola'. *Waterlines*, Vol. 17, No. 2.

Oyo, A. (2002) *Creating Successful Private Sector Supply Chains: A resource guide for rural water supply and sanitation practitioners*. WSP: Washington D.C.

Parry-Jones, S., Reed, R. and Skinner, B.H. (2001a) *Sustainable Handpump Projects in Africa: A literature review*. WEDC, Loughborough University: UK.

Parry-Jones, S., Reed, R. and Skinner, B.H. (2001b) *Sustainable Handpump Projects in Africa: Draft Guidelines for field evaluation of handpump projects*. WEDC, Loughborough University: UK.

Pump Aid (2004) *The Elephant Pump*. Pump Aid, Loughborough: UK. http://www.pumpaid.org.

Reed, R.A. (1995) *Sustainable Sewerage*. Intermediate Technology Publications: London.

Reed, B.J. (2002) *Involving Men and Women in Engineering Projects*. WEDC, Loughborough University: UK (DRAFT report)

Regmi, S. C. and Fawcett, B. (2001) *Men's Roles, Gender Relations, and Sustainability in Water Supplies: Some lessons from Nepal*. IIDS, Southampton University: UK (http://www.soton.ac.uk/~civilenv/postgraduate/eng4dev/water-oxford.PDF).

Rietbergen-McCracken, J. and Narayan, D. (1998) *Participation and Social Assessment: Tools and techniques*. The World Bank: Washington D.C.

RWSN (2004a) *The Handpump*. Rural Water Supply Network: St. Gallen, Switzerland. (http://www.skat.ch/htn/publications/archive.htm, accessed 01/06/04)

RWSN (2004b) *Focus on Africa, a critical need. Rural Water Supply Network*: St. Gallen, Switzerland (http://www.skat.ch/htn/about/partners.htm#focus, accessed 01/06/04).

Sander, P. Chesley, M.M. and Minor, T.B. (1996) 'Groundwater Assessment using Remote Sensing and GIS in a Rural Groundwater Project in Ghana: Lessons Learned.' *Hydrogeology Journal*, vol.4, no.3, 1996.

References

Sansom, K. (2002) Personal communication with the author. WEDC, Loughborough University: UK.

Sansom, K., Franceys, R., Morales-Reyes, J. and Njiru, C. (2001) Contracting out water and sanitation services: Draft final report. WEDC, Loughborough University: UK.

Sarkinnen, P. (1994) *Lessons learned from Kenya-Finland Western water supply programme (1981-1993)* UNDP-World Bank regional Water and Sanitation Group, December 1994.

Schouten, T. (2004) *Scaling up Community Management of Rural Water Supply.* PowerPoint presentation, IRC.

Schouten, T. and Moriarty, P. (2003) *Community Water, Community Management - From system to service in rural areas.* ITDG Publishing/IRC.

Skinner, B.H. (2003) *Small-Scale Water Supply: A review of technologies.* ITDG Publishing: London, UK.

Sohail M. (ed.) (2001) *Public Private Partnerships and the Poor.* WEDC, Loughborough University: UK

Soley, F.K. and Thogersen, J. (2002) 'O&M Audit, A Practical Tool for Sustainability', in Reed, B. (ed.) *Proceedings of 28th WEDC Conference, Kolkata, India, 2002.* WEDC, Loughborough University: UK.
(can be accessed at http://wedc.lboro.ac.uk/conferences/conference.php)

Soley, F.K. and Thogersen, J. (2003) Monitoring and Evaluation System for Rural Water Supply', in Harvey, P.A. (ed.) *Proceedings of 29th WEDC Conference, Abuja, Nigeria, 2003.* WEDC, Loughborough University: UK.
(can be accessed at http://wedc.lboro.ac.uk/conferences/conference.php)

Srinivasan, L. (1990) *Tools for Community Participation: A manual for training trainers in participatory techniques.* PROWWESS/UNDP: New York.

Sugden, S. (2001) 'Assessing Sustainability - The sustainability snapshot', in Scott, R. (ed.) *Proceedings of 27th WEDC Conference, Lusaka, Zambia, August 2001.* WEDC, Loughborough University: UK.
(can be accessed at http://wedc.lboro.ac.uk/conferences/conference.php)

References

Sutton, S. (2002) *Community led Improvements of Rural Drinking Water Supplies*. SWL Consultants: Shrewsbury, UK.

Sutton, S. (2003) *Why Think of Smaller Units for Rural Water Supply? Household and small community solutions*. Overview presentation at the 4th HTN Forum, 2-5 June 2003, Durban, South Africa.

Sutton, S. and Nkoloma, H. (2003) *Encouraging Change: Sustainable steps in water supply, sanitation and hygiene*. TALC: St. Albans, UK.

Tayong, A. and Poubom, C. (2002) *Convincing People to Pay for Water: Nkouondja in Cameroon*. IRC: Delft, The Netherlands.

Teeuw, R.M. (1995) 'Groundwater Exploration using Remote Sensing and a Low-Cost Geographic Information System.' *Hydrogeology Journal*, vol.3, no.3, 1995.

Thomson, M. (2003) *Performance Measurement Framework for Uganda Water and Sanitation Sector*. WELL (WEDC/LSHTM.IRC).

Thorpe, I. (2002) *Participation, Appropriate Technology (Pump Aid and the Elephant Pump) - Zimbabwe*. [Cmup2-35] Contribution to 'Beyond the Community' E-conference on Scaling up of Community Management of Rural Water Supplies: http://www.jiscmail.ac.uk/lists/WSSCMANP.html

Trémolet, S. and Browning, S. (2002) *The Interface between Regulatory Frameworks and Tri-Sector Partnerships*. Business Partners for Development, Water and Sanitation Cluster: London.

UNCHS (2004) *The Maintenance of Infrastructure and its Financing and Cost Recovery*. United Nations Centre for Human Settlements (Habitat). http://www.unchs.org/unchs/english/mainten/contents.htm

van Beers, P. (2001a) 'Leasing, a new Handpump O&M concept', in Scott, R. (ed.) *Proceedings of 27th WEDC Conference, Lusaka, Zambia, August 2001*. WEDC, Loughborough University: UK.
(can be accessed at http://wedc.lboro.ac.uk/conferences/conference.php)

van Beers, P. (2001b) *Supply Chains for Handpump Spare Parts*. Presentation at 'Guidelines for Sustainable Handpump Projects in Africa' Workshop, 24 August 2001, Lusaka, Zambia.

References

van Beers, P. (2003) Personal communication with the author, October 2003.

van Hemert, B., Orozco, O.S., Haemhouts, J. and Galíz, O.A. (1992) *The Rope Pump: The challenge of popular technology*. INAA/Rural Aqueduct Directive (DAR), Region V: Nicaragua.

van Miert, T. and Binamungu, D. (2001) *The Shinyanga Experience: Water user group concept as a sustainable management system for hand pump wells*. SKAT: St. Gallen, Switzerland.

Webster, B. (1999) *Effective Demand for Rural Water Supply in South Africa*. WEDC, Loughborough University: UK.

Wedgwood, A. (2003) *Methodology for Rapid Assessment of Willingness to Pay for Water in Rural Communities (Southern Africa)* Unpublished report, WEDC, Loughborough University: UK.

Wedgwood and Sansom, K. (2003) *Willingness-to-pay Surveys - A Streamlined Approach: Guidance notes for small town water services* WEDC, Loughborough University: UK.

WELL (1998) *DFID Guidance manual on water supply and sanitation programmes*. WELL, WEDC, Loughborough University, UK, 1998, www.lboro.ac.uk/well

Wheat, S. (2000) 'Well Wishers.' *The Guardian*: March 22, 2000.

Whittington, D. (1998) Administering Contingent Valuation Surveys in Developing Countries. *World Development*, 26(1): 21-30.

WHO (2000) *Tools for assessing the O&M status of water supply and sanitation in developing countries*. World Health Organization: Geneva, Switzerland.

WHO (2003) *Guidelines for Drinking Water Quality (3rd Edition)*. World Heath Organization: Geneva. (can be accessed at http://www.who.int/water_sanitation_health/dwq/guidelines3rd/en/)

WHO/UNICEF (2000) *Global water supply and sanitation assessment 2000 report*. WHO/UNICEF: New York.

Wood, M. (2001) *Appropriate technology* Contribution to 'E-conference on Handpump Sustainability' http://www.jiscmail.ac.uk/lists/htn.html (November, 2001).

World Bank (1997) *Mali Rural Water Supply Project*. Performance Audit Report No. 16511, World Bank: Washington DC.

World Bank (2004) *PRSP Source Book*. World Bank: Washington D.C. http://www.worldbank.org/poverty/strategies/sourcons.htm

World Vision (2003) *Ghana Rural Water Project Phase III 1995-2003: Final evaluation June 10 -28, 2003*. Unpublished confidential report, World Vision: Ghana.

World Water Council (2002) *UN Consecrates Water as Public Good, Human Right*. www.worldwatercouncil.org/download/ UN_water_public_good.pdf

WSP (1999) *Sustainability Monitoring: The VIP way, A ground-level exercise*. Water and Sanitation Program: Washington D.C. (can be accessed at http://www.wsp.org/pdfs/sa_vip.pdf)

WSP (2000) *Supply Chains: A global initiative*. Water and Sanitation Program: Washington D.C. (can be accessed at www.wsp.org/publications/global_supplyupdate.pdf)

WSSCC (2002) *Beyond the Community*. E-conference on Scaling up of Community Management of Rural Water Supplies: http://www.jiscmail.ac.uk/lists/WSSCMANP.html

Wurzel, P. (2001) *Drilling Boreholes for Handpumps*. Working Papers on Water Supply and Environmental Sanitation, Volume 2, SKAT: St. Gallen, Switzerland. (can be accessed at http://www.skat.ch/htn/downloads/ bh4handpumps.pdf)

Zambia-Water (2004) *WASHE*. http://www.zambia-water.org.zm/washe.htm

References

References

Annexes

Annexes

Annex A: Advocacy tools

The following information summary sheets are designed to be used for advocacy purposes.

A1.   Institutional support for community management

A2.   Private sector participation

A3.   Local sustainable technologies

A4.   Procurement and importation

A.1 Institutional support for community management

A.1.1 Assertion

Community management requires ongoing support from local Government or an alternative institution if it is to be sustainable.

A.1.2 Objective

To raise awareness of the need for institutional support for community management, and the need to budget and plan for this accordingly, and build support/consensus among policy-makers and managers.

A.1.3 Benefits

The benefits of providing ongoing support to communities that manage their own water systems are:

- Better sustained willingness to pay among users;

- Early detection and remedy of management short-comings;

- Continued capacity building and expansion of CBOs;

- Reduction in system failures and downtimes; and

- Increased opportunities for monitoring and data collection.

A.1.4 Actions

Institutional support for community management should include:

- Monitoring and evaluation;

- Participatory planning;

- Specialist technical assistance; and

- Capacity building.

Governments must develop decentralized strategies for such support, including sustainable financing mechanisms, public sector capacity building and information management.

A.2 Private sector participation

A.2.1 Assertion

Private sector participation provides an opportunity for sustainable rural water services and can be used in place of community management.

A.2.2 Objective

To promote indigenous private sector management options for rural water supplies, including privately managed O&M and privately owned water systems, where community management systems have been unsuccessful.

A.2.3 Benefits

Community managed O&M systems have failed to deliver the levels of sustainability initially desired. The benefits of private sector participation are:

- Greater efficiency by combining facility and service delivery;

- Government regulation is required, but not direct support to communities;

- Private organizations can more easily access spare parts due to greater mobility;

- Rehabilitation needs can be identified and implemented by private entities;

- Development of indigenous private sector and local economy; and

- Taxation opportunities for local Government to derive revenue.

A.2.4 Actions

- Opportunities need to be developed for private sector participation in the delivery and O&M of rural water services.

- Incentives should be created for indigenous private sector participation in all elements of rural water supply, from manufacture to maintenance.

- Capacity building of the local private sector is required, including training in 'hardware' and 'software' activities.

- New models for Public-Private Operation & Maintenance (PPOM) and Private Ownership, Operation & Maintenance (POOM) should be tested.

A.3 Local sustainable technologies

A.3.1 Assertion

Technologies that are easy to understand and locally manufactured using locally available components and materials, provide the most sustainable technical solution for rural water supply.

A.3.2 Objective

To promote low-cost local technical solutions such as the Rope pump and locally developed handpumps, in place of imported technologies dependent on specialist spare parts and components.

A.3.3 Benefits

The benefits of using such 'local' technologies are:

• Support to local enterprise and development of the local economy;

• Low-cost affordable water supply to poor rural communities;

• Minimal problems of spare parts supply;

• Possible increased frequency of breakage but reduced downtimes; and

• Higher overall sustainability levels.

A.3.4 Actions

• Technology choice should not be predetermined. Programmes and projects should seek to adopt the use of simple local technologies.

• Incentives should be provided for local indigenous development and manufacture of water systems and technologies.

• Further research and development of existing local technologies is required, especially for application in areas dependent on deep groundwater resources.

• Technology development should begin with a review of existing components available in local markets in that country.

Annexes

A.4   Procurement and importation

A.4.1   Assertion

The procurement of handpumps should be as local to the users as possible. Importation policies that discourage local manufacture and/or procurement should be abolished.

A.4.2   Objective

To promote the purchase of pumps at rural level, in district capitals and rural growth centres, and to dissuade governments from granting exemption from import duty for handpumps.

A.4.3   Benefits

Local purchase of pumps will be more likely to:

• Lead to unsubsidized private sector provision of spare parts at local level.

Removal of tax exempt status for handpumps will:

• Help ensure that local manufacturers are not disadvantaged.

A.4.4   Actions

• Donors and implementing agencies should purchase pumps and other technical components from local retailers in rural areas.

• Incentives should be provided to national suppliers to develop partnerships with local retailers to supply pumps, parts and technical services (such as pump installation) in combination.

• Incentives should be provided to the local private sector to manufacture technologies in country.

• Importation duties should be applied to water supply technologies and components in line with other imported goods.

Annexes

Annexes

Annex B: Annuity factor table

This table can be used to calculate water facility replacement costs and the amount that should be saved each year to ensure that major repairs are met.

Table B.1. Annuity factor table

No of years (n)	Interest Rate (r)							
	3%	5%	6%	8%	10%	12%	15%	20%
1	0.9709	0.9524	0.9434	0.9259	0.9091	0.8929	0.8696	0.8111
2	1.9135	1.8594	1.8334	1.7833	1.7355	1.6901	1.6257	1.4726
3	2.8286	2.7232	2.6730	2.5771	2.4869	2.4018	2.2832	2.0146
4	3.7171	3.5460	3.4651	3.3121	3.1699	3.0373	2.8550	2.4611
5	4.5797	4.3295	4.3295	3.9927	3.7908	3.6048	3.3522	2.8306
6	5.4172	5.0757	4.9173	4.6229	4.3553	4.1114	3.7845	3.1378
7	6.2303	5.7864	5.5824	5.2064	4.8684	4.5638	4.1604	3.3944
8	7.0197	6.4632	6.2098	5.7466	5.3349	4.9676	4.4873	3.6096
9	7.861	7.1078	6.8017	6.2469	5.7590	5.3282	4.7716	3.7909
10	8.5302	7.7217	7.3601	6.7101	6.1446	5.6502	5.0188	3.9443
11	9.2526	8.3064	7.8869	7.1390	6.4951	5.9377	5.2337	4.0746
12	9.9540	8.8633	8.3838	7.5361	6.8137	6.1944	5.4206	4.1857
13	10.6350	9.3936	8.8527	7.9038	7.1034	6.4235	5.5831	4.2807
14	11.2961	9.8986	9.2950	8.2442	7.3667	6.6282	5.7245	4.3624
15	11.9379	10.3797	9.7122	8.5595	7.6061	6.8109	5.8474	4.4328
20	14.8775	12.4622	11.4699	9.8181	8.5136	7.4694	6.2593	4.6681
22	15.9369	13.1630	12.0416	10.2007	8.7715	7.6446	6.3587	4.7264
25	17.4131	14.0939	12.7834	10.6748	9.0770	7.8431	6.4641	4.7910
30	19.6004	15.3725	13.7648	11.2578	9.4269	8.0552	6.5660	4.8597

Annexes

Annex C: Technical assessments

C.1 Bailer test

The bailer test is a short simple test (adapted from MacDonald et al., 2002) to assess whether or not a borehole can sustain a handpump. The equipment required consists of: two bailers A and B (e.g. 75mm/3-inch diameter steel pipe with a flap at one end holding 4.4 litres in a 1m length) each attached to 20m of rope; a stopwatch; and a well-dipper. The following procedure can be used:

1. Rest water table (RWT) measured in borehole (ideally same day as drilling or development of borehole).

2. Bailer A is lowered down the borehole; as the full bail is removed the stopwatch is started.

3. A second bail is removed using Bailer B as Bailer A is emptied.

4. Procedure continues for 10 minutes during which time 20 - 50 bails should have been extracted, depending on depth to water levels (aim for 40 at a constant rate)

5. After ten minutes of bailing, stopwatch is reset and water levels measured every 30 seconds for a further 30 minutes.

6. Calculate pumping rate in litres per minute by dividing volume of water abstracted (in litres) by the length of the test (usually 10 minutes).

7. Calculate the maximum drawdown for the test by subtracting the rest water level from the first water level measurement after bailing stopped (dmax).

8. Read from the data the recovery time for water-levels to recover half-way to RWT (t50).

9. Read from the data the time for the water-levels to recover three-quarters of the way to RWT (t75).

10. Use the pumping rate and the drilled diameter of the borehole to find the guideline values in Table C.1.

If the maximum drawdown and t50 and t75 are all **less** than quoted in the table (for the correct borehole diameter and pumping rate) then the borehole is likely to be successful. If they are all much **greater**, then the borehole will have problems sustaining a handpump. If some are greater and some are less, then a proper pumping test must be carried out.

The borehole should sustain a handpump if:

- Maximum drawdown during the test is less than 3m;

- Water levels recover to 50 per cent in 15 minutes;

- Water levels recover to 75 per cent in 25 minutes.

- Transmissivity is greater than 1m2/d (using The is recovery method, see MacDonald et al., 2002).

Table C.1. Yield estimation by bailer test[1]

Borehole diameter		Flow rate (litres/minute)				
		7.0 (16*)	10.5 (24*)	14.0 (32*)	17.5 (40*)	21.0 (48*)
4 inch	Max. drawdown (m):	3.5	5.3	7.1	8.8	10.6
	t50 (mins):	6	6	6	6	6
	t75 (mins):	14	14	14	14	14
5 inch	Max. drawdown (m):	2.9	4.3	5.7	7.1	8.5
	t50 (mins):	9	9	9	9	9
	t75 (mins):	21	21	21	21	21
6 inch	Max. drawdown (m):	2.3	3.4	4.6	5.7	6.9
	t50 (mins):	12	12	12	12	12
	t75 (mins):	28	28	28	28	28
8 inch	Max. drawdown (m):	1.5	2.3	3.1	3.8	4.6
	t50 (mins):	19	19	19	19	19
	t75 (mins):	46	46	46	46	46

1. * The number in brackets indicates the number of standard bails removed per minute. A standard bail is a 75mm/3" pipe, 1m in length, holding 4.4 litres of water.

Annexes

This is based on the following success criteria:

- The pump is designed to support 250 people with 25 litres each per day;
- Pumping takes place over a 12 hour period;
- The dry season lasts for six months; and
- Drawdown in the borehole does not exceed 15 metres below the rest water table.

C.2   Well cleaning process

Below is a simple ten-stage process to cleaning a hand-dug well.

Equipment

Stiff brushes	HTH Chlorine powder (or bleach)
Safety helmet	Safety glasses
Strong ropes	Bucket
Generator	Electrical de-watering pump
3-4 Workers	Ladder
Tripod	Pulley system

Stages

1.   Remove any objects floating on the water surface using a bucket and rope. If there is a large volume of oil it will not be possible to clean the well and the attempt should be abandoned. Look out for gas bubbles as this may indicate that it is not safe to enter the bottom of the well without good ventilation.

2.   Lower the electrical de-watering pump into the well on a rope ensuring that the delivery pipe is supported and pumps to appropriate drainage. Pump the well until it is completely empty of water. Alternatively, the well may be de-watered manually using bailers, but in most cases this will not empty the well sufficiently.

3.   One individual should then climb into the base of the well using foot-holes in the well lining. If this is not possible a ladder may be required. S/he should be supported by a rope and should wear a safety helmet. The rope should pass through a pulley system supported by a tripod above the well, and there should be enough people to pull the worker out of the well in case of an emergency.

4.   This individual should remove any solid objects and sludge by using a bucket and rope which is pulled to the surface from above.

5.   The rate at which water recharges the well should be checked regularly. If the water level rises quickly the worker should regularly climb out of the well and the well should be emptied again using the de-watering pump.

6.   Once all waste has been removed, the inside walls of the well should be scrubbed using a stiff brush and chlorine solution. *Safety glasses should be worn*. This process should be carried out along the whole depth of the well if possible.

7.   The well should then be left for several hours (or overnight) to give time to recharge and for the water level to rise to normal.

8.   Once full, the well should be shock chlorinated, i.e. a bucketful of concentrated HTH (high test hypochlorite) solution or bleach should be thrown into the well.

9.   The water in the well should then be pumped out again several times using the de-watering pump to purge the well and ensure that the taste or odour of chlorine will not deter people from using the water.

10. Finally, the well should be left to fill up once again. The water quality can be tested after this if appropriate.

Annexes

C.3   Borehole rehabilitation assessment process

In order to assess the need for borehole rehabilitation the following process should be conducted during monitoring.

1.   Check the output from the pump, i.e. number of strokes/revolutions to fill a 20 litre jerrican. This should be approximately 40 and should not exceed an absolute maximum of 100. If more than 10 strokes are required before the delivery of water there is a significant problem with the pump or footvalve, or there is a leak in the riser pipe.

2.   Check the turbidity of the water, which should not exceed 5NTU. If it is higher than this there is a problem of siltation in the borehole.

3.   Remove the pump, including the down-hole components, and inspect it to ensure that it is working correctly and that no components are in need of replacement. Also examine for signs of incrustation or corrosion.

4.   Check the water level in borehole.

If the pump fails to deliver water as required the following options can be used to determine the cause of the problem and the necessary rehabilitation measure. A borehole camera is essential to conduct this process comprehensively.

A.   Water in borehole, none from rising main

Indicated by no water when pump operated but water detected in borehole using well-dipper.

• *Cause 1:   pump broken or hole in riser pipe*

• Solution 1: remove pump and repair

• *Cause 2:   pump intake (footvalve) above water level*

• Solution 2: add riser pipe(s) to lower footvalve (if borehole deep enough)

B.   Pump OK, reduced output from borehole

Indicated by high pump delivery rate at start of pumping followed by reduced flow rate even though stroke rate remains constant.

- *Cause 1:* *reduced water level in aquifer (indicated by use of well-dipper)*

- Solution 1: hydrofracture, or
  abandon

- Cause 2: blocking of screen and/or filter, or
  poor design of screen and gravel pack
  (indicated by borehole camera)

- Solution 2: try redeveloping using airlift, or if this does not work
  abandon

- *Cause 3:* *incrustation with minerals*
  (indicated by examination of down-hole pump
  components + camera)

- Solution 3: air lift
  swab/surge
  chemical or acid treatment
  recoverable if not too severe

- *Cause 4:* *incrustation with iron bacteria*
  (indicated by examination of down-hole pump
  components + camera)

- Solution 3: air lift
  swab/surge
  chlorine or bleach
  recoverable if not too severe, but will re-grow so need to repeat

- *Cause 5:* *screen corroded , damaged or destroyed*
  (indicated by borehole camera)

- Solution 5: remove and replace - almost impossible
  insert new smaller screen and pack, or screen with pre-bonded
  pack, or
  abandon

- *Cause 6:* *borehole contains foreign objects (indicated by borehole camera)*

- Solution 6: small inert objects remove - difficult
  accept or abandon

Annexes

C. No Water

- *Cause 1:* *filled with silt (indicated by examination of down-hole pump components)*

- Solution 1: bailer or air lift pump
  Redevelop, or
  abandon

- *Cause 2:* *aquifer dried up (indicated by borehole camera)*

- Solution 2: hydrofracture, or
  abandon

D. Highly turbid water

- *Cause:* *poor design or deterioration of screen and pack unscreened section of borehole or unsealed base (indicated by borehole camera)*

- Solution: try redeveloping/hydrofracturing, but may not work
  internal gravel pack
  telescoped design
  introduce filtration system following delivery

Annex D: Sustainability snapshots

Table D.1. Sustainability snapshot[1]

Factor	Statement
Financial	1. No funds available for maintenance when needed. 2. Funds available but not sufficient for the most expensive maintenance process. 3. Funds available and sufficient for the most expensive maintenance process.
Technical skills	1. Technical skills not available for maintenance when needed. 2. Some technical skills for maintenance but not for all. 3. Technical skills for all maintenance processes available.
Spares and equipment	1. Spares and equipment not available when needed. 2. Spares and equipment available but not for all repairs. 3. Spares and equipment available for all repairs when needed.

1.   After Sugden, 2001

Annexes

Table D.2. Sustainability snapshot examples, Kenya (2003)

Factor	Statement	Score
Naitawang Community, Transmara Diocese		
Financial	No funds available for maintenance when needed.	1
Technical skills	Some technical skills for maintenance but not for all.	2
Spares and equipment	Community is not aware of where to get spares and equipment when there is a breakdown	1
Chelelach Community, Transmara Diocese		
Financial	No funds available for maintenance when needed.	1
Technical skills	Some technical skills for maintenance but not for all.	2
Spares and equipment	Community is not aware of where to get spares and equipment when there is a breakdown	1
Kaongo Women Group Water Project, Kisii Diocese		
Financial	Limited funds available for maintenance when needed.	2
Technical skills	Technical skills not available for maintenance when needed.	1
Spares and equipment	Community is not aware of where to get spares and equipment when there is a breakdown apart from visiting RWD for guidance	1
godNyango Water Project, Kisii Diocese		
Financial	No funds available for maintenance when needed. Pump broken for more than a year and no repairs done	1
Technical skills	Technical skills not available for maintenance when needed. Community depends on RWD for assistance	1
Spares and equipment	Community is not aware of where to get spares and equipment when there is a breakdown, depends on RWD for assistance	1
Kanyauke Water Project, HomaBay Diocese		
Financial	Adequate funds available for maintenance when needed.	3
Technical skills	Technical skills available for maintenance when needed.	3
Spares and equipment	Community depends on RWD for spares and equipment when there is a breakdown.	2

Annexes

Table D.2. Sustainability snapshot examples, Kenya (2003) *(continued)*

Factor	Statement	Score
Jwelu Community Water Project, HomaBay Diocese		
Financial	Some funds available for maintenance when needed but not adequate for major breakdown.	2
Technical skills	Technical skills not available for maintenance when needed.	1
Spares and equipment	Spare parts and equipment not available when needed.	1

Table D.3. Expanded sustainability snapshot

Factor	Issue	Statement
Project process	a) Participation	1. The pump was 'given', community not offered chance to participate 2. Community was asked if they wanted to participate 3. The community initiated the project themselves
	b) Capital contribution	1. Community did not make any financial or in-kind contribution towards pump 2. Community made significant in-kind contribution (set by the Project) 3. Community made financial contribution (set by the Project)
Institutional arrangements	a) Management system	1. No community organization has responsibility for the water source 2. Community has organization but is not managing the source satisfactorily 3. Community organization is actively managing the source to everyone's satisfaction
	b) Training	1. No one in community received any training from the Project or government staff 2. Some people trained but cannot remember or apply what was learned 3. Useful training was provided which still benefits trainees now
	c) Major breakdowns	1. Community would not know what to do in event of major breakdown 2. No clear procedure, responsibilities unclear in case of major breakdown 3. Clear procedure - confident that pump would be quickly repaired in case of major 'breakdown
Water supply issues	a) Water use	1. Water never used for drinking 2. Water sometimes used for drinking water, sometimes not 3. Water always used for drinking water
	b) Water quality	1. All the people who use the pump perceive the water is not good for drinking 2. Some of the people who use the pump perceive the water is not good for drinking 3. Everyone who uses the pump perceives the water is good for drinking
	c) Source reliability	1. The water source yield is poor, people have to use other sources all the time 2. Sometimes (dry season) the yield is inadequate to meet needs 3. The water source always meets everyone's needs
Maintenance	a) Technical skills	1. Technical skills not available to community for maintenance when needed 2. Some technical skills available for maintenance and repairs, but not all 3. Technical skills for all maintenance processes and repairs readily available
	b) Equipment and spares	1. Maintenance equipment and spare parts not available 2. Some availability but not for all repairs 3. Equipment and spares available for all repairs
	c) Preventative maintenance	1. No preventive maintenance being carried out on pump 2. Some preventive maintenance being carried out, but not regularly 3. Regular programme of preventive maintenance carried out
	d) Maintenance funds	1. No funds readily available for maintenance when needed 2. Some funds readily available but not sufficient for most expensive repairs 3. Funds readily available and sufficient to cover most expensive repairs

Annexes

Table D.3. Expanded sustainability snapshot *(continued)*

Factor	Issue	Statement
Community and social aspects	a) Access/ exclusion	1. Some people never get access to the pump even when they want to use it 2. Some people sometimes do not get access to the pump 3. All the people who want to use the pump can gain access all the time
	b) Impact	1. There is no improvement in the community quality of life after the handpump installation 2. There is some improvement but not sufficient to solve all water problems 3. Quality of life of the community has substantially improved
	c) User satisfaction	1. Community does not like the handpump and would prefer other water sources 2. Like the handpump but worried about sustainability 3. Happy with the handpump and expect to be able to sustain it
	d) Hygiene awareness	1. No one in the community is aware of the link between dirty water and diseases 2. People are generally aware of need to use water in a hygienic way but often ignore it 3. All the people are aware and use water in a hygienic way

Annexes

Table D.4. Expanded sustainability snapshot grid (filled out for four villages in Ghana)[1]

		Afram Plains		Volta Region		
Project name:						
Village name:		Odumase	Somsei	Yordan'nu	Fesi	Ave score
Date:		04/06/02	04/06/02	04/06/02	04/06/02	
Handpump and reference number:		India Mk3 (two pumps)	India Mk3 (two pumps)	India Mk3 (one pump)	India Mk3 (five pumps)	
Component	**Issue**					
Project process	Participation	1	2	3	3	2.25
	Capital contribution	1	3	3	3	2.5
Institutional arrangements	Management system	3	3	3	3	3.0
	Training	2	2	3	3	2.5
	Major breakdowns	3	3	3	3	3.0
Water supply issues	Water use	3	3	3	3	3.0
	Water quality	3	3	3	3	3.0
	Source reliability	3	3	3	3	3.0
Maintenance	Technical skills	3	2	3	3	2.75
	Equipment and spares	3	3	3	3	3.0
	Preventative maintenance	2	2	3	3	2.5
	Maintenance funds	2	2	3	3	2.5
Community and social aspects	Access/exclusion	3	3	3	2	2.75
	Impact	3	3	2	2	2.5
	User satisfaction	3	3	3	1	2.5
	Hygiene awareness	3	3	3	3	3.0
	Average score:	**2.56**	**2.68**	**2.94**	**2.75**	

1. Average column score can be used to evaluate overall level of sustainability in each community, and average row score can be used to evaluate overall effectiveness of different project components.

Annex E: Handpump data sheet

Table E.1. Handpump data sheet

Date of visit and location/name of village:				
Information on handpump maintenance				
Number of Households/Population				
Number of handpumps in village				
Active organization for handpump management				
Number of men in committee				
Number of women in committee				
How/when is money collected for O&M?				
Do they currently have funds set aside for O&M?				
How much money is available at present?				
Who, if anyone, does preventive maintenance?				
Who fixes broken pumps?				
Where are spare parts available from?				
Who buys spare parts when needed?				
Who owns the pump(s)?				
Details of each handpump in village	No. 1	No. 2	No. 3	No. 4
Type of handpump (model, make, country of origin)				
Type of source (drilled borehole, hand-dug well)				
Date of source completion (and by whom)				
Depth to cylinder (m)				
Date of installation (and by whom)				
Riser pipe material (uPVC, steel, GI)				
Currently functioning?				
When did it last break down/fail?				
What was the problem?				
How long was it broken?				
Who fixed it?				
Who paid and how much did it cost?				
How many times has it broken: 1) in the last year? 2) Since it was installed?				

Annexes

Table E.1. Handpump data sheet *(continued)*

Date of visit and location/name of village:				
Details of each handpump in village (continued)	No. 1	No. 2	No. 3	No. 4
Approximate yield (litres/second)				
Does this vary with seasons?				
How many users/households use this pump?				
Is rationing or restriction in place?				
Is the pump lockable?				
Is the taste satisfactory?				
What is the water used for?				
If it functions but is not used, what is the problem?				
Condition of apron				
Drainage adequate				
General quality of construction/installation				
General observations and comments on pump quality, operation, usage, problems etc				

Annexes

Annex F: Background to research

This book is the primary output from a research project funded by the Department for International Development (DFID) entitled 'Guidelines for Sustainable Handpumps Projects in Africa'.

The overall purpose of this project was:

Improved benefits from communal handpumps in Africa through an increased application of factors affecting sustainability of new projects.

The research aimed to collect data from successful projects and synthesize it into a set of guidelines that can be used by planners, implementers and decision-makers to prepare future handpump projects which will have an improved chance of long-term sustainability. The project was divided into three phases: the first to collect baseline data, establish a peer review panel and identify key issues to be addressed; the second to collect data from the field and prepare guidelines; and the third to disseminate the project outputs.

An advisory panel consisting of sector professionals was formed to guide the research process. Governments, NGOs, consultants, the private sector and academia were represented on the panel. An extensive literature review and an international workshop and e-conference on handpump sustainability were conducted early on in the project. On the basis of this, fieldwork methodologies were developed and field research visits undertaken to five countries in sub-Saharan Africa, namely, Ghana, Kenya, South Africa, Uganda and Zambia. The field visits were conducted through collaboration with in-country governmental agencies, ESAs, NGOs and research institutions.

The research indicated that there is a huge spectrum of approaches and solutions to water service delivery using handpumps. Sustainability is affected by actions and issues at all levels from government policy to community perceptions. For these reasons it became apparent that the project could not realistically expect to produce finite guidelines for all levels; the scope was simply too large. It also became clear that rural water supply should be based on programmes and services considering a wide range of technologies, rather than projects dealing with only one (the handpump).

Annexes

Following the field visits and consultation with Advisory Panel members and other project stakeholders it was decided to avoid the term 'Guidelines' for the final research output. The need for information on specific but interrelated issues was recognized and it was decided that the final project output should consist of 'building blocks' for sustainability targeted at specific end-users. It was also agreed that the scope of the project should be widened to consider rural water supply services in sub-Saharan Africa in general. The need for the output to act as an advocacy tool to promote sustainability at policy, management and practitioner levels was also recognized.

Outputs from the research include:

• Literature review;

• Field evaluation guide;

• Workshop report;

• E-conference synthesis report;

• Interim report; and

• Field visits for five countries.

Details of the research project and all research outputs, including an electronic version of this book. (can be accessed at http://www.lboro.ac.uk/wedc/projects/shp/index.htm or http://wedc.lboro.ac.uk/projects/new_projects3.php?id=47)

Index